ECONOMIC REVOLUTIONS IN BAHAYA HISTORY

Dr C. M. Tibazarwa, BA, MA, MA, PhD.

MERLIN BOOKS LTD.
Braunton Devon

First published in Great Britain, 1994

British Library Cataloguing in Publication Data

Tibazarwa, C. M.
Economic Revolutions in Bahaya History
I. Title
306.08

ISBN 0–86303–630–9

Printed in England by
Antony Rowe Ltd., Chippenham, Wilts.

Map I AFRICA

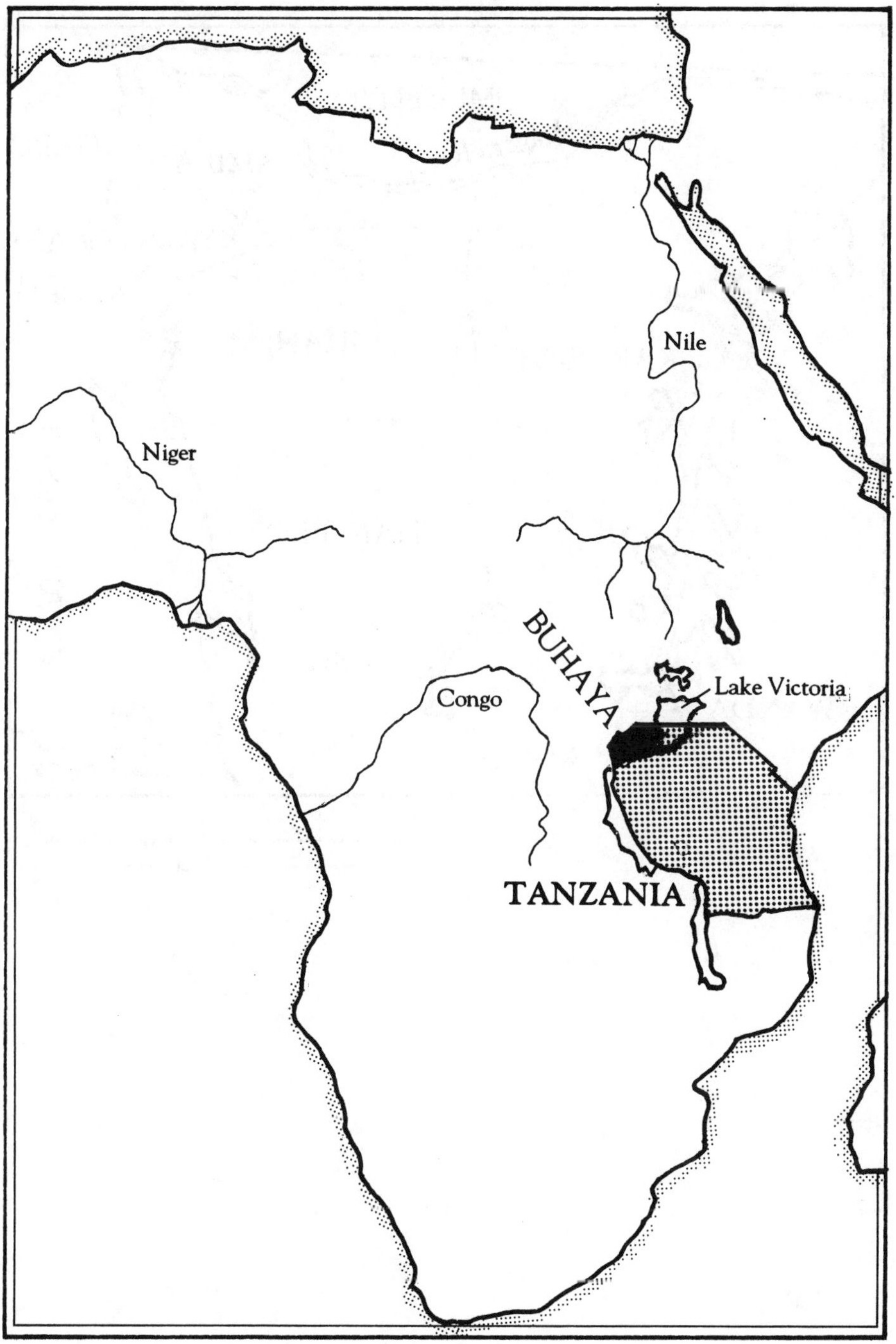

Map II BUHAYA

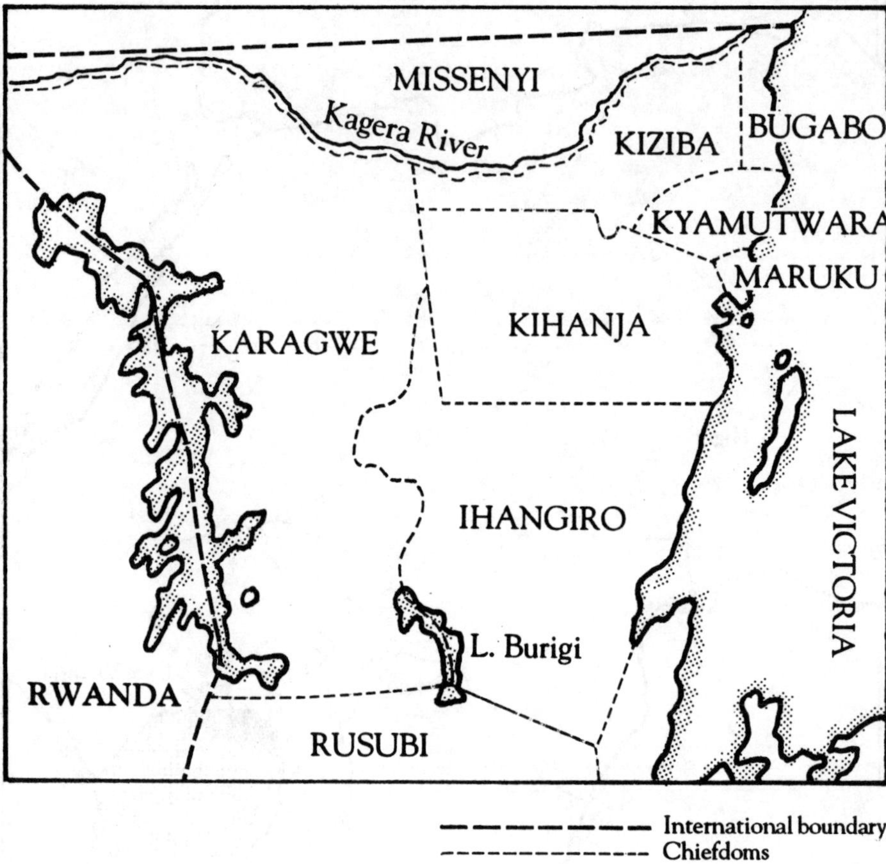

ACKNOWLEDGEMENT

This work is not the result of a one-time survey or research, but rather an expression of a lifelong experience. As such, I am indebted foremost to my parents and relatives for initiating me to the historical phenomenon of my tribe from childhood. The academic interest in the subject, however, took definite shape when I taught history at Ihungo Secondary School, where I benefited from the challenge of my ex-students and the collaboration of my fellow teachers. To them I owe a great deal and mention should be made of Joseph Kiiza (Missenyi), Andrew K. Tibandegabe (Karagawe), John Mutasingwa (Kyamutwara), and the late Ferdinand Basimaki (Ihangiro).

When I began to put down my thoughts, however, I found myself discussing the subjects at various places ranging from the traditional huts in the remote areas of Muleba District to the great halls of Oxford University. Not only did I have to re-examine the places of my childhood in Buhaya, but I found it necessary to visit such places as the Royal Museum of Natural History in London and the Natural History Museum in Geneva with a view to improving my understanding of prehistory, zoology, Egyptology, etc.

The number of people with whom I discussed this subject is too large to reproduce here. Mention, however, should be made of the late Raphael Kyandyoga, Otto Sulemani Kolomba, Benedicto Babi, all of Ijumbi, the late Benedicto Kikoba Rwamarungu of Kihanja and Goti Ntambala of Ihunga. At BALIMI headquarters, I interviewed the General Manager, Gervas Ishengoma, the Statistician, M. Mukamba, and the Company Secretary, Philbert Mutagahwa. Useful information was also obtained from Burchard R. Baisi, former employee of BUKOP. Sylvester Bandio furnished an analysis of the fishes of the lakes and rivers, while E. Munseri, former editor of *Bukya Na Gandi*, covered a number of issues of a political nature. It is to my niece, Sister Pancratia Kaganda, however, that I owe special thanks for her encouragement and material help.

Outside Tanzania, I am equally indebted to many people such as Allan Bell of the Rhodes Foundation, Oxford, and the librarians of the King Albert I Library in Brussels. Anasthazia Basseg (Cameroon) and Ami Aminata Maiga-Keita (Mali), both of the ACP Secretariat, assisted with the comparison of the African linguistic forms. Special thanks are due to Derek Quinlan of the EC Commission for reading the manuscripts and for his useful suggestions and to Professor Robert F. Gray (Maryland, USA) for his invaluable help.

However, the views and errors in this work are all Tibazarwa's.

CONTENTS

CHAPTER I

INTRODUCTION TO ECONOMIC REVOLUTIONS IN BAHAYA HISTORY

Introduction

It is topical to reflect that, much as the Bahaya people think of themselves as a unique and socially insular tribe, they owe a lot of their character to many cultures in Africa and elsewhere. Thus, being predominantly Bantu, their bodily characteristics borrow heavily from the early dwellers of the Bight of Benin while, from the people of the Nile Valley, they appear to have gained transfusions of blood and an enrichment of culture. Their copper and iron technology might have been transferred from the Yoruba of West Africa and the Meroe of the Lower Nile. Their language, while qualifying as a dialect of the erstwhile kingdoms of Bunyoro, Ankole and Toro, unmistakably bears affinity to the Kiha, Zulu and Xhosa down south. Similarly, the resemblance of the traditional Bahaya matrimonial rites to those of the Hehe of Iringa, cannot be adequately explained by accident alone. Indeed, one cannot delve far into any tribal history without unearthing additional proof of the truism that 'Africa is one'.

Ideally, the genealogical relationship between the tribes of Africa could be duly determined by a comprehensive survey of the 3,000 tribes of the continent. Needless to say, the exercise would be a mammoth one and undoubtedly lies outside the range of a small book like this one which concentrates on one tribe, not because of its possible uniqueness but, on the contrary, because the conclusions which can be drawn about Bahaya could apply widely to other tribes.

Emphasis on tribal history derives support from its relevance to the African personality and philosophy that exists only in a tribal milieu. Despite the forces tending to transform the African, he still identifies himself essentially with his tribe. Therefore, analyses of tribal structures are pertinent not only to history but also to the modern African as an individual and as a member of society. This study, of a single tribe, is intended to contribute to this understanding.

An equally important objective is that of contributing to the interpretation of the available records on the African tribe. While the problem of the incompleteness of such records is generally recognized, a speedy remedy has not been forthcoming. Indeed, in the post-independence years, there has been a deliberate shift from tribal to national emphasis, thereby increasing the need for tribal records. A related objective is to afford the reader a totally different perspective of the history of the tribe, which hitherto has been dominated by political and military events. Emphasis in this work is on economics, with a view to shedding light on how economic forces influenced the path of history of the tribe. It is assumed throughout, that history is shaped by the interaction of factors in combination or in succession, and that economic elements are among the significant ones. By underscoring the economic angle of the history of the tribe, the analysis will significantly diverge from most of the available literature on the subject, and it is in this respect that this work is expected to make the maximum contribution.

Overall, the report recognizes three fundamental problems in many tribal records and endeavours to examine them in the light of the experience of the Bahaya people: the first shortcoming is the tendency to place historical details in a single narrative with no regard to the role played by different sectors. The second problem involves giving undue prominence to the political and military events while leaving other features in the background. The third is the dominating position of foreigners in the interpretation of tribal history. While more will be said subsequently about these shortcomings, it suffices to stress, right at the outset, that this study also aims to explain the causes of those problems and thereby to contribute to reducing their negative effects.

Basic Concepts

To facilitate the understanding of the way terms have been used throughout this work, we have attempted to define the major ones below. Thus the term 'economic revolution' is used in the same context as 'industrial revolution', meaning a complete reversal in the significance of economic activities in a given society. Such a change usually involves substitution of one type of occupation for another, consequent upon transformations introduced in the basic economic variables of labour, land, capital management and technology.

As a compound word, the term 'economic history' refers to the interplay between history and economics and envisages drawing on historical records to infer economic relationships. The focus is on economics, defined elsewhere as a study of the principles governing the allocation of scarce resources among unlimited needs, and concerned with production, consumption, distribution and the social organization associated therewith.[1] But, more importantly, economics, as a social science, seeks to explain how the above-mentioned variables are transformed over time and how they interact with one another in a society during a given period of time. In the process of revolutionary change, a variable may act as a lead or a lag, depending on the circumstances of the interaction.[2] While history and economics deal largely with the same factors, the former discipline emphasizes the static point of view while economics brings out the dynamic dimensions over time as well as the cross-effects with other elements.

Typically, the Bahaya as a tribe fall within the category of a traditional pre-twentieth century society.

Rostow defines a traditional society as one 'whose structure is developed with limited production functions, based on pre-Newtonian science and technology, and pre-Newtonian attitudes towards the physical world'.[3] By limited production functions he implies that people rely on subsistence activities such as cultivation, fishing or fruit-gathering for their livelihood. While this definition is not applicable to all cases in Africa, it provides a basis for the conceptualization of a traditional society for the purpose of this work. One might add that traditional society was characterized by an unclear division of labour on a sectoral or institutional basis. Implicitly, economic analysis of traditional society is bound to be more inextricably intertwined with the historical account. However, an effort is made to explain economic situations in given periods by tracing a historical path of selected variables, such as the government's role in the production or cultivation of a certain crop. Overall, the incomplete historical records of traditional society have compelled greater reliance to be placed on bold economic assumptions and historical analyses to assist the development of the argument.

Both the simplicity of the peasant economy, based largely on the agricultural sector, and the pre-eminence of a feudal-cum-aristocratic system, have tended to make the history of Buhaya very comparable to that of medieval Europe.[4] One might therefore draw appropriate comparisons from medieval Europe, on which there is ample historical analysis, in so far as most of Bahaya history fits Rostow's definition of a traditional society.

Basic Assumptions

The basic assumption in this work is that Bahaya history, like that of many other tribes in Africa, was largely shaped by economic forces, mainly of an agricultural nature. However, given that Buhaya remained a traditional economy until late in the twentieth century, the dominance of the agricultural influence should not come as a surprise.

Even without causing a revolution, foodstuffs and economic activities can shed much light on history. As underscored by Daniel McCall, 'food plants can tell us a good deal of the past of the people who used them' since, from any point of view, food is mankind's fundamental quest.[5] Indeed, human history is dominated by man struggling to get food. During the Stone Age, his preoccupation was mainly to gather food by hunting, fishing, picking fruits or digging up roots. After developing tools and techniques for facilitating the task of obtaining food, he was able to domesticate animals and to practise agriculture.[6] This stage was followed by the iron and subsequent metal ages during which still more sophisticated tools were used, enabling man to improve his methods of obtaining food. Prima facie, the history of Buhaya tends to fit into this hypothetical evolutionary path of history, as will become apparent later on in this work.

In order to attain the objectives described above, one might also assume that data is available. As has already been reiterated, however, many African accounts, both oral and written, are deficient in reliable data. Though, for years, the Bahaya tribe has attracted historical and anthropological researchers, there are still serious gaps in the record and, for the time being, these can only be dealt with by making assumptions. At best, the available historic construct is a fresco work drawing on records which are still in the process of being placed on firmer ground. Hope of refining the records has been raised by newly discovered techniques including linguistic inferences, economic analysis, carbon dating, serology and the like.[7]

Finally, there is a further assumption that the Bahaya is a tribe. While a brief description of the tribe will be provided subsequently, it is essential to be clear on the very concept. The word is derived from Latin and is defined as a section of the population of the pre-Imperial Roman city. Webster's New Collegiate Dictionary defines a tribe as a social group comprising numerous families, clans or generations together with slaves, dependants or adopted strangers. The equivalent in Bahaya language is 'oluganda', defined by Fr. Ignatius Bonabaisi as brotherhood or kinsmanship.[8] A Swahili dictionary defines 'Kabila', meaning tribe, as a group of people with a common language, customs and culture.[9]

The use of the same word to mean family, clan or tribe, or even race, may reflect the pre-dynastic clan system where the nation or state was just an extension of the clan, which was a group of kinships uniting to form a country or kingdom. During the pre-dynastic period, characterized by loose, centralized political control and cephalous clan-based structures, the nation was like an extended family.[10] Apparently, the concept of a tribe may have undergone an evolutionary change, first to apply to an extended clan, then to a kingdom. Thus, at the dawn of the colonial era, the Bahaya perhaps considered themselves as belonging to a conglomerate of autonomous but uniglot states rather than to one tribe.[11] Indeed, the Bahaya's conception of themselves as one tribe might have been a colonial innovation.

Interpretation Problem

Economic history, like other social sciences, aims to interpret written and oral records so as to facilitate the understanding of events during subsequent periods. Indeed, the dynamism of history stems from its inherent quality as a basic reference of progress made in sectors such as art, music and industry. In a similar manner, this study aims to interpret the history of the tribe from the economic perspective.

The approach adopted for this work is to make use of the available accounts to depict the economic path followed by the tribe from the earliest times. Ultimately, an integrated picture of the tribe's past is given by highlighting the interaction between economic variables and other factors, mainly of a political, geographical and social nature.

Problems of erroneous interpretation in both oral and written history have been attributed to over-emphasis on military conquests and political events.

Such problems can be illustrated by a proposition made by an eminent historian and anthropologist, C. G. Seligman, who argued that:

> The civilizations of Africa are the civilizations of the Hamites, their history, the records of these peoples and their interaction with the two other African stocks, the Negro and the Bushman.[12]

His hypothesis implies that non-Hamitic communities were assumed to be non-existent or capable of playing only a subjective role in the drama of history. Although the hypothesis is manifestly untenable, it nevertheless demonstrates how a faulty basic interpretation can damage subsequent historical constructs.

Another illustration of tendentious interpretation was cited by Iris Berger, who points to the work of Sir Harry Johnston as having had a detrimental effect on the history of Bachwezi origins because his record reflected racial bigotry rather than genuine historical assumption.[13] Thus, subsequent writers using his interpretation tended to go far astray on the wrong path before the records could be set straight.

While historians might make such dangerous faults unintentionally, it is believed that the conquerors deliberately twisted history to reinforce their influence. Concern about the prevalent risk of using the conquerors' account as an historical base was duly expressed by G. I. Jones, who asserted that:

> The African traditions on the other hand, if used alone, are no substitute for historical record. They are not concerned with a time scale and can only be placed in the right historical perspective if they can be correlated with dated historical records.[14]

He further argues that the conquerors tended to adapt their story to suit their purposes. As shown above, it was due to such accounts that Seligman happened to propound a fallacious hypothesis. Similarly, in Buhaya, the falsification of events could be illustrated by numerous examples, one of which was to rename a village after a conqueror's patron instead of a traditional founder.[15]

The accusation of twisting history is not confined to the Hamitic dynasties but to Arab and European conquerors alike. Indeed, G. I. Jones makes a highly plausible analysis of how:

> The records published in the nineteenth century were written to supply information either to a British government department or to the Victorian reading public, both of which had already formed very definite ideas about West African 'Natives'.[16]

The above statement applies to all Africa and indeed to all conquerors of all times. This reflects the danger of history written by foreigners and colonizers for that matter. As a problem, it constitutes a challenge of the first priority to the indigenous historian who ought to provide a balancing element by establishing accurate records in the first place. The danger is all the greater given that the actual oral historians are fast disappearing without effective replacement, as competent would-be apprentices emigrate to the cities where they are preoccupied more with metropolitan affairs than tribal history. As a result, the widening gap in the tribal records is likely to increase this danger, as European research and interpretation continues to dominate African history. In a limited way, therefore, this report might contribute to the indigenous interpretation of history.

Much as scholarly work on African history continues to develop, the preponderance of the foreign viewpoint has tended to grow unabated. The bias dates back to the time of the explorers, missionaries and colonizers whose adventures were motivated by their convictions and who sought to improve what they believed was inferior or lacking in the African. More perplexing, however, has been the dominance of this foreign interpretation of history which has maintained its momentum during the post-independence era. Even if the generosity of foreign-based grants could offer a partial explanation for this tendency, no one can minimize the danger of the African being inclined to visualize himself through foreign interpreted history.

The danger of foreign domination in the interpretation of African history is duly underlined by Immanuel Wallerstein in a recent study. He pointed out that African studies were detrimentally dominated by anthropologists who 'were almost all either university-trained scholars, on the one hand, or colonial administrators on the other'. They were also 'all Europeans and almost always of the nationality of the governing colonial power'. In short, the anthropologists tended to be biased towards colonial masters so as to provide them with information needed in the administration of the dependencies. Though this bias was later attacked by nationalistic and liberation movements, its impact has remained almost intact to date.[17]

Approach and Problems

The analysis in this work relies on the historical record in trying to identify those elements which might have contributed to the economic development of the tribe from earliest times. The attempt involves the tracing of the historical path of the tribe from the economic point of view. In the process, and without embarking on a rigorous analysis, consideration is given to the impact of economics on the historical and other elements. While politicians and personalities could not be avoided in the study, they are brought in only to enhance the economic themes in focus.

The brevity with which this work is presented presumes some knowledge of or interest in tribal history. More than anything else, this brevity was essential, given the need to cover an exceptionally vast period ranging from pre-historic times to today. Above all, emphasis on the economic features alone has meant that events have been treated selectively and thus many details which make up a purely historical account have been excluded.

The overall approach, however, encounters a number of additional problems which are worth mentioning. One of them is the inadequacy of data which is essential for rigorous analysis. This problem is more pronounced in the earlier epochs, where reliance has mainly to be on guesswork or mere hypothesis. A similar and related problem is the incompleteness of the historical accounts. As we know, tribal history is still in the process of being compiled and so there are still many gaps which, in the course of this analysis, can only be filled by heroic assumptions.

In this introductory chapter, an attempt is made to describe the objectives as well as to define the basic terms and assumptions used in the work. Some paragraphs are devoted to the description of historical interpretation which constitutes an aspect of the theme of this work. Chapter II is devoted to the essential details about Buhaya and its people as well as its peculiarities, so as to set the stage for the analysis presented in the substantive parts. The subsequent chapters are arranged chronologically according to the major economic structures based on different crops and their impact on history. Thus, Chapter III deals with the first agricultural revolution in Buhaya, based on the fingermillet grain, and traces the history of the tribe from the early epochs. Chapter IV is entitled the Banana/Engaju era because it features the revolution based on the banana plant and the manure cattle called ENGAJU. Next is the chapter on the coffee revolution, which started with the European colonial era. Emerging from the coffee culture was the exceptionally commercially buoyant period of 1949–60, referred to as the Ezoni Period. Finally, there is a brief chapter setting out the overall conclusions to be drawn.

1. The basic notions of economics can be found in any primer on the subject. For a basic analytical role of economics, *see* Kenneth E. Boulding, *Economic Analysis* (Harper and Brothers, 1953), Part I, pp.3–233.
2. A good reference on the subject of lag and lead variables on economic development is W. W. Rostow, *The Stages of Economic Growth: A Non-Communist Manifesto* (London: Cambridge University Press, 1961).
3. Cf. W. W. Rostow, *The Stages of Economic Growth*, op. cit., p.1. For a historical and developmental perspective, *see* Benjamin Higgins, *Economic Development* (New York: W. W. Norton & Company Inc., 1968), pp.161–87.
4. For a standard account of the times, *see* E. Lipson, M.A., *The Economic History of England* (London: A. Black Limited, 1929). *Also*: S. B. Clough, *European Economic History: The Economic Development of Western Civilisation* (McGraw Hill Book Company, 1968). *See also* Clive Day, Ph.D., *Economic Development in Europe* (New York: Macmillan Company, 1942), pp.1–68.
5. Daniel F. McCall, *Africa in Time Perspective* (New York: Oxford University Press, 1969), p.89. *See also* G. Murdock, *Africa: Its People and Their Cultural History* (New York: McGraw Hill, 1959), pp.17–23.
6. A summary of the historical perspective of African agricultural history is presented by Basil Davidson, in *Africa South of the Sahara 1981–82* (London: Europa Publications Limited), pp.6–7.

7. For more about the new techniques, *see* D. F. McCall, 'Early History of Africa', *Encyclopedia Americana*, 1965, Vol. I, pp.223x–224y.
8. Fr. Ignatius Bonabaisi, *Ikany — Ngambo* (Limburg: Printing Press of the Pallottine Fathers, 1957).
9. *See* Taasisi ya Uchunguzi wa Kiswahili, *Kamusi ya Kiswahili Sanifu* (Dar es Salaam: Oxford University Press, 1981).
10. A presentation of cephalous structures can be found in P. van Pelt's *Bantu Customs in Mainland Tanzania* (Tabora: TMP Book Department, 1974), pp.91–132.
11. A conglomerate can be described as a form of political organization of component states not centralized but otherwise possessing distinct common aspects, e.g. the Balkan States. An exceptionally appropriate analysis of the definition of the term 'tribe' is provided by Elizabeth Colson. She notes, however, that 'because of the general confusion about its implications, it is best abandoned'. *Vide* L. H. Gann and P. Guignan, *Colonialism in Africa 1870–1960*, Vol. I (London: Cambridge University Press, 1969), pp.1–65.
12. Charles Gabriel Seligman, *Races of Africa* (London: Oxford University Press, 3rd edition, 1957), p.85.
13. Cf. Iris Berger, *Religion and Resistance: East African Kingdoms in the Precolonial Period*, Annales, Series In–8° — Sciences Humaines — No. 105, 1981 (Tervuren, Belgium: Musée Royal de l'Afrique Centrale). The work she is referring to is Sir Harry Johnston, *The Uganda Protectorate* (London: Hutchinson and Co., 1902), p.763.
14. G. I. Jones, 'European and African Tradition on the Rio Real' in *Journal of African History*, Vol. IV, No.3 (1963), pp.391–402.
15. Traditionally, each village had a patron who was invoked on special occasions; this was a Bantu custom dating from early times. With the conquest of the Nilo-Hamitics, the patron's name was replaced by one from the conqueror's group.
16. G. I. Jones, op. cit., p.392.
17. From Immanuel Wallerstein, 'The Evolving Role of the African Scholar in African Studies', in *Canadian Journal of African Studies Revue*, Vol. 17 (1983), pp.9–16.

CHAPTER II

PHYSICAL AND SOCIAL FEATURES OF BUHAYA

Introduction

This is an extension of the preceding chapter and it aims to describe places which will be referred to in the course of this work. By providing a separate chapter at the outset on the exotic sounding names of physical aspects peculiar to Buhaya, the non-local reader can be spared the trouble of having to make too frequent use of the atlas. The first part of the chapter describes the places closely associated with historical events and, to this effect, notes are provided on the geographical elements likely to have figured prominently in the shaping of the tribe's history. Later in the chapter, the social background of the Bahaya is presented to facilitate the examination of the tribe's development through the centuries.

This chapter will also seek to evaluate the role of geographical factors in shaping the history of the region. While the geography inevitably influences those coming to settle, the land, the weather, soil fertility and topography play no minor role in determining the pace of development. These roles, however, changed from period to period, corresponding with the different stages attained by man in civilization. Thus, at times, lakes and mountains provided invaluable shelters which, for generations, allowed cultures to grow. At other times, the same features became important means of communication linking the region with distant places. Thus, to cave dwellers, the forests and valleys very probably provided ideal shelters against intruders or waves of emigrants. However, during later civilizations of agriculturalists and pastoralists, Buhaya became either the route they traversed over the centuries of migrations or, being attracted by the geography, their final destination.

Buhaya in the Context of Tanzania

The most relevant context in which Buhaya should be considered is the country of Tanzania, of which it forms a constituent region. Comprising an area of 5,950 square miles, Buhaya claims 1.6% of the area of the country and about 3.7% of its population.[1] Historically, Buhaya is but a chapter of the ethnical and social struggle and evolution of the country.

Tanzania, a country known before the union with Zanzibar as Tanganyika, covers an area of 364,000 square miles (945,087 square kilometres) and shares borders with Kenya, Uganda, Rwanda, Burundi, Zaire, Zambia, Malawi and Mozambique. Its history, as a unified state, dates back to

Map II–1 EAST AFRICA

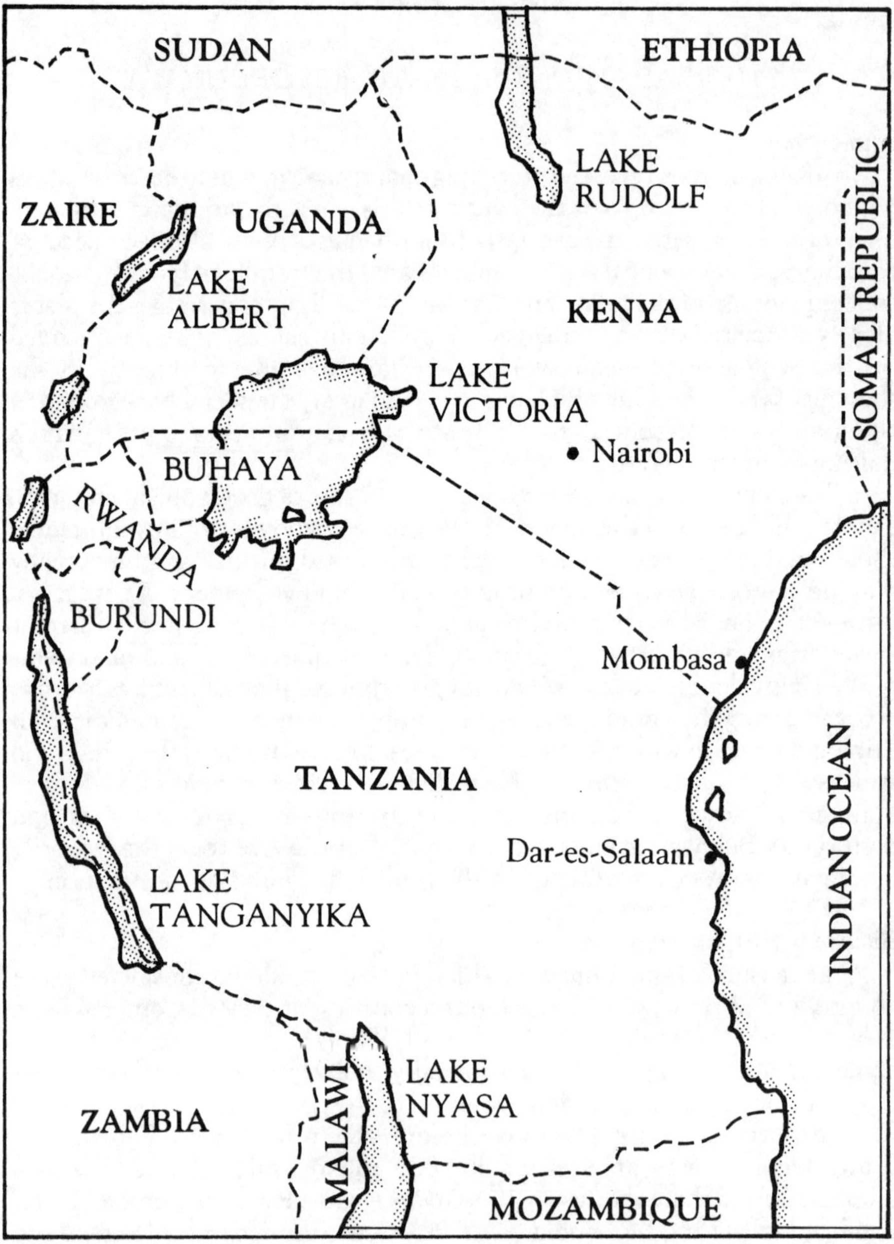

the European conquest at the turn of the century, commencing with German colonial rule, which was terminated by the British who remained in power until independence in 1961. From as early as the ninth century, however, Arabs and Portuguese were making conquests of the coastal areas of the country though there is no evidence of attempts to create a single political unit as we know it today.

Prior to the twentieth century, therefore, the history of Tanzania is to be found in separate accounts of the tribes into which the population is mainly divided sociologically. Despite the 120 tribes, there is no single dominant one, the largest being the Sukuma located to the east of Lake Victoria, the Nyamwezi to the south of the lake, the Chagga around Mount Kilimanjaro, the Hehe of Iringa, the Makonde of Mtwara, the Gogo of Dodoma and the Haya of Buhaya. The history of each tribe, however, goes back over many centuries of migration, inter-tribal warfare, dynasties, famine and folklore. In a way, tribes were related genealogically through the process of small tribes forming offshoots of big ones or merging with others through migration, intermarriage and warfare.

Broadly, the Tanzanian tribes can be divided into the Western Bantu, occupying the highlands and basins of the Great Lakes and the central and the south-western areas of the country. Another group is the Eastern Bantu, which includes the Chagga, Pare, Bondei, Luguru and Nyika and the coastal tribes. The third group comprises the Nilotics, represented by such tribes as the Masai and Tatoga. The fourth is the small group of Khoisan tribes, best represented by the Sandawe and the Haza, whose language is characterized by click sounds. In Tanzania, the Bantu groups are the most prominent, both numerically and culturally, and the Bahaya happen to fall into the Bantu-dominated tribes.

Geographically, Buhaya lies in the north-western corner of Tanzania, some 1,000 miles away from the capital, Dar es Salaam. Such a location has always spelled problems for transport and communication with the capital during both the colonial period and after independence. Buhaya is linked to Dar es Salaam by a steamer service through Mwanza and further on by rail to Tabora and the Ocean coast. There is a road linking the area with Dar es Salaam through Nzega, Singida and Dodoma.

Topographically, Tanzania can be divided into three zones, commencing with the low-lying coastal belt along the Indian Ocean and encompassing the islands of Zanzibar. Having a good rainfall, the region is important agriculturally and is densely populated. Lying to the west of the coastal belt is the central plateau, running along the Rift Valley, marked by low rainfall and covered by savannah shrubbery. The plateau supports herds of livestock and wild animals and, in this way, it is important economically. The third zone comprises the highlands around the northern mountains, the great lakes and the south-western area, and it is in this region where Buhaya is situated, occupying the western highlands of Lake Victoria.

Geographical Features of Buhaya

Buhaya comprises the region covered by the eight Bukoba chiefdoms: Bugabo, Ihangiro, Karagwe, Kihanja, Kiziba, Kyamutwara, Maruku and Missenyi. This area is more or less rectangular in shape, a bit narrower from east to west, and covers about 5,950 square miles. Roughly, it is bisected by longitude 31.5° east, which passes through Maputo and Cairo, and latitude 0.5° south. The 1° east parallel, which passes through the northern frontier, cuts the southern tip of Somalia, while the entire region lies well within longitudes 30° east and 32° east. The boundaries of the region with Uganda, Rwanda and Burundi can be described as 'along the first parallel of latitude until it strikes the Kagera River about 70 miles west of Lake Victoria. From this point, the western boundary follows the Kagera River to approximately 2°25', and thence along the eastern boundary of Urundi to the Malagarasi River, which flows to Lake Tanganyika.'[2]

To the east, the region is flanked by Lake Victoria, so named by Captain John Hanning Speke in 1858, but hitherto known locally as Rweru (White Sea). To the north is Uganda and to the west Rwanda. Bihalamuro district, which used to form one of the Buhaya states, is now the southern border. The capital of the region, Bukoba, is located to the north, just on the shore of Lake Victoria at the mouth of the Kanoni River. Both name and site were a result of the imagination of two German adventurists, Emin Pasha and Dr Karl Peters, the name of the town having been associated with the fishermen of the Bakoba clan who used to frequent that shore at the time of the first German visit. Since then, the hinterland of the town has often been referred to as Bukoba, which might also from time to time be used to signify the Buhaya region.

Climatically, Buhaya falls within the same region as southern Uganda. The climate is normally described as mild, with temperatures averaging 20°C (68°F) and, though the variations from month to month are insignificant, there is a considerable difference between the day's and the night's maxima and minima from noon to midnight. July tends to be both the driest and the coolest month of the year. Rainfall is otherwise well distributed throughout all the seasons with the heaviest precipitation occurring in March/April and October/November, averaging 80 inches a year.[3] Geographically, the rainfall is not all that evenly distributed; the average drops rather abruptly towards the south and the west, with Ngote (Ihangiro) and Bugene (Karagwe) averaging less than 40 inches a year. Thus, the coastal plateau receives the highest rainfall. The skies are generally overcast more than 260 days in a year and this greatly reduces evaporation. Overall, the relatively cool weather with a good rainfall constitute characteristics favourable to economic and cultural development.

The ecology of Buhaya is determined largely by the rainfall, which is well above the average for Tanzania. Typically, the region is evergreen with thick forests on the hilltops and valleys and tall grass on the slopes. Due to over-cultivation and erosion, however, the forests have disappeared, having

Map II–2 BUHAYA: PHYSICAL SKETCH

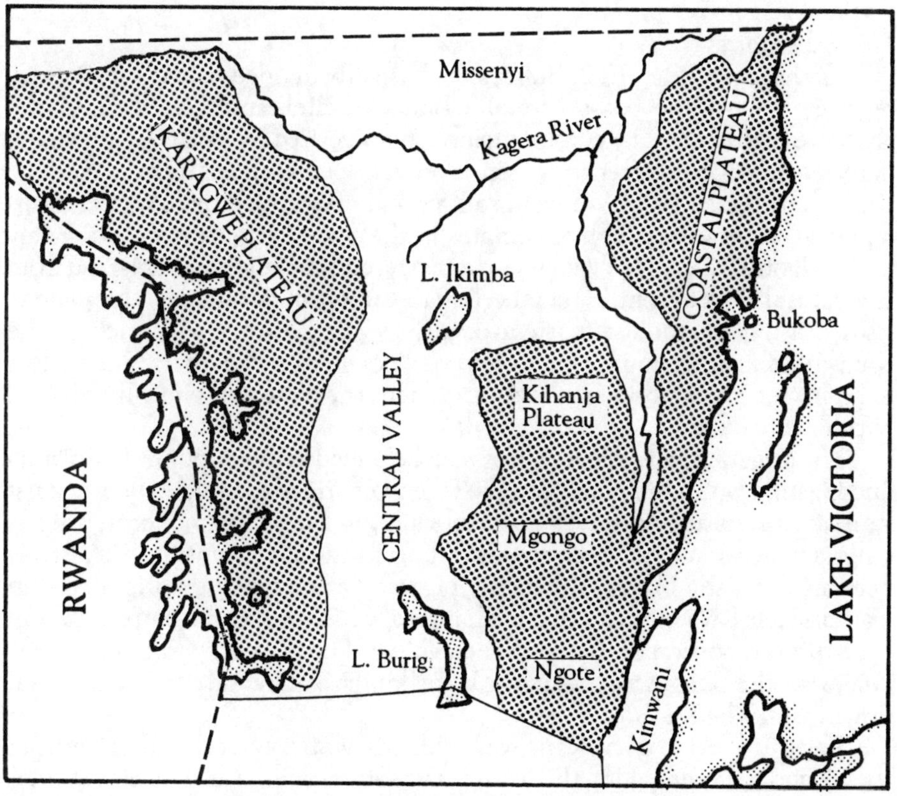

been replaced by plantations. For similar reasons, the animals which used to roam the area have migrated to distant places and the former hunters' favourite waterbuck (enjobe) and the springbok (ensa) have moved from the densely inhabited parts of the region. Overall, today's ecology is dominated by the banana/coffee farms, interspersed with open common grassland (orweya). In fact, a village is made up of stretches of individually owned plots of banana plantations, each of which contains a homestead. The resulting scenery, then, is that of banana farms dotted with dwelling houses, which gives the Bahaya village its unique economic and ecological characteristics. These, in their turn, give rise to what is called the banana culture complex, implying that the plant is central to the economic and social activities of the inhabitants of the region. A more detailed insight into the banana-based culture is made in a subsequent chapter.

Physical Features

As shown on Map II–2, Buhaya is physically divided into three distinct regions, namely the coast (literally Buhaya), the central valley and the Karagwe highlands. The coastal region, characterized by a plateau averaging between 4,000–6,000 feet above sea-level, rises perpendicularly from the lake shore on the east. From Kimwani to Kemondo Bay, the coastal region forms a plane tilting west, which terminates in the one-edged, canyon-like valley of the Ngono River. This valley separates the eastern edge of the plateau from the central ridge. From Mubembe Bay to the Ugandan border, the plateau rises still higher, though it is cut deeply by fast flowing rivers such as the Kanoni, Maiga, Kyamunene and Ntoro. Though from weathering the edges expose huge Precambrian rocks and boulders, the plateau is typically covered with fertile red soils.

The Kagera River, whose sources can be traced in Zaire, Burundi, Rwanda and Uganda, and which has a unique characteristic of tending to flow against its main tributaries, crosses the central valley in the north and forms marshy valleys which have not been important agriculturally. Mention has already been made of the Ngono River, the biggest Kagera tributary originating in Tanzania, at Rwamilinga Hills in Ihangiro, which forms the eastern part of the southern portion of the W-shaped valley. The western part of the valley comprises the Burigi Lake basin, the Lake Ikimba Valley and the Mwisa River, flowing into the Kagera.

The third region is the Karagwe highlands, which extend all the way from the Ugandan border along the west to the south of Buhaya. The elevation is an extension of the Rwanda and Ankole mountain ranges and plateaus, standing on average at a height of 4,000 to 5,000 feet above sea-level. The geological texture is a Precambrian folded structure with bold ridges which are less weathered than those in the coastal zone, though they have a north-south trend corresponding to the drainage of the area by the upper Kagera and the Burigi-Mwisa rivers. The eastern edge is marked by a sharp scarp which, while not strictly continuous, is well marked right from the northern border with Uganda to Biharamulo. Owing to lower precipitation in Karagwe, the ridges are covered with grass and shrubs rather than with luxuriant vegetation.

The People

Ethnically, the majority of the Bahaya people are of Bantu stock, which comprises up to 90% of the population, while the remaining portion consists of Nilo-Hamitics from Bahr-el-Ghazal and the Horn of Africa.[4] The interaction between the Nilotic and Bantu groups was a major feature of the history of Buhaya.

In 1948, the population was quoted at 299,860, giving an annual rate of increase in population of 2.6% between the years 1948 and 1979. The distribution of the population according to the eight chiefdoms is well indicated in Table II–1.[5] Using 1948 as an example, and as shown in Table II–1, the population was distributed as follows (in percentage): Bugabo (6.46), Ihangiro (23.53), Karagwe (15.90), Kihanja (25.22), Kiziba (13.73), Kyamutwara (9.06), Maruku (2.60) and Missenyi (3.50).[6] The table also shows that the distribution changed considerably over the 1912–48 period.

TABLE II–1 *DISTRIBUTION OF THE POPULATION OF BUHAYA ACCORDING TO CHIEFDOMS*

CHIEFDOM	1912	%	1926	%	1948	%
1. BUGABO	19,106	9.74	21,183	9.92	19,378	6.46
2. IHANGIRO	39,237	20.00	45,524	21.32	70,566	23.53
3. KARAGWE	27,837	14.19	27,106	12.69	47,671	15.90
4. KIHANJA	48,576	24.76	52,655	24.65	75,621	25.22
5. KIZIBA	38,878	19.82	39,203	18.35	41,185	13.73
6. KYAMUTWARA	22,541	11.49	20,260	9.49	27,191	9.06
7. MARUKU	–	–	7,643	3.58	7,772	2.60
8. MISSENYI	–	–	–	–	10,476	3.50
TOTAL	196,175	100.00	213,574	100.00	299,860	100.00

Sources: *Engoma Ya Buhaya*, Vol. III, No. 1, January 1950. Ralph A. Austen, *Northwestern Tanzania under German and British Rule* (Yale University Press, 1968), p.268.

The demographic structure in 1948 showed that the sex ratio was 1.18, with females numbering 162,577 as against 137,283 males.[7] Children or infants numbered 48,923 girls and 50,635 boys, which makes a total figure of 99,558, accounting for 33.20% of the population of 299,860. (For the same population, there were 90,100 tax payers or 30.15% of the population.)

The geographical distribution of the population varied with economic occupation, which also influenced land availability. This phenomenon is duly developed by D. N. McMaster.[8] Thus, in a grain-based economy, the population concentration was more marked in the Karagwe area, whereas the banana culture necessitated the shift of demographic density to the forested highlands bordering Lake Victoria. Among the basic factors influencing population distribution were rainfall, soil fertility and the physical features of the landscape. To these should be added agricultural activities which influenced land availability. With the pre-eminence of the banana, settlement was mainly on the forest areas which were rather limited but where the shortage was mitigated by permanent farm agriculture relying on intensive cultivation. Eventually, the banana culture led to the formation of villages with a higher population density similar to that of today. The introduction of the coffee tree did not bring about a significant change in the population distribution because it is grown on the same farm as the banana and therefore does not require the extension of farms or emigration to new areas for growing coffee.

With regard to the political and social structure, there are no indications that the Bahaya ever formed a single tribe under one indigenous ruler in pre-colonial times. To date, the tribe is divided into small kingdoms (chiefdoms) which, prior to the arrival of the Europeans, used to wage war against one another. The salient common features of the tribe are the clan system, the language, the customs and the geographical unity of the region. Some attempt to establish political unity was made by the British Administration in 1926 when the Bakama Council (Lukiiko), comprising the eight chiefs of Buhaya, was instituted.

The Lukiiko co-ordinated the activities of the chiefdoms but had no political status of its own other than the collective power of semi-autonomous chiefs. Despite the initiatives of a capable secretariat headed by Mr Francisco Xavier Lwamugira, the Council had only limited success in forging the unity of the Bahaya. After all, the Council, like other para-tribal political systems of the time, was exogenous and based outside the area.

In general, to date, the Bahaya have always tended to identify themselves with the political divisions, that is, the chiefdoms. For centuries, strangely, the tribe also had temperamental divisions whereby people from a locality were attributed with a given dominant character trait. These character references, which comprised such terms as 'The Outspoken', 'The Over-courteous', 'The Stingy', were not taken seriously, though they underscored a sense of community that has always tended to prevail throughout the Bahaya tribe.

Socially, however, the Bahaya think of themselves as one group, though they cannot easily identify what binds them together other than language and region. Outsiders, however, whether within Tanzania or outside it, tend to make a more comprehensive and realistic assessment of the tribe. Thus, Sir J. F. Cunningham, who observed the tribe at the turn of the century, made the following comments on the Bahaya, to whom he referred as Baziba, and whose land, he said, extended for a hundred miles along the west and south-west of Lake Victoria Nyanza:

> The Baziba (Bahaya) are a tribe of remarkably good physique, and have no objection whatever to leaving their country in large numbers to seek employment elsewhere. Their requirements in regard to feeding and housing are extremely simple, and as they are industrious and fearless, they should be good raw material as native soldiers or general labourers.
>
> ... They are a strong, hardy race, very enterprising, and are always ready to turn their hands to any kind of work. At one moment you meet them carrying water-pots between Victoria Nyanza and the Europeans' houses and gardens; at another you meet them hawking round loads of coffee for sale to Europeans or Indians; and, again, preparing fibre, or carrying loads for some firm or other — always busy, never loitering, and always good-humoured and happy.[9]

1. According to the 1957 census of Tanganyika.
2. *Report by His Majesty's Government of the United Kingdom of Great Britain and Northern Ireland to the Council of the League of Nations on the Administration of Tanganyika Territory for the year 1929.* Colonial Paper No.46 (London: His Majesty's Stationery Office, 1930), p.4.
3. For a precise description of the Bukoba weather, see Priscilla Copeland Reining, 'Haya Land Tenure: Land Holding and Tenancy', *Anthropological Quarterly*, Vol. 35 (April, 1962), p.60.
4. Iris Berger, *Religion and Resistance: East African Kingdoms in the Precolonial Period*, op. cit., p.9.
5. According to *Africa South of the Sahara 1981–1982* (London: Europe Publications Limited), the population of the Kagera region, that is Buhaya plus Biharamulo and Ngara Districts, was 1.009 million in 1978. The two non-Buhaya districts normally form about a third of the total population.
6. *Engoma Ya Buhaya*, Vol. III, No.1, January 1950, p.12 (percentages calculated by the author).
7. Source of figures: *Engoma Ya Buhaya*, op. cit.
8. D. N. McMaster, 'Change of Regional Balance in the Bukoba District of Tanganyika', in *Tanganyika Notes and Records*, No.56 (March 1961), pp.79–92.
9. Sir J. F. Cunningham, *Uganda and Its People* (London: Hutchinson & Co., 1905), p.283.

CHAPTER III

THE FINGERMILLET REVOLUTION UP TO AD 1500

Introduction

The period examined in this chapter extends from the beginning of recorded time to AD 1500. Ideally, such a vast span of time should be treated in many volumes to adequately describe the geological, economic, political and other types of events which must have taken place. Scanty information on prehistoric Buhaya, however, can permit only a discursive consideration of the tribe's past. Besides, despite its vastness, the whole period is examined mainly from the point of view of its relevance to the evolution of subsequent periods and, to this effect, an attempt is made to highlight the features which might have significantly influenced later civilizations. By emphasizing the socio-economic aspects of the period, a good link can be established between the two epochs.

Conveniently, the epoch is divided into two, the first part ending in AD 300 and the second in AD 1500. While the division is rather arbitrary, it represents, on the one hand, prehistoric times, about which little is known, and the earlier civilization of the agriculturalist Bantu settlers on the other. Because information on the first period is meagre, it is examined only briefly, and the analysis is based largely on assumptions. Although earlier prehistoric times of the ice ages are taken to be less relevant to economic history, it is assumed here that human development is a continuous process and therefore that each period influences subsequent ones.

A greater part of the chapter is devoted to the period after AD 300, during which it is estimated that the agricultural Bantu people settled the land of Buhaya and thereby established the nucleus of the tribe of today. The migrants are assumed to have arrived from Bunyoro in Uganda, though it is believed that they originated in the Benue Valley located on what is currently the Nigeria/Cameroon border. In this connection, reference will be made to the different hypotheses on the migratory waves of the Bantu and other ethnic groups which might have influenced the early history of Buhaya.

The life of the early settlers underwent a fundamental transformation because of the cultivation of a small seed grain known as FINGERMILLET (ELEUSINE CORACANA).[1] Economic reliance on the grain might have culminated in the transition of the early Bantu structure from mainly a hunter-gatherer type of existence to farming. By enhancing the agricultural pattern of life, the transition provided an opportunity for human advancement, introducing a measure of control over the production of food supply. The quest for food having been the main preoccupation of prehistoric man, a shift to a systematic food supply ought to have constituted a change of revolutionary magnitude. Arising from this transition was the change in lifestyle, political structures, technology and so on. The form taken by the change, as well as its impact on tribal life, is described in the subsequent paragraphs.

Buhaya During the Stone Age

Given that economic history is about man's behaviour in a given social framework, consideration of the prehistoric hominids is beyond the range of this work. The period of relevance emerges more clearly during the Stone Age, when man managed to live in sizeable social communities.[2] Above all, man had by then learned to use tools which were essential to his economic life. For East Africa, a simplified classification of Stone Age epochs divides them into three: the Earlier Stone Age, lasting until 55000 BC, the Middle Stone Age, which ended about 10000 BC, and the Later Stone Age, which ended about 500 years ago.

Archaeologists, however, tend to agree that Africa south of the Sahara was among the regions of the world where prehistoric cultures thrived. Various studies on prehistoric Africa point to the possibility that several places on the continent were inhabited by Early Stone Age people or ape men. Recent excavations at the Olduvai Gorge in northern Tanzania, for example, indicate that the *Homo erectus*, Zinjanthropus, lived in the area more than 500,000 years ago. Similar excavations at Omo in Ethiopia revealed another form of *Homo sapiens* which existed 130,000 years ago.[3] This reinforces the hypothesis that the African plateau might have nurtured the earliest form of *Homo sapiens*.

If the period before 55000 BC is of more relevance, it is because it developed in the *Homo erectus*, the predecessor of the *Homo sapiens* who is more pertinent to economic history. However, it was during this Middle Stone Age that the *Homo sapiens* (Rhodesiensis) might have spread in sub-Saharan Africa, during which time the Bushmanoids and allied stock emerged. The Negroid stock might have appeared around 11,000 years ago, just at the beginning of the Later Stone Age. The emergence of the Bantu stock, however, has not yet been adequately established, nor their morphological and phylogenetical characteristics, which are different from those of Bushmanoids and Negrillos.

The evidence of the culture of the Stone Age man in Buhaya, however, restricts the likelihood to the Later Stone Age men like the Pigmies, the Bushmen and the Hottentots. Although the three ethnic groups were significantly different from the point of view of physical attributes, their cultures might have reached their zenith at the same time. Besides, it is possible that the features of these cultures were comparable.[4]

An obvious difference among the three racial groups mentioned was their geographical preferences: the Pigmies inclined towards dwelling in thick equatorial forests, the Bushmen preferring cooler highland grasslands, while the Hottentots confined themselves to the arid zones of southern Africa.

Apparent similarities and the contemporaneity of the Bushman and Pigmy did not preclude a basic difference in the skin pigment nor different environmental preferences. Mention was made that the Pigmies preferred to live on the outskirts of thick forests, while the Bushmen close cooler, high-elevation areas. It might be assumed, however, that these cultural differences and experiences were put to good use by succeeding civilizations. The sectors which benefited most were hunting, pottery and wood-carving. However, it can be assumed that a positive contribution also extended to such areas as language and intermarriage. Regrettably, subsequent cultures were unable to develop the art of drawing and writing, which was established by Stone Age people and which has survived to date, though only in the caves.

According to *Zamani Mpaka Siku Hizi*,[5] legends and stories make reference to the presence of Pigmies in the forest of the Congo River Basin, Rwanda and Burundi and even in central Tanzania and Kenya. Occupation-wise, they are believed to have been itinerant hunters with little interest in agriculture or permanent settlement.[6] It is also alleged that they intermarried with other peoples arriving in successive migratory waves and consequently produced mixed breeds of people whose culture borrowed from both the invaders and the Pigmies.

It was in the field of hunting skills that Pigmies contributed most significantly to later cultures. To them is attributed the bow and arrow as well as the poison applied thereby. The Pigmies are believed to have invented the bowstring, made from the small intestine of the lion, and the wooden arrowhead. In pottery, Pigmies introduced techniques for using various types of clays to make water-pitchers, bowls and cooking pots. They also invented techniques for trapping animals, e.g. using ditches, bush fires, fall traps and pits, stakes and ropes as well as driving animals over cliffs or into swamps.

Evidence of the caveman in Stone Age culture in Buhaya is provided by certain tools which are still in wide use, an example being the grindstone or quern used for milling fingermillet.[7] A flat stone measuring roughly two square feet and hewn out of a hard rock (granite) is usually used in unworked form. The grinder, or top-stone, a smaller piece of rock fitting into the palm, crushes the grain by sliding it over the flat surface of the grindstone. Various other examples of the use of unworked stone can be cited to show that the Bahaya people benefited considerably from Stone Age technology.

The second type of evidence of the presence of the caveman in Buhaya comes from the painting on the walls of caves found in several places in the region. In fact, similar cave drawings can be seen in many parts of Africa. In Tanzania, for example, the paintings found on the rocks in the caves of Singida are among the most revealing as to the cultural attainments of Stone Age man.[8] In Buhaya, such drawings are found in the Ihungo Hills, about two kilometres to the north of Bukoba town and in the highlands of Ihangiro. The archaeological discoveries at Nsogezi near the Kagera River and the Karagwe have boosted the available evidence. The drawings reveal to some extent that the major occupation of the time was hunting. However, equally enamouring is the technology of preparing multicoloured, or polychromatic, and indelible ink as well as the artistic refinement attained at such an early stage of human history.

Overall, archaeological evidence points to the significant contribution to culture made by the three ethnic Stone Age groups. Besides the normal evolutionary mingling of races, there was a gradual improvement in the techniques of adapting to the environment. Early Stone Age man had already displayed versatility in improving his stone tools and, above all, he learned to master fire, which marked a major step in human development.

After all, it was during the latter part of the Middle Stone Age and the early part of the Later Stone Age that the Bushmanoid cultures dominated the African continent, and Buhaya was no exception. From that culture, man was able to advance techniques of hunting small and big animals, reptiles and birds as well as gathering fruits and nuts. Among the tools used were stones, bone gouges and sticks. Some indications suggest that the life of Stone Age man in Buhaya was relatively productive, as can be indicated by cave drawings. He should have found the land of Buhaya abounding in food obtainable from the forest, rivers and grassland. Equally significant was the salubrious climate with a heavy rainfall but low relative humidity owing to altitude and moderate temperatures, which discouraged such pests as mosquitoes and tsetse flies, thus rendering the area ideal for habitation during the Stone Ages.[9] The third factor was the natural protection of the region against invaders. To the east was Lake Victoria, which could not be easily crossed at that time. In the west was the upper Kagera River, which forms numerous lakes along the border with Rwanda. To the north was the Kagera River, which was also difficult to cross. To the south were Lake Burigi and the foresty jungles which form a border with Biharamulo District (Rusubi as it was known then).

By and large, it seems that Buhaya played an important role in the Stone Age period by forging ahead in Pleistocene technology. There are reasons to believe that the Nsongezi civilization reached other parts of the world when the Bushmanoids spread throughout the length and breadth of the continent. It is no wonder that later immigrants found some base on which to build their own civilizations.

Nsongezi, located in Uganda around the north-west point of the Kagera River, seems to be the source of Buhaya's Stone Age innovations. Whatever developments took place at Nsongezi, they can be assumed to have been felt not only in the Kagera valley but also in other parts of Africa and the rest of the world. Nsongezi and Sango Bay culture apparently flourished in the first part of the Middle Stone Age, i.e. about 35000 BC.[10] Assuming that this dating can be substantiated, Buhaya would boast one of the most ancient civilizations. D. N. McMaster describes Nsongezi as 'one of the greatest hearths of African history'.[11] He cites millions of artefacts discovered in the Nsongezi area, making it probable that the place had attained a remarkable level of Stone Age development. While apparently much work has yet to be done to collect more information about the site, referred to sometimes as the Nsongezi 'factory', one might allude to the contribution of Buhaya to the development of man during the early years of civilization.

The Arrival of Bantu in Buhaya

This section appears to be a digression, taking us into a controversial field of anthropology relating to Bantu origins and migrations. The digression, however, is considered inevitable since the tribal structure of today cannot be amply explained without reference to its ethnic structure and origin. Migrations would help us to understand the technological attainments as well as the cultural components. In any case, reference to the anthropological theories will be confined to what is essential to the understanding of the foundations of the tribe.

Theories of Bantu Origin and Migrations

Being largely a Bantu group, the Bahaya should trace their origins in the southbound migratory waves which characterized the African communities of the first centuries AD. It is estimated that the first batch of Bantu had probably established itself on the western shores of Lake Victoria by AD 400 and their uninterrupted presence to date constitutes an important element in the character of the tribe. Some knowledge of Bantu origins would therefore facilitate an understanding of the cultural foundations of the Bahaya. In this connection, an examination needs to be made of Bantu roots, which were founded in cultures of these migrations and the cultural changes likely to have taken place then.

The term 'Bantu', which tends to defy unequivocal ethnical definition, has remained a linguistic classification connoting a group of African people using a language of the same etymological origin. Attempts to delineate the Bantu people solely on the basis of their physical characteristics, such as hair texture and complexion, has led to contradictory conclusions. Thus the linguistic criterion, incomplete as it might be, remains the only base for categorizing the Bantu.

According to *Zamani Mpaka Siku Hizi*,[12] the term 'Bantu' derives from the suffix –ATU (ANTU) used almost invariably by the linguistic groups of the race when signifying the word 'human being', examples *Muntu*, *Mtu*, *Munhu*, meaning the same thing in three Bantu tribal groups, and it is mainly on the basis of this word that the language group derived its name, BANTU. However, there is more in common among the Bantu languages than just one word; the prefixes, the suffixes and even the roots of words. Take the example of the word 'elephant', which in Beti (Cameroon) is *Zok*, Swahili (Tanzania) *Ndovu*, Haya (Tanzania) *Enjoju* and Kikuyu (Kenya) *Njogu*. As shown in Table III–1, the incidence of the core of the word is no accident but a fundamental relationship of the different languages.

TABLE III–1 *WORD RELATIONSHIP IN SELECTED AFRICAN LANGUAGES*

	SWAHILI	ENGLISH	HAYA (Tanzania)	BETI (Cameroon)	KIKUYU (Kenya)	SOTHO (Lesotho)	BAMBARA (Mali)	LUNYORO (Uganda)
1.	KIBOKO	HIPPO-POTAMUS	ENJUBU	HIPPO		KHULU	MALI	ENJUBU
2.	CHUI (JIKE)	FEMALE LEOPARD	ENGWE-ENKAZI		NGARI	LENGAU	WARANIN-KALAN	ENGO
3.	MTU	HUMAN BEING	OMUNTU	MOT	MUNDU	MOTHO	ADAMADEN	OMUNTU
4.	KULA	TO EAT	KULYA	NDIAN	KURIA	KOJA	DUMINI	KULYA
5.	NDOVU (TEMBO)	ELEPHANT	ENJOJU	ZOK	NJOGU	TLOU	SAMA	ENJOJU
6.	SIMBA	LION	ENTARE	MBWEMBWEM	MURUTHI	TAU	WARABA	ENTARE
7.	MTI	TREE	OMUTI	ELE	MUTI	SEFATE	JIRI	OMUTI
8.	ENDA	GO	GENDA	KELEK	THII	TSAMAEA	TAKA	GENDA
9.	ULEZI	FINGERMILLET	OBUROI		OCEMBE	MABELE	SANYO	OBURO
10.	MKONO	ARM	MUKONO	WOO	JUOKO	SEPHAKA	BOLOTEGE	MUKONO

According to J. H. Greenberg's analysis, the Bantu languages belong to the category of Niger–Congo languages, the other important members of the groups being West Atlantic, Mande, Voltaic, Kwa, Adamawa–Eastern and Benue–Congo.[13] Examples of languages in the subgroups are West Atlantic (Fulani), Mande (Bambara, Voltaic, Mossi), Kwa (Yoruba, Ibo), Adamawa–Eastern (Sango), Benue–Congo (Swahili, Kongo, Xhosa, Lingala). It is estimated that the Benue–Congo subgroup comprises about 600 languages spoken from the Bight of Benin to Zululand, the majority of which are Bantu. The non-Bantu *Congo–Benue* major languages are Efile and Tiv, found in Eastern Nigeria. Accordingly, the Bantu area covers a great part of Africa south of the Sahara, indicating that the term 'Bantu' has at least linguistic and geographical connotations and dimensions.

If the ethnical criterion of skin pigment, hair texture, etc., has proven inconclusive, it is because the hybrid theory, purporting that Bantu are a mixture of Negroids, Nilo-Hamitics and Negrillos, is untenable since it could not explain the linguistic affinity of the group. The only categorization base remaining is linguistic, confining the definition of Bantu to etymological inference. Attempts to move too far away from linguistic criteria have yet to establish a convincing case.

Archaeological and other historic research methods which offer a good alternative to linguistic criteria, must first establish a correlation between technological spread and social development, since technology can still be transferred irrespective of ethnic, geographical, linguistic or political boundaries.[14] However, archaeology and other disciplines can be used to test the hypotheses derived from the linguistic criteria.

Apparently, the Bantu group has much more in common than linguistic affinity. While the morphological identity has not been able to stand up on technical grounds, there are common bodily features traceable among the majority of the Bantu. From the point of view of sociology, the analysis of *Bantu Customs in Mainland Tanzania*, by P. van Pelt, concluded that, to a significant extent, the Bantu people share religious beliefs, kinship, habits, ceremonies and even the philosophy of life.[15] Though their customs might form part of cultural traits shared by other African ethnic groups, the Bantu identity has tended to remain tenacious over the centuries.

Two related questions of relevance to this study have attracted researchers, namely the original place of the Bantu stock and the migrations made to settle in the various parts of Africa. In the quest for the origin of the Bantu race, J. H. Greenberg also analysed the linguistic relationships of the tribes south of the Sahara.[16] By examining the etymological connections of the tribal languages, he concluded that the core source of the Bantu appears to have been around the Eastern Nigeria/Cameroon plateau and the Benue plateau; that is around the Adamawa Mountains, located between the Cameroon and Nigeria. Classifying African languages into four, namely, Niger–Congo, Afro-Asiatic, Sudanic and Clicks, he concluded that the Bantu languages fall within the Niger–Congo group and, by studying its composites, he inferred that the core origin of the Bantu was in the area around the watershed of the Niger and the Congo rivers.

D. F. McCall renders further support to Greenberg by pointing to the plausibility of the hypothesis that the Bantu origin might well have been in the region around the Benue River.[17] Christopher Wrigley supports the hypothesis by remarking that 'Greenberg's scheme of classification is taken as the basis for discussion because there is no other of equal comprehensiveness and plausibility'.[18]

George Peter Murdock feels that 'on linguistic grounds alone, it is impossible that the Bantu could have come from anywhere else' than the Cameroon–Nigeria border.[19] Basil Davidson also asserts that 'Negroes of the Bantu language group began a long and complex process of expansion and dispersal, launched several years ago from an original homeland in the country of the Niger–Benue confluence of modern Nigeria and Cameroon'.[20] This area corresponds to what is now known as the Adamawa region.[21]

Direction of the Migratory Waves

The second question which is as intriguing as the definition of the term Bantu and their origin, relates to the course of their migratory movements.

From the available data, Bantu migrations fall into three categories of hypotheses, based largely on the direction of movements. Firstly, there is the hypothesis of spontaneous growth of autonomous clusters of Bantu communities located in different parts of the African continent south of the Sahara.[22] Supposedly, the clusters started to snowball into larger communities and to intermix through migrations and warfare.

According to the second category of hypotheses, Bantu movements were from the south to the north or north-east. D. A. Wilson, for instance, writes that the Bantu might have arrived from the Congo (Basin) forests and the south.[23] Similarly, Zoe Marsh and G. W. Kingsnorth assert that the Bantu core-source is the Congo–Zambezi watershed.[24] More vague is the parallel proposition in *Zamani Mpaka Siku Hizi* that the Bantus originated from Uganda and Kenya from where they spread to other parts of Africa, including the West Africa region.[25] J. E. G. Sutton, too, feels that 'Bantu migrations into East Africa were probably from south, south-west and west'.[26]

The buttress of this south-to-north hypothesis, however, is contained in the work of Malcolm Guthrie, who postulates that Bantu origins are in the south, around the area which is now called Katanga, from where they spread in all directions to the Great Lakes.[27] In his 1962 article, Guthrie summarizes his classic contribution to the theory of Bantu language, origin and migration. Like Greenberg, he seeks to establish a relationship between etymological variations and historical events. He samples 200 Bantu languages from which he established 22,000 sets of cognates, each being a derivative from a selected number of words representing reflexes, or variations of such as suffixes and prefixes. A basic set of common words in the given languages was established, against which each sample language was compared, and the outcome was evaluated. By mapping the scores of sampled languages, deductions were made as to which ones were older or younger:

> The state of affairs revealed by the map includes a belt of high figures, termed the nucleus, stretching right across the Bantu area on both sides of the boundaries between the regions.[28]

The results point to the core around Katanga and give Swahili a high position in the centre. Guthrie goes on to conclude that Bantu might have spread from there to the north, south and east. Overall, however, despite the results obtained, it seems that the analytical techniques used need to be placed on a sound footing for their application to social sciences.[29]

The third hypothesis follows on Greenberg's basic conclusion that the cradle of the Bantu race is the Bantu/Congo watershed, as already discussed. Even assuming the origin was somewhere else, stress here is on the migration movement being in a southward direction.

By and large, the southbound direction of migration appears most plausible as the probable course of the Bantu race, even assuming that they were pushed by the Nilotic and Semitic invaders. While northward bound waves might have taken place, they ought to have been more of an exception than the rule. The problem of direction could have been compounded by the slow pace of migration, taking generations to cover a relatively short distance, thus making backwash migrations possible without reversing the general southward trend.

The Bunyoro Pass

Assuming the origin of the Benue–Niger watershed and the southward movement, Bantu migrations might have initially trekked south-eastwards to avoid the dense equatorial forests, then southwards, along the Nile valley to the highlands of Bunyoro. To reconstruct the route, one just needs to look at Map V–1.[30] From the Adamawa Mountains the eastward route would be along the watershed between the Chari and the Ubangi Rivers up to the border between Sudan and the Central African Republic. The journey would then be south-east along the watershed separating the numerous tributaries of the Ubangi River and those of the Nile in the Bahr el Ghazal region. The narrow, corridor-like watershed ought to have provided a better alternative route to the impassable marshes of the Bahr el Ghazal, bordered by the precipitous Abyssinian Mountains and the Lolibai Mountains further to the east and south. Emerging from the pass-like Nile Valley in Bunyoro, the migrating group had once again several choices of direction, to the south, east and south-west.[31]

The likely influence of Bunyoro in the migrations of the Iron Age Bantu groups might also be accounted for by its geography.[32] A large part of Bunyoro comprises a plateau of an average elevation of between 2,000 and 5,000 feet above sea-level, where the temperatures are relatively cool. The region is

Map III–1 NILE-CONGO WATERSHED

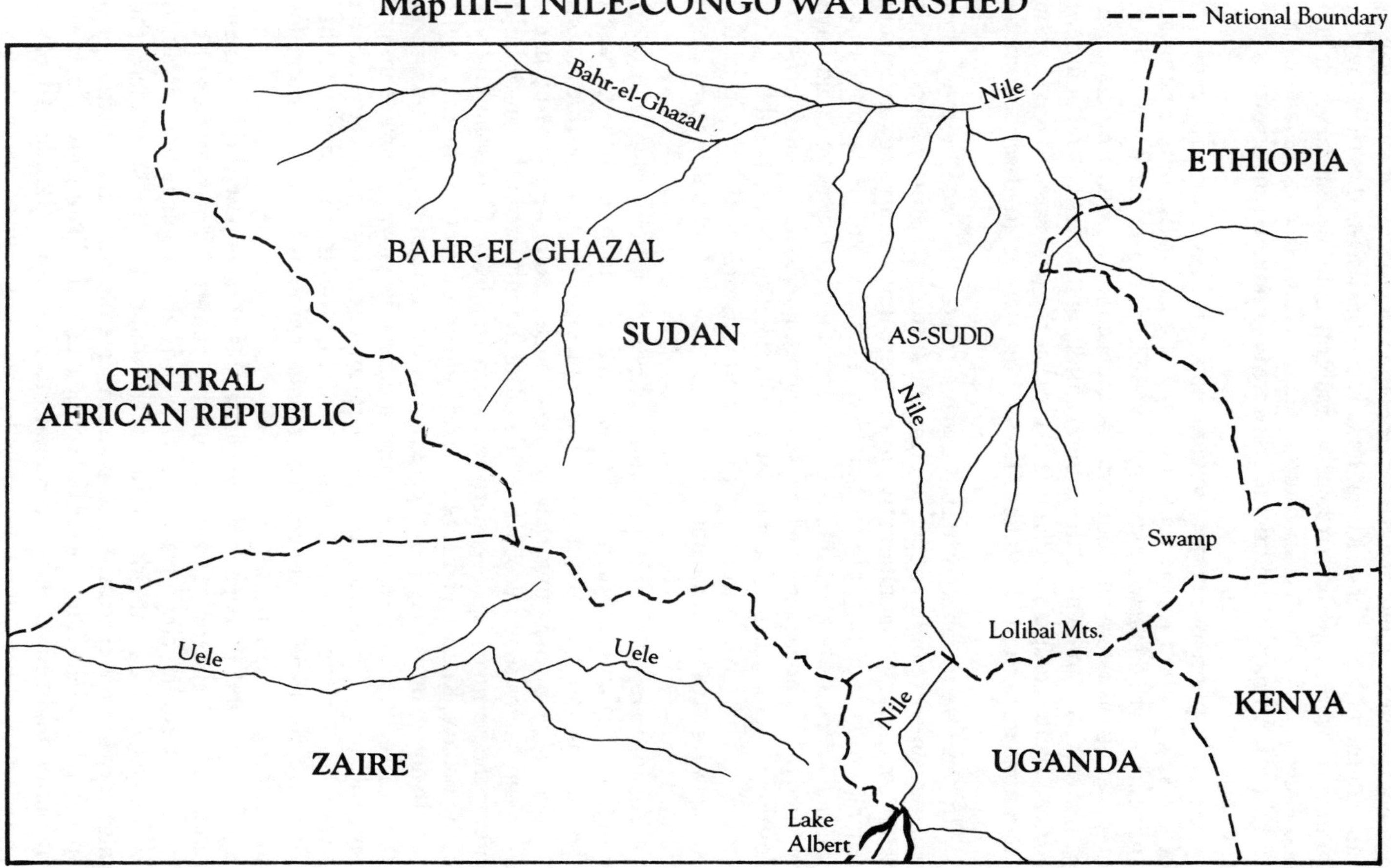

bordered to the west by Lake Albert (Mobutu) and to the east by the marshy valley of the Nile and Lake Kioga. Its soils can be described as rich, suitable for many types of crops, both tropical and subtropical. The natural vegetation of the region is savannah grass, interspersed with forests along the ravines and on hilltops. Among the traditional crops are fingermillet, yams, bananas and potatoes.

Several a priori assumptions tend to support the possibility that Bunyoro held a key position in the southward migrations. Firstly, most southward migratory waves had few good alternatives except to use the Bunyoro 'pass' in spreading to eastern and southern Africa. Secondly, the narrowness of the path might have influenced the cultural affinity of the Eastern and Southern African Bantu groups. Thirdly, it is likely that the pass was also used by the migrations from the Nile Valley. These three themes are described briefly below.

In the first instance, whilst the actual routes followed by the Bantu emigrants might not have been as clear-cut as the reconstructed account, it is not conceivable that alternative routes were limitless. Indeed, an equally tenable proposition might be that some waves followed the Atlantic coast to southern Africa while settling the land *en route*. Such a wave could have reached the Katanga plateau where, one may assume, a strong cluster of Bantu developed before dispersing further in all directions. Yet, possibly, some groups might have penetrated the equatorial forests directly from the Adamawa area to found the Equatorial Bantu tribes still inhabiting the Congo Basin.

Again, here, Sir Harry Johnston makes a firm proposition that, after mingling, the Bantu 'made their first great expansion in the countries between the Victoria and Albert Nyanzas',[33] thus implying the interiacustrine region.

Secondly, by assuming that Bunyoro might have been used by many migratory waves, support could be rendered for the cultural and linguistic links among the Bantu groups of eastern and southern Africa. Thus, some customs of the Bahaya, Kikuyu, Hehe, Shona and Zulu are closer than the case might be with non-Bantu groups, as reflected in the linguistic affinity. A comparison of some words among selected groups and Swahili provides further insight into this link. Table III–1 reveals more linguistic closeness between the Nyoro, Haya, Hehe and Sotho than, say, to the Swahili or Mandingo, further suggesting the likelihood of common migratory routes and a core source for the former tribal group.

Thirdly, and perhaps more relevantly, is the support the hypothesis renders to the coherence of interlacustrine culture.[34] The closeness of the language, customs, crops, traditional gods and beliefs could not be explained by the geographical integrity of the land surrounded by the lakes. Here, the migratory route comes in. At no point in time did the interlacustrine area appear to have been a homogeneous political unit; the likely cause of cultural similarity might have been a common migratory route. Besides, there are indications that the cultural waves had one direction, namely southwards.

Bunyoro and Buhaya

The bearing of 'the Bunyoro migratory pass' assumption on the history of the Bahaya is supported by some related events. In the first place, the early settlers in Buhaya formed part of the Bantu stock presently found in eastern and southern Africa, as could be explained by linguistic affinity. Within the interlacustrine group, the Bantus have close cultural identities including a language which can be understood without translation, common religious beliefs, gods and philosophy. Furthermore, there were unmistakable similarities in the economic activities of the tribes involved, including agricultural preferences, techniques and socio-economic systems.

In the second instance, the fact that Bunyoro was assumed to be a common station for many migrations, may shed light on the direction of the Bantu movement. Based on the research by Hans Cory, for instance,[35] seven of the original clans that settled in Buhaya originated in Bunyoro, as is indicated in Table III–2. As the table shows, indigenous clans in Buhaya came from Bunyoro or Uganda. Indeed, Bishop J. Kibira more categorically points out that 'at the time of migration from Bunyoro into Buhaya and Karagwe they came in clan groups each claiming to be of one ancestry and being under one clan head'.[36]

TABLE III–2 *ORIGIN OF BANTU CLANS*

Clans in Buhaya	Country or Region of Origin	Clans in Buhaya	Country or Region of Origin
1. Batundu	Bunyoro, Uganda	5. Basaizi	Bunyoro, Ankole
2. Bahunga	Bunyoro	6. Bakuma	Ihangiro
3. Banyuma	Buganda, Bunyoro	7. Baihuzi	Bunyoro
4. Basimba	Bunyoro	8. Bagombe	Bunyoro

Conclusively then, the migratory movement with respect to Buhaya at that time was from north to south, that is from Bunyoro to Buhaya. Given that several clans were involved, and the unlikelihood of the migrations occurring at the same time or originating from the same locations, the assumption of the southward direction of the Bantu migration is thereby given convincing support. The conclusion also adds evidence of close kinship among the interlacustrine tribes, in this particular instance, the Bahaya, Banyoro, Banyankole and the Baganda.

A supplementary argument needs to be introduced here, relating to whether Bunyoro itself might have been the core source of the migrations. As discussed already, however, Bunyoro was like a reservoir for the migrations from the north-east and north-west and, as such, it might not have been an ideal place for sustaining a strong and stable Bantu culture for centuries. Caution has to be exercised before making definitive conclusions which might contradict researched evidence on the origin of the pioneer settlers of Bunyoro. However, Sir Harry Johnston has contributed to the answer by pointing out that, some two or three thousand years earlier, the area comprising Uganda was settled by 'a horde of West African Negroes speaking a mother tongue of the Bantu languages'. He further observed that the source of the Bantu was possibly 'the north-west, from the region along the water-parting between the Congo and the Nile systems.'[37]

Early Bantu Settlers and the Clan System

From the foregoing analysis, there is no firm conclusion as to whether the first Bantu settlers in Buhaya were part of the southbound migratory waves; however, the probability is high. Oral history, together with written record, tends to put the major Bantu migrations in the second and third century AD, thus tending to confirm the estimated arrival of the first batch of Bantu stock in Buhaya around the fourth century AD.[38] Initially, the migrants might have been much closer in language, customs, technology and economic tendencies. In the course of migrating, none the less, one may imagine that the migrants acquired other cultures encountered *en route*. To trace the source of migrations, one has to examine social, cultural and linguistic traits and relate them to the path of the migrants.

Available evidence points to the probability that the early settlers of Buhaya came from the north, mainly from Bunyoro and Ankole. Assuming that the eastern part of Buhaya was covered with thick forests, it is likely that the first settlements took place in the western part, namely in Karagwe. Since the main foodstuff of the time was millet, preference in settling might have been given to grassy highlands which were similar to those in Bunyoro. Indeed, unwritten accounts tend to point to many clans in the east of Buhaya having had ancestors who migrated from Karagwe or Ankole.[39] Oral accounts tend to support the story of Karagwe having had a civilization much earlier than those on the east coast of the region. The reasons appear to be geographical. The possibility of the early migrations reaching Buhaya by boat from the east is rendered improbable by the primitive technology of the time. The land route through Karagwe remains the only logical alternative.

The numerous fast rivers and marshes along the west coast of the lake rule out the likelihood of migrants having arrived from the north or north-east. The remaining possibility might have been along the watershed between Lake Albert/George/Kivu on the one side, and the Kagera/Lake Victoria on the other.

Organizationally, the settlers grouped themselves into units, the most important being a *CLAN*. Normally, the necessary condition for membership was patrilineal kinship, though marriage and rituals might have bestowed affiliation. Simply, a clan was a group of people claiming the same patrilineal ancestors. Three characteristics identified one clan from the other. First was a clan name, e.g. Bahunga, Bakoba, etc., second was the totem or an animal taken as the clan symbol and third was a taboo which was an animal or a thing which members were forbidden to eat or even touch. As an illustration, the Bahunga clan has the frog (or other tail-less animals) as a totem while their taboo is the small intestine of a sheep. For the Basiita, the totem is chicken while the taboo is bushbuck. Another important feature of a Bahaya clan is that its members are totally forbidden to marry from within the clan itself and are expected to observe strict obligations as if they belonged to one family. The number of clan members is unlimited and, when the tribe comprised three-quarters of a million people, it reckoned about a hundred clans.[40]

Another general feature of the clan is that members claim the same ancestry or direct lineal descent from one source. A number of writers agree that a clan-cluster would share a lineage of seven or eight generations.[41] Though as a category of people, they claimed common totems, taboos, kinship, mutual obligations and civic duties, the membership did not form a close-knit economic unit. As a sociological unit, the clan provided a structure or community through which production and consumption could be influenced. Similarly, a clan sometimes acted as a political faction or party in influencing governmental action. Within its jurisdiction, the clan head had powers to impose any form of punishment on any of its members.

So far among the recorded descriptions of the Bahaya clan systems, the best is that of Hans Cory and M. M. Hartnoll, where clans are grouped into pure Hima, bastard Hima and Bairu.[42] In their analysis, the issue of the exogamous clan relationship, special names, totems and a compendium of Bahaya clans and their major features are presented. Their classification into three, however, is not as generally acceptable as one of the following pairs, Enfura/Abairu, Abengoma/Abahangoma, or Enfura/Abantu. A useful insight into the Bahaya clan system can be gained by reading Bishop Kibira's analysis of the clan concept. He effectively points to the definition of a clan as the answer given to the question 'OLI MUKI' meaning 'what type of category are you?'[43] The political system of the Bahaya clan fitted what Dr Lucy Mair categorized as a diffused government.[44] In case of emergency, the jurisdiction of the country was entrusted to the head of the leading clan, or chief, who co-ordinated activities until conditions returned to normal. Gradually, the position of chief and leading clan was institutionalized, thus becoming the central government.

During the period under discussion, it appears that the Batundu clan was dominant in many Buhaya localities, to the extent that the period between AD 400 and AD 1500 is sometimes referred to as the Batundu era. In Ihangiro, however, the ruling clan was the Bahutu, in Karagwe, the Basiita, and in Kiziba, the Bakuma.[45] The Batundu, associated largely with Kyamutwara, are believed to have established a very advanced system of clan rule, characterized by recognition of equality among clans. Though co-operation was expected whenever the situation so demanded, each clan was otherwise left free to operate autonomously during normal periods.

Besides the Batundu clan, which was perhaps the most outstanding, other pioneer groups are the Bahunga, Bagombe, Banyuma, Basimba, Basaizi and

Bakuma.[46] While it is unlikely that these clans arrived at the same time, it has already been indicated that they generally immigrated from the north, namely from Bunyoro, Buganda or Ankole. It is believed that the Bahaya culture owes a great deal to the characteristics of each of these clans as well as to the miscegenation among them.

In practice, a clan was more than a group of kith and kin for it constituted a social, economic and administrative unit. Socially, each individual identified himself fully with his clan and, through it, interacted with other people at the village and national level. The clan in turn demanded unqualified loyalty from each member. Honours gained from hunting, military or other public duties were received in the name of the whole clan. Besides administering justice, the clan facilitated liaisons with other clans. Inter-clan disputes would be settled by elders' courts, a practice which was upheld by the colonial powers and which survives to the present day. In short, the clan system constituted the social, economic and cultural tribal structure which underwent transformation in the process of economic changes from loose type government to dynastic centralized control.

Economic Revolution Based on Fingermillet

Both the Stone Age cultures and the early waves of migrations appear to contain an element of relevance to the roots of the Bahaya tribe. Preoccupied with the quest for food, and lacking specialization at the individual and community level, prehistoric man led a low level of life which hardly varied from one locality to another. Cultural differentiation emerged when occupation began to change according to environment, food availability, technology and social structures. The differentiating process itself depended on many factors. Very likely, at the time of the settlement of the Bantu stock, agriculture was still of a primitive or transitional type, undergoing a change from a gatherer-hunter category of occupation to a predominantly farming activity, which accounted for a greater portion of food supply.[47] The change implied that the tribe was able to concentrate on farming and, for that matter, on fingermillet agriculture, which was facilitated by hoe-cultivation and good land.

One can imagine that, on arrival, the settlers would try to create living conditions which were similar to those prevailing in the areas of origin or of transit. Being basically an agricultural people, they would have tended to cultivate such crops as yams, bananas and millets. Owing to the primitive techniques available then, shifting agriculture was commonly resorted to; a cultivated piece of land would be abandoned for some years before being used again. Such an agricultural system encouraged people to shift their farms and habitation frequently.

The economic highlights of the period under consideration derive from a number of factors, foremost being the preceding culture of the Stone Age, Pigmy and Bushman. The second was the geography of Buhaya, characterized by rich soil, heavy rainfall and cool, equitable temperatures. The third was the Bantu culture which had benefited from the long route of migration from the Bight of Benin, through Uganda to Buhaya. Fourthly, there was the dominance of fingermillet which revolutionized the way of life and led to the development of the tribal character, out of which grew the culture existing there today. These factors are reviewed briefly in the following paragraphs.

To a significant extent, the Stone Age cultural heritage facilitated the adjustment of Bantu immigrants to Buhaya. The superior hunting techniques of Negrillos also proved a major benefit which was derived from the contact of the two cultures. The use of the bow, the poison-arrow, as well as ditch traps was acquired by the settlers. Equally useful were the methods of gathering fruits and collecting edible insects.[48] It is also assumed that Bantus benefited from the advanced pottery skills of the Pigmies. Whatever was developed by Stone Age man, however, enriched the life of the settlers who improved upon it as well.

Features of the Fingermillet Revolution

In a way, the agronomic characteristics of the Eleusine explain its economic importance. As a millet, it does not require heavy rainfall and can flourish on different soils, though it does better in areas at an altitude of 2,300 metres above sea-level. The grass-like plant, which grows no higher than 1–2 metres, produces an inflorescence of six spikes each about 10 cm. long, which, in the early stages, look like fingers — hence the name fingermillet.

Its small-sized grain protects it from destruction by pests and this renders it easy to store for up to seven years without damage. As it dries quickly in sunshine, its storability, durability and handling is relatively easy. Other advantages include a high yield, of about 450–900 kg. per acre on normal unfertilized soils. Above all, its flour forms an excellent food which can be prepared in different ways, such as a soft porridge-type pudding, as well as bread and meal. To date, it is estimated that about 200 million people in different parts of the world depend on it for sustenance.

When exactly the Eleusine Coracana reached Buhaya, or even where it came from, has yet to be established. However, by carbon dating, J. Esmond Clark has indicated the existence of the crop in Eastern Ethiopia between 1063 and 83 BC.[49] Basil Davidson observes that '... the hoe cultivation of millet and some varieties of sorghum ... appeared in eastern and central Africa some two thousand years ago, and spread gradually southwards with the extension of early Bantu cultures'.[50] Since these dates are well ahead of the estimated arrival of the Bantu stock in Buhaya, there is a possibility that fingermillet might have originated in Ethiopia and possibly had reached Bunyoro from where it was brought to Buhaya and later taken further south of Tanzania and beyond.[51]

However, many accounts, both oral and written, consistently tend to support the existence and dominance of fingermillet in pre-dynastic Buhaya. Oral accounts teem with episodes and sayings which indicate that fingermillet was the main crop of the tribe. Similarly, stories about the conquest of the

Nilo-Hamitics consistently show that the invaders established their influence by giving out fingermillet during times of famine and that the early ruling clans traded their kingdoms for the grain. A. G. M. Ishumi asserts that, during the period of early settlers of Kiziba, the 'staple food was fingermillet'.[52] Rehse also refers to fingermillet as having been an important foodstuff in traditional Kiziba.[53] Equally significant is that, until a few decades ago, the grain continued to be widely used for food in some parts of Ihangiro and Karagwe.[54]

If the crucial revolutionizing element of fingermillet was attributed to its storability, a complementary and necessary condition was its production, which depended mainly on good soil, altitude and the availability of arable land. Its harvest ensured food supply, thus reducing the threat of famine and making time available for cultural, political and other activities. The change affected all aspects of life, to the extent that it deserved to be termed a revolution.

For the early Bantu, the possibility of settling permanently in one location was enhanced by the storable quality of fingermillet. With granaries of storable millet which could last for years, there was no longer cause for shifting about, as the case might have been during the period of primitive agriculture, fruit gathering and hunting. Consequently, people settled in one place and larger communities evolved, necessitating more sophisticated forms of government and economy.

It was in terms of cultural development that the transformational effects of the crop appear to have been most pronounced. Thus, eating and working habits had to be adjusted to fingermillet-centred developments. With the time saved from itinerant agriculture, cultural activities were stressed, in particular as regards formal education, dancing and political discussions. Among other aspects affected by the revolution was the daily routine. Thus, the periods of the day were divided up according to the time for grinding the grain, boiling the water and taking the meal. Similarly, the seasons of the year were expressed in terms of activities relating to the agriculture of fingermillet, examples being the seasons for clearing the bushes, tilling, sowing, flowering of the plant and harvesting.

Planted in September, millet would be ready for harvesting in February, the period referred to as *Amagesha* or the harvest season. To vary and supplement the fingermillet diet were sweet potatoes, yams, *enumbu*, peas, beans, groundnuts and bananas.[55] The banana, however, was not intensively cultivated and might have been planted along the streams or in marshy places where it would grow without requiring regular care.[56] Sweet potatoes, groundnuts and *enumbu* were annual crops which could be grown on common land and were usually the woman's specialization; the yield reflected not only a higher level of consumption for the family but also the level of diligence on the part of its women members. Peas, beans and yams were cultivated along with other crops or even around the hut and could thus be tended by men, women or children. The bitter millet or *sorghum vulgare* was grown widely and used in brewing malts and wines. Owing to its bitterness, the vulgare was not in competition with Coracana as a food item although it took up a good part of the cultivated land otherwise devoted to fingermillet.

The impact of the changes associated with fingermillet is reflected in the development of economic sectors, commencing with agriculture. Other sectors, however, were also significantly affected, mainly commerce, industry, pottery, textiles, etc., as will be discussed briefly in the following paragraphs.

Commerce

There were two especially significant aspects of commerce in ancient Buhaya. First was the formative stage as man was evolving from an isolated individual jack-of-all-trades to being a member of a society based on the division of labour and economic specialization. Irrespective of the occupation, whether farming, fishing or hunting, and regardless of the level of production, there had always been the urge to exchange products so as to increase the variety of goods consumed. Commerce associated with the early stages of human development can be defined as 'subsistence-oriented trade confined to the neighbourhood and villages',[57] since it lacked specialization at the production and market level. It can be supposed, therefore, that the commerce carried on by the early Bantu settlers in Buhaya was of a subsistence type, featuring such local goods as yams, beans, mushrooms, fish and livestock, as well as metal, wood and basketwork items.

With the predominance of agriculture, the early immigrants made precocious advances not only in production and trading in foodstuffs but also in making related agricultural tools and implements. At some stage, the region must have undergone some form of economic specialization enabling a higher level of attainment of commercial exchange of these items.

Even in commerce, the supremacy of fingermillet was evident mainly in that it was the medium of exchange. Owing to its quality of durability or storability as well as its divisibility, fingermillet had the essential qualities of a medium of exchange. The commodity was measured in bundles (ekitende) which consisted of dried but unshredded crop wrapped in banana fibres. While the size of a bundle was not standard, its weight was such that a person could carry it about easily on his head while hawking it. When shredded, the grain would be measured in a basket container called *akaibo*, the contents of which varied between a kilo and two kilos. When in meal form, the commodity would be measured using ladles or *emiiko*, a unit of which was assumed to be adequate for a normal meal for one person.

A number of Bahaya proverbs are associated with fingermillet, a relevant one here being that 'he who is present cannot count the number of ladles to be obtained from a pot of fingermillet'. There were generally accepted rates of conversion, from the unshredded bundle of fingermillet to the retailer's container and even to the ladles. Wealth was also reckoned in terms of the number of fingermillet bundles in one's possession as well as the age of these bundles. The crop which had passed six or seven years would usually be discarded to give way to the fresh harvest and this was taken as a sign of abundance in the country. The bundle was also an important component in formal transactions such as the bride price and the payment of the tribute due to the chief.

Apparently, by the sixteenth century, trade in the region had already been linked to that of the central part of the African continent. Indeed, Brian M. Fagan argues that the stage of globalizing tribal trade might have commenced much earlier.[58] He cites the extensive and rapid growth of crops originating from other continents during the period where there was hardly any record on trade as proof of widespread commerce in Africa before European colonization.

Many other types of commodities entered the market, common instances being salt and iron. That salt was highly prized in Buhaya is evidenced by stories and expressions which also attributed its source to Kisumbwa, from where it was transported by hawkers to Buhaya. Sold in banana-fibre packets of about a kilo, salt would be used for almost any transaction. Prior to the sixteenth century, it appears that Kisumbwa was the single major external supplier though later, during the Arab trade, alternative sources might have been located.[59]

Iron was in adequate supply in Buhaya and its products probably formed a significant commodity of trade. Iron mines, seemingly dating back to the pre-dynastic period, are to be found in several parts of the region, thus indicating that the industry had perhaps been prevalent in Buhaya for centuries.

The ore was extracted from opencast pits though there were some deep and extensive mines. Complementary to mining were smelting and smithery which produced iron products such as knives and spears which were among the inter-regional export items of Buhaya. For the domestic market there was a big demand for the bushknife, used in clearing areas destined mainly for planting fingermillet.[60] Besides, there were the heart-shaped hoes produced in varying sizes for digging and weeding, while small knives were made for different purposes, including harvesting, peeling and shaving.

As a basic commodity, fingermillet gave rise to joint demand for such agricultural products as meat, fish and peas, used to make the accompanying relish. Equally importantly, it boosted the demand for the tools necessary for its production and consumption, as will be discussed further on.

Industry and Other Sectors

A good part of the industrial activities were basically influenced by fingermillet culture. Thus, among the industries of the period were blacksmithery, bark-cloth beating, pottery, metalwork, salt distillery, woodcarving and construction. Blacksmithery mainly involved the manufacture of agricultural implements and military tools, namely hoes, knives, sickles, spears and arrow-heads. The industry was vertically integrated, involving mining, smelting and hammering into shape. However, there was specialization on the basis of villages or clans and with respect to the type of industry.

Specialization in pottery depended to a large degree on the availability of clay and therefore clay-work was to be found normally in certain villages which had easy access to raw materials. Sometimes clans were specialized in pottery, in which case they benefited by handing down skills from generation to generation. Despite the likelihood that demand was high, given that each household needed utensils and that production was intensive, there is no evidence of the development of special technology for the process, such as the use of the wheel.

The work involved kneading the clay by treading and then making pots or other items which were baked. The items produced included large-mouthed pots for cooking fingermillet meal, long-necked pots for carrying water, small recipients for bowls, and extra large ones for storing fluids or brewing alcoholic drinks.

Barkcloth beating constituted an important aspect of the textile industry, involving the hammering out of barksheet into cloth, but excluded the growing of the tree, which constitutes a different undertaking altogether. Another type of industrial activity related to making leather apparel, which entailed scraping, cutting and sewing all types of apparel from dried animal skins. The third sector was based on weaving fibres into skirts by using raffia (obuhunge), banana and other forms of fibres.

Besides iron, other metals also gave rise to industries, the most important being copper, from which wire and rings for ornamental purposes were manufactured. The major chemical industry was the extraction of cooking salt from certain plants. This process involved burning leaves to obtain ashes which were then dissolved, filtered, boiled and evaporated before a concentrated solution of salt could be obtained. As salt was required for daily cooking, production was significant, although the operation was on an individual small-scale basis and no mechanized means were invented to facilitate large-scale production.

As residential houses had to be bigger and more comfortable to accommodate increasing and permanent settlement, the art of construction grew more specialized. The main common building was a conical hut (MSHONGE) thatched with special grass and which had walls made of polished elephant grass bound together by large cables of stick, the whole structure being supported by poles, some of which measured 30 feet high. The poles had to be carved in a certain way and the walls had to be woven by a craftsman to avoid leakage and to ensure artistic presentation.

Woodcarving required the use of the steel adze or knife for work on such objects as pillars or handles. An important object of woodcarving was the milk-can, the average contents of which were about one gallon; a special wood was used to ensure that the milk would not absorb its smell. Other carved objects were the bow and arrow, and the zither box or African harp. Every household had a wooden ladle for stirring the dough when preparing the millet meal.

Recapitulation

Examination of the Stone Age culture shows that the origin of the Bahaya is not unique when compared to interlacustrine or other tribes, or even the rest of mankind. The founders of the tribe were most likely straying migrants from the southbound waves of migrations that for centuries were prevalent throughout the continent of Africa. It is unlikely that the early years of settlement witnessed a tribal character which was markedly different from that of many other tribes. It was only after generations, when fingermillet became the predominant cultivated crop, that the tribal identity began to emerge.

The survey further underlines the often-stated need for placing prehistoric Buhaya in the context of other regions of Africa. The chronological remoteness of the period, however, allows only a general examination of the Stone Age culture which prevailed in the whole of sub-Saharan Africa, since Stone Age man belonged to no tribe nor was he confined to a single region.

The various techniques developed by Stone Age people enabled later civilizations to adapt to the changing environment; for instance, with the mastery of fire and the use of certain plants and creatures for food and medicine. In later epochs, man made greater strides in harnessing nature for obtaining food and shelter. He had invented techniques for hunting animals, birds and insects as well as for gathering fruits and berries from the forests. Genuine evidence of the existence of Stone Age man in Buhaya makes his achievements of greater pertinence to the cultural foundations of the tribe. The remoteness of the time of Stone Age cultures should in no way diminish their contribution to the civilization of the Bahaya.

If emphasis has been placed on the Stone Age, the major objective is to describe the period when the Bantu stock settled in Buhaya, around AD 300. It is presumed that the settlers originated from the interior of the Benue valley and migrated southwards to Bunyoro from where they dispersed, some groups settling in Buhaya and others going to other areas of the eastern and southern plateau of Africa. The arrival of Bantu stock laid the foundation of the tribe whose social organizations were based on the clan system. The claim on the land of Buhaya made by the original Bantu clans has been respected to this day through the communal land ownership system.[61]

The economic life of the tribe, however, changed radically with the introduction of fingermillet. The crop, by proving to be a reliable source of food, mainly owing to its quality of storability, constituted an assurance against famine and allowed for cultural development. It led to the strengthening of a loose type of governmental structure whereby clans or village groups acted autonomously except in the case of external invasion or emergency. Cultivation of fingermillet became the central activity which influenced industrial manufacture, pottery and other commercial activities. The fingermillet culture, however, was cut short by the arrival of a non-Bantu wave of migrants and we shall return to this question in the next chapter.

1. A zoological description of the fingermillet is provided later in this chapter. The grain is sometimes called Ragi or African Millet.
2. The Pleistocene era commenced about 2.5 million years ago and was characterized initially by the *Homo erectus*, e.g. Zinjanthropus, Australopithecus Africanus and Robustus.
3. For an original work on the prehistoric, *see* L. S. B. Leakey, *Stone Age Africa: An Outline of Prehistory in Africa* (London: Humphrey Milford, Oxford University Press, 1936). Useful notes are provided by Basil Davidson, in 'Africa in Historical Perspective' in *Africa South of the Sahara 1981–82* (London: Europa Publications Ltd., 1981), pp.3–18.
4. A brief comparison of the African racial groups is provided by the Institute of Swahili Research, *Zamani Mpaka Siku Hizi* (Arusha: East Africa Publications Limited, 1981), pp.2–7.
5. Institute of Swahili Research, *Zamani Mpaka Siku Hizi*, op. cit., pp.4–5.
6. An elaborate ethnic grouping is attempted by H. Mapunda, *Historia ya Mapambano ya Mwafrika* (Dar es Salaam: Tanzania Publishing House, 1976), pp.14–22.
7. Reference to the grindstone as a neolithic tool is to be found in the article of J. Desmond Clark, 'The Spread of Food Production in Sub-Saharan Africa', *Journal of African History*, III, 2 (1962), p.217.
8. Interesting accounts of cave drawings can be found in B. A. Ogot (ed.), *Zamani, A Survey of East African History* (Nairobi: East African Publishing House Ltd., 1969), pp.65–6.
9. *See* Priscilla Copeland Reining, 'Haya Land Tenure: Landholding and Tenancy', op. cit., p.58.
10. Cf. B. A. Ogot (ed.), *Zamani, A Survey of East African History*, op. cit., p.59.
11. D. N. McMaster, 'Change of Regional Balance in the Bukoba District of Tanganyika', *Tanganyika Notes and Records*, No.56, March 1961, pp.79–92.
12. Institute of Swahili Research, *Zamani Mpaka Siku Hizi*, op. cit., p.5. The word 'Bantu' is an answer given to the question 'what are you?' or 'who are you?'
13. J. H. Greenberg, *Studies in African Linguistic Classification* (New Haven: The Compass Publishing House, 1955). *See also*, by the same author, *Africa as a Linguistic Area* (University of Chicago Press, 1963). The strength of his analysis lies not only in his basing his work on previous research in the field, but also on common sense focusing on linguistic evidence.
14. For a plausible attempt to link archaeological and linguistic criteria, *see* A. A. Mturi, 'Ancient Civilisation of the People of the Great Lakes, the Linguistic and Archaeological Evidence: An Overview', in *La Civilisation Ancienne des Peuples des Grands Lacs. Colloque de Bujumbura* (Paris: Editions Karthala, 1979), pp.430–9.
15. P. van Pelt, *Bantu Customs in Mainland Tanzania*, op. cit., pp.33–42.
16. *See* J. H. Greenberg, *Studies in African Linguistic Classification* (New Haven, 1955), *Africa as a Linguistic Area*, op. cit. *See also*, by the same author, 'Linguistic Evidence Regarding Bantu Origins' in *Journal of African History*, Vol. XIII, 2 (1972), pp.189–216. For a more recent work, *see* Theophile Obenga, *Les Bantus* (Paris: Presence Africaine, 1980).
17. David F. McCall, *Africa in Time Perspective: A Discussion of Historical Reconstruction from Unwritten Sources*, op. cit.
18. *See* Christopher Wrigley's article, 'Linguistic Clues to African History' in *Journal of African History*, Vol. III, 2 (1962), p.269.
19. G. P. Murdock, *Africa: Its People and Their Cultural History* (New York: McGraw-Hill Book Company Inc., 1959), p.21.
20. Basil Davidson, 'Africa in Historical Perspective' in *Africa South of the Sahara 1981–82*, op. cit., p.3.
21. The region of Adamawa mentioned above lies between 10°E and 14°E and between 6°N and 8°N of the Equator and is shared between Cameroon and Nigeria. It is shielded in the south and south-east by the Adamawa Ranges, to the east by the Mandara

mountains and to the north by the Bauchi Plateau. Flowing in a south-westerly direction, the Benue River is fed by the tributaries Gongola, Pai and Waise from the north and Benue Far, Taraba and Donga from the south. As a watershed, the Adamawa is drained to the south by the Sanaga River and the tributaries of the Congo, mainly the Mambere and the Kadei. Its north-west drainage system has already been described above. The valley is extensively flat, between 0–200 metres above sea-level, and lies within the isohyet of 25 cm.–51 cm. and the savannah belt.

22. This viewpoint is shared by some indigenous African groups who, through oral traditions, claim to have been living in the region from time immemorial.

23. D. A. Wilson, *East African History 1000–1970* (Nairobi: Evans Brothers Limited, 1976), p.1.

24. Zoe Marsh and G. W. Kingsnorth, op. cit., p.7.

25. Institute of Swahili Research, *Zamani Mpaka Siku Hizi*, op. cit., pp.7–8.

26. B. A. Ogot (ed.), *Zamani, A Survey of East African History* (Nairobi: East African Publishing House, 1969), p.90.

27. M. Guthrie, 'Some Developments in Prehistory of the Bantu Languages', *Journal of African History*, Vol. III, 2 (1962), pp.273–82.

28. Ibid. p.277.

29. Among the obvious problems to be tackled in Guthrie's analysis is how to relate cognation with the chronology of tribal migration. To reduce the risk of application of statistical analysis to social behaviour, it might be necessary to know the languages rather well before comparing only the grammatical variations, including the false cognates. One such problem could be illustrated by a comparison between Dutch and Afrikans (South Africa), the latter having more archaic terms than Dutch. Similarly, words tend to move forwards and backwards over a period of time. *See also* Robert G. Armstrong, 'Glottochronology and African Linguistics' in *Journal of African History*, Vol. III, 2 (1962), pp.283–90.

30. An attempt to reconstruct the route was made by Sir Harry Johnston, *see*, *The Uganda Protectorate* (London: Hutchinson & Co., 1902), p.763.

31. *See* Maps III–1 and II–1.

32. Notes on the geography of the region are provided by B. W. Langlands, 'Uganda: Physical and Social Geography' in *Africa South of the Sahara 1981–82*, op. cit., p.1077. S. R. Karugile also concludes that Bunyoro became the principal link between the Nilotic north and the Bantu south because it was a centre for the salt trade; cf. *A Political History of Uganda* (Nairobi and London: Heinemann, 1980), p.26.

33. Sir Harry Johnston, op. cit., p.763.

34. The interlacustrine group is located within the area surrounded by Lakes Albert, Edward, Kivu, Tanganyika and Victoria, and includes the following tribes among others: Banyoro, Batoro, Baganda, Babuddu, Banyankole, Bahaya, Banyarwanda, Barundi, Baha, Bazinza and Bavinza.

35. Hans Cory and M. M. Hartnoll, *Customary Law of the Haya Tribe* (Cass Library of African Studies: Library of African Law No.7, London, 1945), pp.350–88.

36. J. M. Kibira, *Church, Clan and the World* (Uppsala: Almquist & Wicksell, 1974), p.24.

37. Sir Harry Johnston, *The Uganda Protectorate*, op. cit. p.763.

38. Basil Davidson estimates that the Bantu had spread to Central Africa by the beginning of the Christian era: *see* his article 'Africa in Historical Perspective', in *Africa South of the Sahara 1981–82*, op. cit., p.3.

39. It should be pointed out that Bahaya clans claim that their customs originated from Karagwe, Ankole and elsewhere; *see* Hans Cory and M. M. Hartnoll, *Customary Law of the Bahaya Tribe*, op. cit., p.255.

40. A description of totems and taboos is presented by Hans Cory and M. M. Hartnoll, *Customary Law of the Haya Tribe*, op. cit., p.287. The scientific and social explanation of totems and taboos has yet to be established.

41. Cf. Lucy Mair, *Primitive Government*, op. cit., pp.16–17. *Also* P. van Pelt, *Bantu Customs*

in Mainland Tanzania, op. cit., p.93, and Iris Berger, *Religion and Resistance*, op. cit., p.6.

42. Hans Cory and M. M. Hartnoll, *Customary Law of the Bahaya Tribe*, op. cit., p.287.
43. J. M. Kibira, *Church, Clan and The World*, op. cit., p.18.
44. Lucy Mair, *Primitive Government*, op. cit., p.78. Elsewhere it is called the amorphous system, cf. E. Colson, op. cit., pp.51–3.
45. An original analysis of the Bantu clan political system is presented by J. F. Mbwiliza, 'The Hoe and the Stick: A Political Economy of the Heru Kingdom c. 1750–1900', in *La Civilisation Ancienne des Peuples des Grands Lacs, Colloque Bujumbura* (Bujumbura: Editions Karthala, 1979), pp.100–14.
46. For a list of the main clans in Buhaya, *see* Hans Cory and M. M. Hartnoll, ibid., pp.287–349. *See also* Padre Willibald Mupapi, *Amakuru G' Abaihuzi Ba Buhaya* (Bunena: Rumuli Press).
47. The transformation of primitive agriculture in Africa is described by Basil Davidson in his article 'Africa in Historical Perspective', in *Africa South of the Sahara 1981–82*, op. cit., p.6.
48. Three kinds of insects are used as food by the Bahaya: grasshoppers (ensenene), termites (obushwa) and sandflies (eishami). Traditionally, Bahaya do not eat any poultry, though chickens were kept for telling the time and because of superstition. The latter implies cutting open the abdomen of the chicken and prognosticating the future by examining the intestines. Cf. J. F. Cunningham, *Uganda and Its People*, op. cit., p.286.
49. J. Desmond Clark, 'The Spread of Food Production in Sub-Saharan Africa', *Journal of African History*, Vol. III, 2 (1962), pp.211–18.
50. Basil Davidson, 'Africa in Historical Perspective', in *Africa South of the Sahara 1981–82*, op. cit., p.6.
51. The Wabena and Wahehe have known the culture of fingermillet for many years. Indeed, the Wabena (Wulesi) derive their name from Kubena = to harvest fingermillet with bare hands without using a knife. *See* Michael Musso, *Mukwava Na Kabila Lake* (Arusha: Eastern Africa Publications Limited, 1968), p.6.
52. Abel G. Ishumi, 'The Kingdom of Kiziba', *Journal of World History*, Vol. XII, 4 (1971), p.718.
53. Hermann Rehse, *Kiziba Land und Leute* (Stuttgart: Verlag von Strecker & Schröder, 1910), p.25.
54. The areas where fingermillet continued to be in wide use were Ngote in Ihangiro and Burigi in Karagwe. For additional evidence on fingermillet, *see* Fr. Paul Betbeder in *Journal of African History*, Vol. XIII, 4 (1971), p.739.
55. For an insight into food crops in Sub-Saharan Africa, *see* J. Desmond Clark, 'The Spread of Food Production in Sub-Saharan Africa', op. cit., pp.211–18.
56. More precise specifications of some of the crops show that the Latin names of the crops were: sweet potatoes = ipomea batata (enfuma), earth nuts = voandzeia subterranea (enshoro), big yams = imonea batata (ekirai), oblong potatoes = coleus (enumbu).
57. Richard Gray and David Birmingham (eds.), *Colonial African Trade* (London: Oxford University Press, 1970), p.3.
58. Ibid.
59. In Uvinza, which is the same region as Kisumbwa, salt mines were located at Bulebe, Isanga and Bukene; *see* Andrew Roberts in Richard and David Birmingham, op. cit., p.40.
60. Bushknives are called 'Mahyo' and this is the origin of the greeting 'Mahyo' which a passer-by addresses to one working the land. In fact, the greeting 'Mahyo' means 'I wish you (farmer) bushknives to facilitate your work!'
61. The system is known as Buharambwa and it is described by Hans Cory and M. M. Hartnoll in *Customary Law of the Bahaya Tribe*, op. cit., pp.113–15.

CHAPTER IV

THE BANANA/ENGAJU REVOLUTION AD 1500–1890

Introduction

The period covered in this chapter extends over four centuries, starting from AD 1500. Given that a single chapter cannot do justice to such a long period, an attempt will be made to deal briefly with the historical account while aiming to highlight the economic aspects. Economically, the period stands in contrast to the preceding fingermillet centuries it displaced and from which it germinated. The transition from one epoch to the other was marked by a switch from fingermillet, as a dominant food crop, to bananas. Concomitantly, social and cultural changes were taking place, mainly as a result of the invasion of the Nilo-Hamitics who established dynasties and political structures. Given the incomplete historical records, the overall objective is to describe and portray the economy of Buhaya during the period.

Background to the Title

The banana constitutes the staple food for the Bahaya and gives rise to the habitation known locally as kibanja (plural: bibanja). While the plant may have been introduced in Buhaya a long time prior to the Bantu settlement, its intensive cultivation is generally attributed to a later wave of settlers of Nilo-Hamitic stock who allegedly arrived in the sixteenth century. It is this banana-based culture which constitutes the focus of this chapter.

The cut-off points for the period under consideration are not watertight, as the commencement date of 1500 is an estimation rather than a fact derived from accurate records. The year 1890 is certainly arbitrary, given that the Hamitic influence in Buhaya is still alive and strong, and forms an important ingredient of the culture and history of the tribe. The economy of this period derives from three elements, namely the Nilo-Hamitic migrants, the dynastic political structure and the agricultural revolution based on the combination of the banana and the longhorn breed of cattle. Prima facie, the elements of governmental structure outweighed the others, though a closer look would reveal a significant correlation among all the three factors. Thus, the arrival of the Nilo-Hamitic stock assumes a special economic significance based on cattle ownership which distinguishes them socially and occupationally and identifies them with prosperity attributed to cattle manure. With increased banana production resulting in enhanced governmental control, both the dynasty and economic growth were assured of continuing symbiotic survival.

During the period, the economy of Buhaya was influenced by the cultivation of the banana plant, which depended on cattle manure for sustained good yield. Considering the plant and the manure as joint inputs for banana production, the economy of the time had to be explained in terms of both variables, whose significance was about equal. For this reason, the title of the chapter is shared between bananas and the longhorn cattle breed locally known as *engaju*.

In a way, the importance of the period 1500–1890 derives from a more recent and reliable historical record kept by the Arabs and the Europeans who visited the area for the most part in the nineteenth century. But equally important is its dynastic characteristic of strong centrally organized kingdoms, which encouraged more conspicuous military, political, economic and cultural events that are easier to remember. Above all, the dynasties themselves can facilitate the dating of events.

The Nilo-Hamitic People

The term 'Nilotic' or 'Nilo-Hamitic' is as imprecise and misleading as 'Bantu' when referring to a racial group. Literally, it connotes the people who inhabit or inhabited the Lower Nile Valley from the Mediterranean Sea to the Ghazel region in the south of Sudan. Accordingly, among distinct ethnic groups, one could count the Caucasians, the Semitics, the Nubians, Cushitics, Omotics and Nilo-Saharans, the major tribes of which were the Shilluk, Nuer, Azande, Dinka, Anuak, Bari, Baggaka, Topotha, Loturo, Acholi, Moru-Madi, etc.[1]

Attempts to group the Nilotics on purely ethnic lines have been frustrated by miscegenation and intermigration over the centuries, as well as by the lack of differentiable physical attributes which tend to vary widely even within the same tribe. An account published by the Brooklyn Museum of Antiquity concludes that racial division is almost impossible since the differences are gradual and, as one moves southwards from the Delta to the Upper Nile, skin colour gets darker and the waviness of the hair diminishes.[2]

The linguistic classification is more confused, given that the Nile region was a frequent victim of non-African invasions of cultures and languages.

Geographically, the Nilotics belong to the Nile Valley but their culture varies not only from locality to locality but also from period to period and both elements should be taken into account when talking about the Nilotic invasion of the south. The Lower Nile, including Northern Sudan, had closer cultural ties, owing to its accessibility from Asia Minor and Europe. The marshy region which now forms the Southern Sudan was thus inaccessible from the north and was ideal for autonomous civilizations which, from period to period, have had to overflow southwards in migratory waves, thus giving rise to cultural collision between the Nilotics and the Bantu. Indeed, there might not have been military invasions as such but rather rivalry for economic or political domination. In those cases where there was no rivalry or shortage of land, as in the case of the Masai, no collision arose. As land seekers, the

Nilotics might have had little to offer in the way of culture, for even their social values were apparently learnt from the Bantu mores-oriented societies.[3] Iris Berger argues convincingly that the Bachwezi culture itself, on which the Nilotic dynasties based their domination, might have been stolen from Bantu mythology. This argument is supported by the experience of the Masai and the Nandi who have tenaciously stuck to a traditional culture which is different from that of the surrounding communities. Even Nilotic superiority in iron and steel working appears to have originated from the Bight of Benin, where development in the use of iron, copper and other metals had advanced significantly from as early as the first century BC.

History, however, has not yet advanced convincing arguments as to why the Bantu tended to fall easy prey to Nilotic invasions. Speculation might suggest that the scarcity of land and the hostile surroundings of the Upper Nile homeland could have forced the Nilotics to fight desperately, whenever conditions so demanded, against the Bantu, who were described as peace-loving, nature-pampered communities. However, the war techniques of the Nilotics might provide a more acceptable explanation.

An equally important explanation lies in the fact that the Nilotics were not primarily empire builders but rather interested in seeking good land for settlement. It appears that they would fight to get land for agriculture or for livestock.[4]

Indeed, some oral accounts relate how the Nilotics ingratiated themselves with the Bantu communities, won their confidence through gifts including milk, meat and cattle, and finally took over the political reins.[5] The Nilotic ethnic tenacity was then deployed to sustain their political dominance.

The apparent difference in character orientation between the Nilotics and the Bantus might have had some bearing not only on the military conquests of the past centuries but also on the political factions in Buhaya, as well as in the majority of sub-Saharan states. Struck by the character of the Bantu, Speke remarked that when they see a stranger in their area, they 'allow him to do and see whatever he likes. They desire his settling amongst them, appreciate the benefits of commerce and civilization and are not suspicious, like the plundering pastorals, of every one coming with evil intentions towards them'.[6]

The Development of Enfura Rule

Two groups of Nilo-Hamitic migrations are of direct interest to this account. First is the group from which the Bachwezi dynasty was established. Second is the Luo group, arriving from what is now known as Southern Sudan, who migrated about AD 1480–1500 to north Madi, Acholi, Lango and further on to Busoga and the Kavirondo Gulf. The earliest Hamitic group to deal with the Bahaya was the Bahinda, who claimed Egyptian origin and Bachwezi ancestry. The salient features of the Bachwezi legend include the divine myths and the diversity of the contradictory versions of these myths. Among the elaborate attempts to unravel the details of the legend are the works of Iris

Berger and Dr Israel Katoke.[7] The important genealogical links of the legend tend to commence with ISAZA, the last of the Batembuzi clan which ruled Bunyoro, who married NYAMATA, daughter of an underworld god called NYAMIYONGA, and begot a son, ISIMBWA, who grew up to become king. The latter was involved in two historic marriages. The first was in Bunyoro to NYINAMWIRU, daughter of Bukuku, a commoner regent, by whom he begot a son, NDAHURA. The second was to NYABIRYO, daughter of Mukidi, who lived in the eastern part of Uganda, and by whom he had a son, KYOMYA. The two half-brothers, NDAHURA and KYOMYA, are the key characters of the Bachwezi legend.

NDAHURA, who succeeded Bukuku as king, later abdicated his throne in favour of his son, WAMARA. For reasons which are not very clear, WAMARA abandoned the throne and vanished into the underworld and this marked the end of the Bachwezi dynasty. It is further claimed that among WAMARA's famous sons were MUGASHA and RUHINDA KIBONABAGABE, founder of the Bahinda dynasty, as will be discussed later.[8] With the arrival of the Babiito invaders, the sons escaped to other regions to found other kingdoms.

As for KYOMYA, legend has it that he travelled widely in the eastern part of Uganda and that he begot twin sons by a woman he encountered while touring the area around Mount Elgon. Some accounts identify the woman as NYATWORO, daughter of Rabongo Omukidi, who was of Nilotic extraction.[9] To the twins, ISENGOMA RUKIDI MPUGA and KATO KIMERA (KINTU), was attributed the founding of the Babiito dynasty of Bunyoro, Kitara and Kiziba. RUKIDI MPUGA was supposed to have invaded Bunyoro and to have taken over the throne from WAMARA. KINTU pushed southward to establish the Babiito empire of Kitara, Buganda and Koki. KINTU's son, KAGANDA, is believed to have conquered the area around the Kagera River, including Kiziba where he killed NTUMWA, the popular leader of the Bakuma clan, thereby earning himself the name 'Kibi', meaning 'the Wicked'.

The relevance of the Bachwezi–Babiito legends to Buhaya is their influence on the thinking of the ruling families. The Bahinda and Babiito attributed their supremacy to the divinity of their ancestors, who allocated the monopoly of power to certain families. Equally important, the legend fits Buhaya into the political and historical matrix of the interlacustrine communities. Further, it sheds light on the political dimension which played an important role in shaping the history of the region during the period AD 1500 to 1900.

Salvaging the remnants of the Bachwezi dynasty, RUHINDA conquered Buhaya, Karagwe, Burundi and Buzinza.[10] The Bahinda dynasties, named after the founder, RUHINDA, have survived to date and their stories contain accounts of his adventures. Most of his success, however, is attributed to his personal qualities, in particular his exceptional physical and intellectual capabilities. It is said that he could cover long distances in a short time and had a flair for negotiating with governments and people who came his way. Part of the account tells how he travelled to Buddu, Koki, then to Karagwe, Ihangiro and Uvinza and was returning home through Kiziba when he died.[11] However, history here is so intricately intermingled with legend, superstition and politics that focus should be on the consequences and not on the events, whose accounts vary from locality to locality.[12] The bold attempt of Dr I. Katoke to organize the tales about Ruhinda has, however, greatly facilitated the discussion of the subject, including the mapping of the trips from Bunyoro to Karagwe, Buzinza and Ihangiro (known in these tales as Kiziramuliro, ruled by NKOMBYA EYA KAIRU).[13]

In Kiziba, the Babiito was the last invading dynasty from the north before the European era and it has retained its lineage to date, thus giving Kiziba a political orientation which is significantly different from that of the rest of Buhaya where the Bahinda and Bankango have been the ruling families. Perhaps this difference might partly explain some cultural deviations between Kiziba and the other kingdoms, possibly caused by the rivalry between the Bachwezi and the Babiito rulers. Furthermore, Kiziba has significant cultural attachments to Kitara and Buganda.[14]

Even after the arrival of the Bankango as the third major dynasty sometime in 1750, there was no significant change in the existing political structures, at least from the point of view of the ruled. Therefore, one can generalize about the period 1500–1890 as having been dominated by the dynastic Nilo-Hamitic clans referred to as ENFURA,[15] who shared a number of characteristics, the first and basic one being their place of origin. The latter might explain the similarity in the political systems that were established and the economic bias. As a non-Bantu ruling minority, their presence implied fundamental and cultural conflict.

The term 'ENFURA' came to refer to a social group of three components, one being the reigning clans of the Babiito in Kiziba, the Bankango in Kyamutwara and Bugabo, and the Bahinda in the remaining kingdoms.[16] The second component was the Hima clans who were Nilotics as well but whose occupations were mainly cattle rearing. The third component was the Bantu clans, elevated by the Mukama to the status of Enfura in recognition of such feats as prowess and marriage to members of ruling clans. Membership of the Enfura group entailed obligations and rights. Thus, members were under an obligation not to intermarry with commoners, nor to sit at the same table or drink from the same containers. Their conduct was to be marked by grace, a sense of honour and unqualified loyalty to the king.

Their most important right was to be first class citizens, a privilege which was exercised with restraint during the takeover from the Bantu but which intensified during the nineteenth century, to such a degree that they were entitled to a different code of justice and could even usurp property. Above all, they controlled the economy through cattle, and later through feudal land, and demanded servitude from the non-aristocrats.

As a social cluster, the Enfura were identified with domination over the

Bantu clans, whose members were collectively referred to as ABAIRU or serfs who, by definition, were second-rate citizens. Several factors, however, combined to extenuate this domination. Foremost was that the class division was not on ethnic lines. The Nilo-Hamitic stock, having travelled through Bantu kingdoms in the north before arriving in Buhaya, where they took up a farming-cum-pastoral way of life, had intermarried to the extent that physical differences were no longer a distinctive mark. Secondly, they were in a minority and therefore were absorbed culturally into the century-old Bantu social systems.[17] Thirdly, the Bantu clans were very coherent and deeply attached to their culture and had developed a leadership and wealth which easily rivalled that of the Enfura. This rivalry might partly explain the tendency towards dynastic tyranny later in the period under consideration.

Iris Berger tends to contrast the above-mentioned factors in Rwanda, Burundi and Uvinza. The percentage of Hamitics was 16.59%, 12.39% and 2% respectively, the Uvinza figure being closer to that of Buhaya. The divisions between ruler/ruled clans tended also to be ethnically pronounced in Rwanda (Hutu/Tutsi), Uvinza (Abaha/Abatusi), Ankole (Abairu/Abahima) and Buhaya (Abairu/Enfura). She also notes a close correlation between ethnic coherence and occupational adherence.[18] The Tutsi, by remaining a pastoral group, safeguarded their culture and physical attributes and therefore their ethnic group. In Buhaya, however, the Enfura group could not claim ethnic distinction and their main occupation of keeping cattle was abandoned to the Abairu in return for tribute or servitude. Thus the group suffered from lack of ethnic and occupational identity and depended only on economic and political status, both of which were fluid and challengeable by the Bantu. Above all, the servitude role in Buhaya was only token, since most toil was undertaken by migrant labour from surrounding kingdoms. The only base of Bahinda monopoly to power was religious; they claimed that the gods had so ordained. But the argument could not have convinced the Bantu who had their own gods long before.

Undoubtedly, the economic base was a shaky one but it may explain the political system in many ways. Firstly, the dynasties were uncertain of their powers because the ruled were not convinced of their autocracy. Therefore, the kingdoms in Buhaya remained manageably small to ensure control over a highly intriguing tribe.[19] Secondly, this explains the tendency towards tyranny on the part of the Enfura rulers who strove to tighten their grip on the ruled. How far these forces might have gone if Europeans had not arrived will remain a historian's conjecture.

The Nilotic domination was distinguished by a number of unique features, the foremost being dynastic political systems where the ruling clans were of Nilo-Hamitic stock.

The second characteristic was the similarity in the political techniques and system established. The strangers would initially befriend the Bantu clans and later usurp power. Legends are congruous on this approach specifying that conquests would be undertaken once the dynasties had established their reign.

An illustration of this approach is the ascent to power of the Bachwezi in Bunyoro, the Bahinda and the Bankango in Kyamutwara.[20]

There is evidence to prove that the dynasties negotiated their way upwards rather than subduing the Bantu by military power. In the first instance, the original clans retained their right of ownership to all the tribal land through the Muharambwa system. Under this system, the members of the original clans owned the soil and all communal land in the name of the Bahaya people and foreigners would be allowed ownership only with the consent of trustee clans in whose name was vested the tribe's right. Thus, the inalienable claim of the Bantu clans over the soil was recognized by the Enfura as a precondition for their settlement and became institutionalized through the *Muharambwa* system.[21]

The third characteristic lies in the manner in which the dynasties were perpetuated. The king, Mukama (plural: Bakama), could be succeeded only by his clan relatives, who, together with the aristocracy, were discouraged from intermarrying with the Bantu, thereby sustaining the monopoly of the ruling few. To strengthen the dynastization process, the sovereign claimed divine powers by which he could influence people's lives even after his death. This belief in the aristocracy of the dead, known as thanatocracy, constitutes the basis of the BACHWEZI dynasty.[22]

Further dynastic dimensions can be illustrated by the experience of Ihangiro. Firstly, succession was restricted to the male offspring or heirs of the Mukama.[23] The public property inherited included land, palaces, drums, places of worship, tenants and slaves, all of which had to be administered in accordance with the custom of the nation. The Mukama's personal property, however, would remain separate from public property so as to give him the necessary security when no longer occupying the throne. It was also his prerogative to choose the capital of the kingdom and, given that only light infrastructure was involved in establishing such headquarters, the capital changed with nearly every new reign. In the case of Ihangiro, kings were identified by the location of their 'head offices', as illustrated in Table IV–1.

Table IV–1 shows the major kings of Ihangiro commencing with Nkombya, the last Bantu king, who was subjugated by Ruhinda, the offspring of the Bachwezi dynasty. One counts twelve Bakama between Ruhinda and the arrival of the Germans in 1890; that is over a period of four centuries. On average, a king ruled some 33 years, which is possible since many of them might have assumed the throne at a relatively young age.[24] It is possible that long reigns were as common during the precolonial period as they were during the subsequent period. As shown in the table, only five Bakama are likely to have occupied the throne during the 100 years following the beginning of German administration in Buhaya.

A still better example of the dynastic development is the experience of Kyamutwara, as can be seen in Table IV–2. For one thing, it has a greater variety of ruling clans. Thus, there were at least three Bantu clans which ruled the kingdom in pre-Nilo-Hamitic times, the Bahutu, Batundu and Bahunga.

TABLE IV–1 *BAKAMA BA IHANGIRO*

	MAJOR NAME	LOCATION OF CAPITAL	REMARKS
1.	NKOMBYA EYA KAIRU	NSHAMBA BUNYAGONGO	Last of Bantu kings, conquered by Ruhinda.
2.	RUHINDA KIBONABAGABE	NO CAPITAL	Founder of Hinda dynasty. Remnant of Bachwezi.
3.	RUHINDA	MUSHULE	First effective Bahinda king.
4.	NYARUBAMBA	KICHUMU	
5.	RUHINDA	MISIKILA	
6.	NTARE	KATWELERE	Powerful.
7.	MULAMILA	KIKONGOLO	Civil wars between Mugongo and Ihaya.
8.	BHUTTO	MAHANE	Imbecile and blind king.
9.	NYARUBAMBA	BUGARAMA	
10.	MUGUNDA	ITONGO	
11.	NTARE	BUGEMBE	
12.	KATANAGI	NTUNGAMO	
13.	NYARUBAMBA	MULEBA	Arrival of Germans.
14.	RUHINDA (HENERICO)	MULINZI	Start of British rule.
15.	MUGINDA (PETRO)	RUBUNGO	Democratic and progressive (see Chapter VI).
16.	NTARE (SILVESTER)	KABALE	
17.	NYARUBAMBA	RUBUNGO	Titular chief only.

The last Bantu Mukama was Kashale of the Bahunga clan, whose headquarters was at Muhutwe.

Bahinda rule arrived there rather later than in Ihangiro, with Bwogi bwa Ngarama as the first in the dynasty. It should be noted that, by then, Kyamutwara encompassed Kihanja, Maruku, Bugabo and 'the smaller' Kyamutwara of today. Of equal historical significance was the ousting of the Bahinda by the Bankango clan who were still in the process of consolidating their dynasty when German rule was established.

A general idea of the arrival of the Nilo-Hamitics is provided by Hans Cory when he wrote: 'The entrance gate of the Lake Province for the Hamitic immigrants was Bukoba and they probably arrived there about three hundred and fifty years ago. They were Bahima also called Bahuma or Batusi ... Ruhinda gave his name to the ruling class of Bukoba, the Bahinda. The Hinda invasion was in the main peaceful.'[25]

The Administrative System of the ENFURA

The economic system of the time was greatly influenced by the political and administrative innovations of the Hamitic dynasties. Apart from despotism and tyranny, their rule was characterized by strong central control superimposed on the local administrative structure. By having each subject identify himself with a village or clan, the competitive spirit during war and

TABLE IV–2 *BAKAMA BA KYAMUTWARA*

	MAJOR NAME	LOCATION OF CAPITAL	REMARKS
1.	IRUNGU	BWIGURA	Last Mutundu clan.
2.	KASHALE	MUHUTWE	Last Bahunga clan Mukama.
3.	BWOGI	NGARAMA	First Muhinda king, son of Ruhinda of Karagwe.
4.	NYAMIGELA	NGARAMA	Died prematurely.
5.	NYALUBAMBA	KAJUMILO	Consolidated Bahinda rule.
6.	KALEMERA ENTWAGU YA MAGANGO	BITUNTU	The cruellest of Hinda kings.
7.	RUKAMBYA (BWOGI)	BITUNTU	
8.	LUGOMORA MAHE	MARUKU	
9.	KAHIGI I	MARUKU	
10.	BWOGI II	MARUKU	Arrival of Bankango.
11.	KALEMERA IV	KABALE	Married to two sisters of Rushuma, important ancestors of Bankango dynasty.
12.	KAJURUNGA	KABALE	Son of Kalemera.
13.	KINYONYI	BULEMBO	Divison in the kingdom of Kyamutwara. He later fled to Uganda leaving Kitekere and later Kaitalba in control.
14.	KAMIRO (BWOGI)	KABALE	Kajurunga's son.
15.	KITEKERE	KABALE	Bankango.
16.	KAITABA	KABALE	
17.	MUKOTANI	KABALE	Arrival of Germans. First strong Bankango Mukama.
18.	BWAHAMA	KABALE	Exiled by the Germans.
19.	MUNTU	KABALE	Imprisoned by Germans during World War I.
20.	RWAIJUMBA (BONIFACE)		
21.	LUGABANDANA (GABRIEL)	KABALE	
22.	RUKAMBA (EMMANUEL)	KABALE	Titular Mukama.

peacetime alike was enhanced and this made for loyalty to and control by the government.

The administrative system of the kingdom can be demonstrated by the example of Ihangiro whose dynasty dates back from Ruhinda and has continued uninterrupted to date. As indicated earlier, the other original Hinda dynasties were Karagwe, Uvinza and Burundi. Later kingdoms emerged including Kyamutwara, Kihanja, Maruku and Ngote. Thus, corresponding to the administrative units were the military groupings. To fight a war, the king himself would take direct charge of the army. Taking the example of Ihangiro, the army would automatically fall into two divisions, corresponding to the *Omwihaya* or coastal region and the *Mugongo* or plateau region. For Kihanja, the divisions would be *Kihanja* Eiguru (plateau) and *Bujumba* and so on for other kingdoms. On assembling, the troops would group according to their political reference, for example soldiers from Ngote would be referred to as ABAHENZANGARO (those who break with bare hands) while those from NSHAMBA would be called ABAASHAMI (the shouters).[26] Both the warrior group name and regional identity proved very effective in generating fighting morale. The honours gained in battle were also enjoyed according to the divisions down to the region, the village and, above all, the clan.

Both the political and military systems were strengthened by a communication network between the palace and the villages with public and private surveillance and a daily information exchange between the palace and regional capitals. Communication with the palace was further encouraged by the unwritten oath whereby each subject had a duty to report any behaviour likely to be detrimental to the security of the realm.

The earliest recorded description of a Mukama and his court can be found in the account of the explorers. Speke provides a day-to-day account of his visit to Bweranyange, the capital of Karagwe, where he was received by the powerful king Rumanyika Orugundu.[27] The orderliness of the kingdom, the pomp of the palace, the wisdom of the king and his awareness of international affairs were unbelievably advanced, not because they excelled those to be found elsewhere in the world, but because they were present in the heart of Africa.

On arrival, Speke was met by a special group dealing with foreigners, and was accommodated in a special hut reserved for strangers. The food presented to him, the way it was cooked, the variety of meat and the civilized way it was served, were all beyond his imagination. More impressive, however, was the etiquette with which the hospitality was administered and the serenity and cultivated manner with which the king held his court with Speke and his entourage.

Overall, the economic and military structure reinforced the economic system, which in turn brought additional strength to the centralized feudal system. Thus, the speed with which the army could be mobilized was not only an assurance against external invasion but also an effective instrument of tyranny and suppression over the non-aristocratic masses whose lot had been reduced to serfdom.

It is not certain whether tyranny was generated by governmental enthusiasm for security though, apparently, it tended to increase with the passing years. To accede to power, it is generally believed the Enfura used enticing Machiavellian tactics. It is also believed that the early kings were fair and just rulers who counted on the confidence of the majority of their subjects. But as kings felt secure on the throne with respect to succession, they succumbed to untold cruelty. Thus, open dissents with kings or nobles would lead to instant execution. Wanton and aimless killing also occurred frequently, as illustrated by Zoe Marsh and G. W. Kingsnorth, who cite incidents concerning the shooting of a palace valet merely to test the power of a gun and the execution of a queen simply because she offered, in jest, a fruit to her husband.[28]

Power intoxication by the later kings of the dynasties is perhaps best exemplified by the rule of Kalemera, Entwagu ya Magango,[29] King of Kihanja, who lined up and butchered hundreds of people simply to amuse himself by creating a stream of blood to flow from where he was seated to the River Muleleizi, a couple of kilometres away.

A more recent case is that of Kakoko, regent of Karagwe from 1882 to 1886, who proved excessively ruthless and tyrannical even though he had succeeded a highly benevolent father, Rumanyika. Kakoko's wayward behaviour, however, had been detected and chronicled by Stanley while the latter was visiting Buhimba on 30 March 1867, where, as a prince, Kakoko was training to be a king.[30]

The Economy

Among the important elements which might have influenced the economic activities of the period, banana cultivation was foremost, followed closely by the raising of the longhorn cattle, which in turn was instrumental to sustaining the banana based economic revolution.

If the banana had been cultivated at all prior to the Enfura period, it must have been on a casual basis around the huts for its shade, leaves and fibres, or along the ravines where it required no tending. During the Enfura period, techniques of tilling the soil and the selection of healthy suckers for planting were developed. Among the far-reaching innovations was the mulching of the banana garden, usually by means of pruned leaves, rotting stems and peelings. From time to time, grass fetched from open meadows was spread to make a thicker mulching carpet. Through mulching, weeds would be stopped, moisture retained and, above all, soil erosion reduced. In a hilly region with rainfall of more than 80 inches a year, soil erosion can be economically disastrous; thanks to the mulching techniques, the fertility of the same area could be preserved and the land could be used for centuries without requiring the opening of new farms. Consequently, migratory farming, necessitated by the search for virgin or fallow land, was eliminated, thereby further encouraging permanent settlement. Thus, small villages grew in membership and combined with neighbouring ones to form stronger regional communities under monarchical government.

In conjunction with farming techniques went the longhorn cattle which were closely identified with Nilotic domination, if not actually introduced by them. The kings were called BAKAMA (singular: Mukama), in recognition of their role in milking cattle.[31] The importance of the longhorn breed lies not so much in the production of milk or meat but rather in generating manure which has proven ideal for banana production. With its tall legs, boat-shaped body and lyre-type horns, this species can voraciously devour large quantities of grass and drink several gallons of water a day. As a result, it can generate a large quantity of manure by which the yield per acre of bananas can be increased. A technical analysis by A. O. Anacleti and D. K. Nagala posits that, at one time, cattle in Buhaya became the centre of a culture/economy or 'complex'.[32] Their conclusion is acceptable if the complex is qualified as a subordinate and not a dominant 'complex' like that of the banana or the cattle *à la* Masai. Notwithstanding this qualification, the banana culture depended fundamentally on the cattle.

Equally instrumental in tightening the grip over the economy were the cattle. As pointed out earlier on, the Enfura identified themselves with cattle as their major economic mainstay and symbol of power. At first, pastoral pursuits appeared harmless to the indigenous society which was primarily agricultural. Indeed, when the pastoral Hamitics began to distribute the cow manure among the peasants, the initial feeling ought to have been one of exuberance in that the Hamitics had ushered in an era of salubrious economic symbiosis. As in other instances, however, advantage was taken of the manure to strengthen the aristocratic grip on the economy. They thus rented out their cattle to peasants who, in exchange for manure, had to give servitude to herd-owners. This later developed into a situation whereby the Enfura usurped the property of the peasants and turned them into serfs. As a result, one of the strongest forms of feudalism, called nyarubanja, was established and continued to exist until 1960.[33] Other methods were used in seizing land and property. Among these were punishment for offences, the issue of a royal decree and the right of inheritance from heirless peasants.

Cattle also enhanced the economic power of the aristocracy when the animal became the medium of exchange. As transactions were conducted by using cattle as a standard value, the owners, who were mainly Hamitics, reaped windfall gains. With cattle, they could make outright purchases of plantations, slaves, wives and even political power. The overall effect of the monetary position of cattle was to enhance the economic supremacy of the Enfura.[34]

The Revolutionizing Process of the Banana and the Ankole Cattle

The banana plant, a herbaceous tuber type belonging to the genus *Musa*, has more than 60 identified species falling into four main categories, *Musa*

Expentium (grown mainly in the Caribbean), *Musa Cavendishii* (found in the Canary Islands), *Musa Acuminata* (found in the East Indies) and *Musa Paradisiaca* (of the plantain type). Supposed to be native to the East Indies, the banana might have reached the Great Lakes via the mouth of the Zambezi.[35] However, this proposition needs to be qualified because, firstly, some species grow wild in the forests of the Congo Basin, which suggests the possibility of their being indigenous. Secondly, East Africa has the widest variety of the banana species and therefore possibly a longer history than that suggested by an East Indies origin. In any case, whether indigenous to Africa or not, some evidence exists to show that the plant might have arrived before the Bantu settlement in Buhaya.

For the Bahaya, however, the genus of relevance is plantain or *Musa Paradisiaca*, believed to have more than 20 species falling into two broad categories: the bitter type used for juice and the more plentiful kind for cooking.[36] They do well on rich soils, though a rainfall of more than 60 inches a year is a necessary condition. The plantain is largely a horticultural crop requiring individual and regular attention throughout the year to ensure weeding and pruning. However, it has the advantage of being a perennial crop and, as such, requires relatively less labour of the sort which must be systematically applied.

As a tuber, the banana has shallow roots which require a moist soil, usually so maintained by means of mulching, using leaves pruned from the plant itself. The bunch consists of clusters or hands each comprised of fingers. An average good bunch bears nine clusters, though the number can be influenced greatly by the type of manure used. Cow manure has been proved to give the best yield, by increasing the number of hands as well as the quality of each fruit. This is where the Ankole longhorn cattle become relevant, by providing the manure necessary for sustaining the high yield of banana plants and therefore maintaining a concentration of population in a relatively small area.

With increased yield per acre, the tribe was better assured of food supply and fear of famine was considerably reduced. Secondly, more time was available for leisure and cultural activities and this further enhanced the social character of the tribe. Thirdly, increased food production may have led to faster population growth, resulting in more concentrated settlements without necessarily extending the village acreage. The overall effect was to transform social habits and organization generally. Also, parallel political developments emerged, making the growth of the banana culture an agent of feudalism, giving the aristocracy increased domination over the economy. By owning more cattle, the lucky few found themselves in an advantageous position to purchase farms or to loan cattle to peasants, thereby claiming more profits and servitude. In general, the changes caused by increased productivity in the banana sector led to economic prosperity although the influence of the aristocracy was enhanced.

With greater recognition of banana farms, *bibanja*, as permanent property and an investment asset at the same time, a code of law was developed to deal with tenure and the transfer of ownership. We shall return to this theme when discussing the feudal system, though it suffices to say that the bibanja were not only considered as property in the commercial sense, but also as a symbol of social status and as a mark of affiliation to the tribe. These features gave rise to a special sentimental attachment to the bibanja, as will be explained later.

Laws were established to deal with purchasing, selling, inheriting and nationalizing bibanja.[37] A parallel code was later developed to deal with the acquisition of new land to be farmed into bibanja, a process known as *kushemba*.[38] Most of the new legal developments were exploited by the aristocracy, who further strengthened their control over the economy.

Mention should also be made of the replacement of fingermillet by bananas as the staple food. The former receded to the background and was used only occasionally, usually only for breakfast porridge and occasionally for other meals. As the new staple food, the banana featured more centrally in the life of the Bahaya. The major farm task became tree pruning and weeding (of the plantations), since planting is done once, for all time. Division of work on the plantation assigned weeding to the women while the men's task was pruning. In contrast to fingermillet, however, banana culture is less demanding. In terms of timing of activities, the tasks are relatively less rigorous and the overall effect may have left the tribe with a reduced sense of hard work involving physical exertion.

Economic Development

It was the agricultural sector which underwent the most dramatic changes when the banana dethroned fingermillet as the staple food of the tribe. Other activities in agriculture, however, are worth mentioning. Similarly, a brief survey is made of other economic sectors, particularly fishing, industry and commerce.

Agriculture

The supremacy of the banana in the agricultural sector implied that most activities centred around its production and that, as far as possible, land was put to growing bananas, which had become the major food of the tribe. Other food crops were spinach, peas, beans and yams, which were planted in the space between banana trees. On communal land, millets, groundnuts and peanuts were cultivated, to mention but a few. On the whole, it appears that food was in abundant supply in Buhaya, especially that obtained from farming or that gathered from the natural habitat, such as fish, wild animals and insects. Agriculture throughout remained peasant in form though it benefited greatly from the progress in iron technology, by which various tools were made. Thus, for clearing bushes, there was the bush-knife and the hoe, the small planting spade, the big banana-uprooting spade (ekiosho), the long-handled banana-leaf sickle (oruabyo), and peeling or general purpose knives. All these tools contributed to a fast development of the banana-based agriculture.

Cultivation of the banana was facilitated by the horticultural characteristics of the plant which do not require or encourage sophisticated farming techniques, such as large-scale tilling or fast techniques of sowing. Its expansion depended mainly on the availability of enough hands to tend the plantation. Being labour intensive, the industry was able to cater for a big population increase without involving any technological transformations.

Fishing

As an industry, fishing provided an additional source of protein, whose deficiency in the tribal diet had been exacerbated by overvaluing cattle as a monetary unit. Happily, the Ngono and other rivers and the Burigi, Ikimba and Rweru (Victoria) lakes teemed with good fish.[39] During the Enfura period, however, the fish industry was discouraged for two apparent reasons. The first was that the occupation of fishing could not readily be placed under the control of the king and his aristocracy. In other words, fishing was looked upon as a sector which encouraged disloyalty to kings and, to combat it, fishermen were disdained as a group in the tribe. This social attitude, however, was a blessing in disguise, for the fishermen were able to develop an independent character which mitigated the oppression of the government. The second reason was that fishing was in direct competition with the cattle-based economy. As an alternative food relish to the banana diet, fish was widely used as it could be purchased in small quantities and could be easily stored when dried. The consumption of fish, which was an effective substitute for meat and milk, was discouraged and, in this connection, it was taboo for Enfura to eat fish under any circumstances.

The fishing industry was encouraged by the demand for fish and by traditional organizational fishing units known as Ikokooro.[40] This was a group of fishermen jointly operating and owning boats, nets, ropes, baskets, drying and smoking beds and other necessary equipment. The members would work together and share the benefits equitably. Furthermore, there were no restrictions on fishing in the lakes or rivers.

Industry

Industrial development reflected society's sectoral priorities. The manufacture of agricultural implements received high priority, as did the production of military equipment. As pointed out earlier, the making of hoes, knives, sickles and similar items made relatively fast progress. Similarly, the production of spears, fighting knives and arrows may have given rise to technological advances in the whole iron industry. As stated earlier, although iron work dates back to the early Bantu settlement, there are reasons to believe that significant developments in the industry took place during the Enfura period.[41] Thus, techniques of manufacturing better steel and better tools may have followed the lead of the military sector, which was emphasized during the dynastic years. Some kings, not satisfied with manufacture of weapons, attempted to build steel 'towers of Babel' but, unfortunately, they were unable to leave reliable records about the architecture used or objectives aimed at.[42]

Besides, there was also the copper industry which was mainly confined to the production of ornaments, principally rings worn by both men and women around the limbs and neck.[43] The technique involved mining the ore, smelting it and pulling it into wire. However, as Arab trade grew, particularly during the nineteenth century, copper was imported from other parts of Africa, mainly to the south of the region.

Conforming to the same sectoral emphasis as above were other industrial activities such as woodwork. This produced handles for weapons and civilian tools like milk cans, wooden mortars and pestles. For ferrying soldiers and fishing, dug-out canoes were manufactured from the *Terminalia Superba* (omulehe). Articles produced from basketwork included shields, containers and other items for military or domestic use.

Commerce

An anonymous book written by the Greeks in the first century AD, known as the *Periplus of the Erythraean Sea*, gives an account of commercial transactions along the East Coast of Africa, which involved trade in lances, hatchets, daggers, ivory, rhinoceros horn, tortoise shell and little palm and, of course, slaves. As far as the interior of Africa is concerned, however, there is no equivalent description of trading activities from any reliable source of information.[44] Before AD 1500, inter-regional commerce was further discouraged by the self-sufficient pursuits of the fingermillet-based peasantry.

In the eighteenth and nineteenth centuries, however, both internal trade and external commerce increased considerably. As village clustering gained momentum due to the banana revolution, the exchange of goods increased, owing to local specialization of crops and the need to take advantage of trade. Secondly, with cattle as a medium of exchange, transactions were significantly facilitated. The items which might have featured significantly in the market were bananas, fish, bitter millet, basketwork and carved articles, including agricultural implements, ornaments and weapons.[45]

The external commerce of Buhaya was influenced by a number of factors including the region's location between the strong kingdoms of the Great Lakes and the Ocean Coast. The trade caravans which left Bagamoyo would pass through Unyanyembe (Tabora), Bweranyange (Karagwe) and proceed to the kingdoms of Buganda, Bunyoro, Ankole and Rwanda. The caravans, organized mainly by coastal Arabs, would bring cowrie shells, cloth, metal tools, ornaments and beads to the interior. In exchange, they would receive ivory, rhino-horn and foodstuffs. Later on, emphasis was on the slave trade.

For centuries, there had been a lively trade between Buhaya and

Kisumbwa, a region located in what is known as Kahama and Kigoma. The main commodity was salt, which was obtainable from rock and was very much in demand in Buhaya at the time. It is from trade that the Bahaya developed the proverb: 'the Sumbwas stink but salt is sweet', implying that, while the Bahaya would readily take salt as a rare relish, they did not socially welcome the people who peddled the commodity.

Buhaya suffered its own share of the ravages of the slave trade. Located on the main route for the caravans from Rwanda, Burundi, Ankole, Buganda, etc., Buhaya witnessed the passing chained gangs which were reinforced at Bweranyange (Karagwe) by cargo from its own territory. Trade in slaves was intensified by tyrannical kings who sold away potential rivals and despised subjects in exchange for weapons and articles of pomp. The aristocracy took advantage of the trade to terrorize the peasants, seize their property or drive them away by selling them as slaves. Overall, the disruption caused locally might have been worse than that caused by the activities of the Arab traders themselves. Thus, the social system was deeply disturbed and, as a result, the economy suffered a series of adverse consequences.[46]

The Social-Cultural Sector

Socio-culturally, a system of strong central government developed during the period with local divisions and ministries being set up to carry out the administration. In a typical case, the king (Omukama) would reign over the kingdom with the assistance of the prime minister (katikiro), whose nomination would depend on capability and not on social class. The major departments or ministries were responsible for rain-divining, war, hunting and religion.[47] The nation was divided into regions called Gombolora, headed by a Mwami, and within each gombolora were three or four Nkungus, each comprising several villages headed by a Mukungu. A village was the smallest unit and was administered by the village headman. As already mentioned, the coherence of a kingdom would be enhanced by an efficient communication system involving drum messages and messengers to systematically convey reports between the national capital and the local headquarters.

The educational system of the time was known as Omukimala. At the age of 11, boys would already have been initiated in the techniques of looking after cattle and goats. At 14, they were required to live at the palace (kikale), to be taught the history of the tribe and, above all, to participate in military training and the manufacture and use of military tools, such as the spear and the shield. Military training, considered to be the most important, involved physical exercises of spear-throwing, battle formation, shield fending and charging. The exercises were undertaken in an atmosphere of strict discipline in the name of the king. The common motto of the soldiers was to be lucky and die for the king. Before completing the training, young men would be taught skills for manufacturing and repairing military tools.

Other cultural aspects worthy of note included sports, which were also greatly influenced by military preoccupations. Thus, the warrior dance featured among the most popular items, with young men mimicking a combat while dancing to drum tomtoms. Wrestling constituted another popular sport.

Story-telling was enjoyed both during leisure time and in the context of serious learning. Mention was made earlier of the importance of oral history which, in the process of teaching and learning, constituted an important educational medium. Each story was expected to convey a moral lesson in the same way as the parables in the Bible. Besides, the exercise inculcated the art of delivery, presentation and public speaking. As in the case of Bunyoro or other interlacustrine cultures, stories featured animals, including the leopard, lion, hyena, tortoise, etc., while the birds commonly referred to were the crow, the sparrow, the crown-crane and the stork.[48] However, the hero was the hare (Nyakami), which corresponded to the fox or wolf in European legends. Story-telling, apparently, had the same effect as the radio or television on leisure in modern times. What history has yet to explain, however, is why neither the Bantu communities, nor the Nilo-Hamitics, much as they had migrated through many civilizations, were not able to develop writing and reading techniques of their own.[49]

The Feudal System, Nyarubanja

As the Nilo-Hamitic political systems developed towards centralized monarchies, the economic pattern assumed the form of feudalism called NYARUBANJA. Literally, the term means a big plantation, bigger than a single household needed for sustenance.[50] The connotation was later extended to cover the overall relationship between the titular owner and the tenant of the plantation. From this point of view, the system bears some resemblance to medieval feudalism, though the aim of this section is to examine the Buhaya type against the background of the European prototype.[51]

As a background, some notes need to be provided on classical feudalism, which Jacques J. Maquet defines as 'complete ownership of the land by the lord and his limited ownership of the labourer, the serf peasant'.[52] As a historical phenomenon, feudalism is sometimes traced back to the times of the Egyptians while others date it back to the end of the Roman Empire, though Maquet estimates the period to be 'from the middle of the ninth century to the beginning of the thirteenth' century.[53] Defining feudalism, however, is rendered more difficult by its many variations from epoch to epoch and from place to place. As Jack Goody puts it, 'there is then a measure of general agreement that "feudal" should be used in comparative work'.[54] This generalization follows from the basic work of Marc Bloch who, after surveying the major characteristics of feudalism, concluded that it was not unique to Europe and that the European variant might have borrowed significantly from other continents.[55] It is on this basis, then, that we can discuss African feudality and nyarubanja.

The European variant was a function of land ownership, seigneurial lordship over vassals and serfs and the manorial administrative pattern.[56] From a purely economic point of view, feudality entailed the renting out by a landlord of his land to a vassal/serf in exchange for a portion of the harvest, servitude and loyalty. Politically, it implied that the central government would cede part of its sovereignty to the aristocracy. Administratively, the lord or landholder assumed jurisdiction over the affairs of those falling within his domain and his responsibilities covered arbitration, the raising of an army for the king and the welfare of his subjects. However, feudalism was all-embracing and equally affected other aspects of life, including religion, thought, society and so on.[57]

Under a typical European seigneurial system, economic considerations remained paramount in the lord–serf relationship. Thus the landlord would demand monetary dues as well as unqualified obedience. In return, the serf would get land utility and social military protection. It should be pointed out that the system was devoid of slavery elements because the relationship was confined to the terms implied in the lord–tenant contract. The freedom of action of the tenant is reflected in the following passage:

> Whatever their legal status may have been, even if it went by the name of serfdom, the peasants who composed a seigneurie were in no sense human livestock, fed by their master and owing the whole of their labour to him. They lived on the produce of fields that they cultivated on their own account, which were usually handed down from father to son; and if the opportunity occurred they could sell or exchange the produce in order to procure other necessaries of life.[58]

The European form of feudality assumed land scarcity through inefficient distribution or sheer inadequacy. Whatever the cause, the landless had to look to clientship as the only available means of earning a living. On the same grounds, it was the land and its use which joined the landlord and the tenant. The clientship contract was usually initiated by the ceremony called homage.

The types of feudality experienced in Africa were summarized by Jacques J. Maquet who, by trying to establish a definition, succeeded in shedding light on the whole concept of feudality as well as in demarcating the domain of the African experience.[59] H concludes that 'if it is to be applied to Africa, the term feudality must be separated from any reference to land ownership'. While on the same point, Dr Lucy Mair posits that East African feudalism was based on a universal need for protection rather than purely economic reasons.[60]

To understand the Buhaya feudal system, one has to take into account the classical type as well as the African variants and a number of special features peculiar to Buhaya. The initial step is to examine the historical development of the Buhaya system, then to analyse the nature of the clientship and, lastly, to consider its political overtones.

As Hans Cory and M. M. Hartnoll put it, nyarubanja evolved from the expansion of a clan and the attempt by its head to keep control over his kin.[61] While the main objective may have been to maintain his influence over the members of the same lineage, the means used were economic, involving token gifts or taxes and compulsory service, known as *nsika*. By linking nyarubanja to the clan period, a proposition could be made that the system had been invented by the Bantu prior to the Nilo-Hamitic arrival. It is equally probable that monarchs exploited the system to tighten their grip on the Bantu element. Thus, as Cory and Hartnoll further argue, the mukama would dispossess the clan-head for the flimsiest reason and assume paternal rule over the clan. To hasten the process of control, monarchs would simply nominate groups of plantations to be held as fiefs and place them under royal agents. Pestilence, wars and famine provided additional opportunities for the monarchy to extend feudality. As the system developed, it grew more complex, so much so that it cannot be fully described here.

From the above flows the second proposition referred to by Priscilla Reining, namely that clientship in Buhaya 'was based on land rather than on cattle, as the case had been in Rwanda, because land is the most important form of property in Buhaya'.[62] Since pastoral activities had not featured as a dominant occupation in Buhaya, it is unlikely that cattle could have formed a basis for a durable system like nyarubanja. While A. O. Anacleti and D. K. Nagala discuss the historical development of the cattle held in the Great Lakes region, they point to the importance of livestock in the social and cultural sector of Buhaya, but not to such an extent that it formed a separate economic mainstay of the region.[63] The topological factors explaining why the cattle complex was bound to remain subsidiary to other sectors is presented by D. N. McMaster.[64] It was the manure from cattle, however, which may have been of great pertinence to the link between the peasant and the monarchy. J. F. Mbwiliza relates the *butekoship*, a feudal system in Buha, to the '... necessity for intensive cultivation which led to the necessity for the use of manure ... paving a slow process of peasant dependency on the pastoral Tutsi'.[65] All these arguments notwithstanding, there was a contradiction in the fact that a peasant would not have given up his land title for cattle manure.

Land, as a factor of nyarubanja, has to be viewed from the angle of scarcity or maldistribution. Shortage of land in Buhaya appears to be a relatively recent phenomenon. With an unlimited supply of land and a simple process for acquiring it, coupled with the peasant's option to emigrate, land scarcity could hardly constitute a basis for tenancy. Nor does the need for protection against invasions present a sound reason for a peasant's wishing to place a feudal yoke around his neck. In all, while the landlord's benefits from feudality are obvious, it is necessary to determine the utility a peasant might have derived from such bondage. Even then, the landlord's benefits need to be stated.[66] Foremost was the recognition of his lordship, second was his entitlement to bananas from the tenant's plantation and third was his expectation of services known as *nsika* from the tenant.

Though failure to fulfil the obligation on the part of the tenant was severely and violently punished, the substantive part of the obligation was light if not token. Firstly, the services demanded of the tenant were casual and not economically necessary, since the landlord's plot was normally of an average size and could be maintained without help from outside the household. Secondly, since the landlord's plantations would have normally provided him with adequate food, the tenants' contribution would have been superfluous. Thirdly, the quantity of other forms of payments would hardly have added much to the wealth of the landlord.

It is very likely, therefore, that the predominant consideration of the landlord was political and psychological, namely subjugation and domination. Dr Lucy Mair attributes this benefit to *clientage*, which is devoid of economic objectives but aims primarily at ensuring subjugation and political confinement.[67] It was in this particular respect that the Bahaya serfdom variant was distinct from the medieval prototype and even other forms of African feudality. In other words, the landlord was content with lording it over a group of peasants. Using the landlord, the king exercised control over the peasants, and over the lord himself, by threatening to dispossess him of the vassalage. Through this 'telescoping clientage', the king kept his domain under full control.

The objective of subjugation in nyarubanja is best illustrated by the tenant's obligation to build his house with the main door facing the landlord's house. Among the obligatory services to be rendered to the lord were menial jobs such as looking after cattle, splitting firewood or pressing banana juice for brewing wine. Overall, the landlord exercised a paternalistic attitude towards the tenants. A pertinent question is why the peasants tolerated the subjugation. Mention was made of the origin of feudality in the clan system. This implied that the peasants had a strong sentiment of attachment to their plantation which was usually located in the vicinity of relatives, and few tried to emigrate. Consequently, the ruling class exploited this feeling of attachment to the traditional plots by demanding subjugation from serfs in exchange for the right to retain the property.[68] While the nature and strength of such a sentiment might be difficult to analyse in a work of this nature, it suffices to mention that the practice can still be found in many African communities today. Additionally, it should be noted that those peasants who had a lesser feeling of attachment to the location, or who were unable to withstand the subjugation, migrated to areas of freedom.

Despite the fundamental difference in the feudal obligation of the nyarubanja and medieval forms, the consequences were similar. Both systems had a stifling effect on developmental initiatives in society. In Buhaya, in particular, the structure of the feudality was organized in such a way as to ensure subjugation of individuals and, therefore, personal or group initiatives, unless they were related to the glorification of the king, were nipped in the bud. As the tempo of technological development increased, other aspects which had been forging ahead since the rule of the Bantu clan, relaxed or even disappeared.[69] Even the agricultural sector suffered as peasants became discouraged by having to share their harvest with the aristocrats, whose own capacity to work on the land was reduced through idleness. By and large, economic development could not advance at an optimum rate. However, as long as productivity of the semi-propelled banana culture continued, the peasant's situation was reasonably tolerable.

With the introduction of the monetary economy, however, a fundamental change occurred in the nyarubanja system which, hitherto a political-psychological phenomenon, assumed economic proportions. Thus, in the era of the slave trade, a landlord would use his fief to capture slaves and exchange them for clothes, ammunition, beads, etc. At that stage, the peasantry could be regarded as a herd from which aristocrats selected beasts for slaughter or sale.

The introduction of money as a medium of exchange aggravated the exploitation of the peasants by the landed aristocracy. The latter, in trying to acquire wealth quickly, extorted increasing amounts of crops and services to the detriment of the peasants, whose position was hardly different from that of slaves. Seeing this, the German administration expressed great concern but was unable to do much about the evil of nyarubanja. The British took more specific steps to deal with the problem though it was not until Tanzania became independent that the system was totally abolished.[70]

The disadvantages of feudalism in Europe were that:

> It gave the ruling class almost complete power over the lives of those who produced food for wealth; it released the nobility from all forms of work except fighting and hunting; it meant privilege for the few, injustice for the majority.[71]

This simplified statement duly summarizes the problem of Buhaya feudalism except that even fighting was left to the serfs. It should be pointed out that feudalism was not unique to Buhaya but that it assumed various forms in many parts of Africa.[72]

In Europe, feudalism emerged and prevailed in the successor states of the Carolingian Empire, particularly during the tenth to thirteenth centuries. Politically, the system implied fragmentation of the powers of the state and their division among the land owners while socially, it meant that lords dominated the workers and exploited them.

Recapitulation

Among the landmarks of the period was the establishment of the Nilo-Hamitic kingdoms by the Bahinda, Babiito and Bankango clans. This process involved the consolidation of the scattered Bantu communities into concentrated villages and regions under a system of local government subject to control by the king. Kingdoms varied from time to time but the most well known were Karagwe, Kyamutwara, Ihangiro, Kiziba and Buzinza. The establishment of the dynasties ensured continuity in the main political territory and eliminated the upheaval which was likely to follow a non-dynastic succession. The latter facilitated the recording of history since events would be associated with a particular king.

The second most outstanding feature of the period was the dominance of the banana in the economy. With increased yield of the fruit as a result of the use of manure and improved husbandry techniques, the danger of famine was reduced, communities became more concentrated and cultural development was enhanced. On the whole, the life of the tribe was transformed as a result of the cultivation of the banana. Thus the seasonal cycle of work revolved around the functions relating to the banana and social status depended upon the quantity of bananas one owned. By manipulating the yield, the king and the aristocracy were able to strengthen their grip on the peasants through a feudal system known as nyarubanja. By this means, the aristocrats claimed ownership of the plantations and thereby extorted rent, payable in goods or services. While the factors which brought it about differ from those which led up to feudalism in medieval Europe, their consequences are surprisingly similar. Generally, they had a repressive effect on the peasants and discouraged the initiative so essential to economic development.

Noteworthy developments could also be recorded in the social and cultural sectors, mainly in the way of sports and the complex educational system. Boys, grouped according to age, were subjected to civil and military training as a preparation for taking up their responsibilities in society.

All the above features contributed to the evolution of the character of the Bahaya today, indeed they constitute that very character. The political system of dynasties established some 500 years ago has survived to date,[73] which vouches for the ingenuity of the inventors of this political mechanism by which disturbances and risks of non-succession were effectively avoided. Other positive features of the period included a strong economy based on banana culture. Often forgotten despite its basic importance is the social impact of the dynastic rule on the people. With the imposition of the Nilo-Hamitic dynasties on the individualism of the early Bantu clan way of life, a new social system was bound to emerge and this is still reflected in the existing social structure of the tribe. In a way, the mingling of the two cultures might have placed the tribe in a better position to confront the events of the twentieth century, in particular the European and Asian cultural invasion.

Finally, the Enfura period served as a bridge between the pure Bantu culture and colonial life. In addition, the nineteenth century in particular might have seen Buhaya at its zenith as a purely African society. Whither this society might have headed if the Germans had not established their administration at the turn of the century will always remain a subject for speculation.

1. A useful account of the Nilotic tribes is presented by B. A. Ogot, *History of the Southern Luo*, Vol. 1 (Nairobi, 1967). Relevant notes are also provided in D. A. Wilson, *East African History*, op. cit., pp.6–9.
2. The Brooklyn Museum, *Africa in Antiquity: the Arts of Ancient Nubia and the Sudan*, Vol. 1, Chapter II.
3. Iris Berger, *Religion and Resistance: East African Kingdoms in the Pre-Colonial Period*, op. cit., pp.27–43.
4. Ibid., pp.8–14.
5. Ibid., p.36.
6. John Hanning Speke, *What Led to the Discovery of the Source of the Nile* (London, Edinburgh: William Blackwood, 1864).
7. Iris Berger, op. cit., pp.45–6, and Israel Katoke, 'The History of the Precolonial States of North-Western Tanzania: Introduction', in *Journal of World History*, Vol. XII, 3 (1971), pp.115–41. For a basic account, *see* Hermann Rehse, *Kiziba Land und Leute*, op. cit., pp.152–262; this happens to be an account of F. X. Lwamugira when he was still a page at King Mutatembwa's court.
8. It is told that Ruhinda's mother was a slave called Njunaki.
9. It is alleged that the woman was of Dinka-Nuer extraction and that the meeting with Kyomya took place under a Biito tree, hence the name Babiito.
10. Buzinza or Buzinja was a name applied to the region east of Rusubi and south of Lake Victoria. It is different from Uvinza which is further south, extending from Kahama to Burundi.
11. Partly derived from local accounts. *See also* the version which has been read widely in Tanzania, in Institute for Swahili Research, Dar es Salaam, *Zamani Mpaka Siku Hizi*, op. cit. pp.15–27.
12. *See* Iris Berger, op. cit. pp.34–6.
13. Israel Katoke, op. cit., pp.524–32. The name Bwirebutakya might have been used by foreigners when referring to Ihangiro. *See* Israel Katoke, 'History of Precolonial States in North-Western Tanzania', *Journal of World History*, op. cit., pp.524–32.
14. Sometimes Baganda refer to Buhaya as Kiziba, *vide* Sir J. F. Cunningham, *Uganda and Its People*, op. cit., p.283.
15. The term Enfura means 'the just' but it later referred to the ruling clans and the aristocracy with exactly converse implications.
16. Other related terms to Enfura included 'mulangira', meaning a lord or a member of the royal family. For more about the social strata in Buhaya, *see* Hans Cory and M. M. Hartnoll, op. cit., pp.281–2.
17. Iris Berger, *Religion and Resistance: East African Kingdoms in the Pre-Colonial Period*, op. cit., Chapter III, pp.5–14.
18. The Masai have defied cultural invasion by sticking to cattle rearing and by staying away from any other social communities except when waging war.
19. Kingship changed easily even if only among the members of the royal family.
20. The Bahinda are supposed to have supplied fingermillet and milk to the Bantu to win their confidence and to encourage them to shift their loyalty from the ruling clans.
21. The deal made by the Enfura and the rights of the indigenous people is analysed in Hans Cory and M. M. Hartnoll, op. cit., pp.249–54. *See also* the analogous *buteko* institution in J. F. Mbwiliza, 'The Hoe and the Stick: a Political Economy in the Heru Kingdom c. 1750–1900', *Journal of World History*, Vol. XII, 3 (1971), pp.100–14.
22. Zoe Marsh and G. W. Kingsnorth, op. cit., p.10. A scholarly analysis is provided by Iris Berger, *Religion and Resistance: East African Kingdoms in the Pre-Colonial Period*, op. cit. It was thus a general belief that murdering the king would bring a curse on the clan or even on the whole nation.
23. There are no instances cited of women Bakama during the Nilo-Hamitic period or before it. In the other neighbouring regions, however, there were women sultanas, *vide* J. H. Speke, *What Led to the Discovery of the Source of the Nile*, op. cit., p.273. Nevertheless, women played an important role in the politics of Buhaya.

24. In the case of Bunyoro, Sir Harry Johnston found that kings reigned for a relatively short period, nine to ten years on average as regards twelve kings. However, he quotes the case of King Kyebambe Nyamutukura who reached such an old age on the throne that his people tried to kill him. Cf. *The Uganda Protectorate*, op. cit., p.597.
25. Hans Cory, 'The People of the Lake Victoria Region', in *Tanganyika Notes and Records*, No. 33, July 1952, p.23.
26. A detailed presentation of the divisions can be found in Hans Cory and M. M. Hartnoll, op. cit., pp.271–2.
27. John Hanning Speke, *Journal of the Discovery of the Source of the Nile*, op. cit., p.318.
28. Zoe Marsh and G. W. Kingsnorth, op. cit., pp.44–5.
29. The term 'Entwagu' connotes ruthless and aimless, paranoic tyranny. *See also* J. F. Kaijage, *Kyamutwara*, op. cit., p.552.
30. H. M. Stanley commented that 'the princes were begging for everything they could imagine', when he visited Buhimba. Kakoko and his brother, Kayenje, were administering the area as subchiefs. When king, Kakoko reportedly tortured many people and many others fled the country. *See* H. M. Stanley, *Through the Dark Continent* (London, 1878).
31. Omukama literally means a milker.
32. A. O. Anacleti and D. K. Nagala, 'The Cattle Complex in the Ancient West Lake Kingdoms', *La Civilization Ancienne des Peuples des Grands Lacs* (Editions Karthala, 75013 Paris), pp.148–59.
33. As a subject relating to property rights, the issue of Nyarubanja is analysed by Hans Cory and M. M. Hartnoll, op. cit., pp.123–36.
34. In the Bahaya language, 'to be rich' is synonymous with 'to own cattle' or *Kutunga*, hence the more cattle one has the richer one is expected to be.
35. Zoe Marsh and G. W. Kingsnorth, op. cit., pp.7–8.
36. About a quarter of all the banana plants in a common Bahaya plantation is comprised of the bitter plantain known as *embüle*. When mature, the fruit is ripened yellow before being pressed to produce the juice which, when fermented by using bitter millet, *sorghum vulgare*, yields banana wine.
37. The legal aspects are analysed by Hans Cory and M. M. Hartnoll, op. cit., pp.260–2.
38. Kushemba means literally 'to cover with something'. In practice, it was applied to the procedure of negotiating for the land title and payment of a fee to the authorities in return for ownership.
39. The major types caught are tilapia, carp, catfish and sardines.
40. For all intents and purposes, an *Ikokooro* was a craft guild with an efficient administrative system. The head of the group organized the group members so as to ensure the regular supply of fish. More importantly, the *Ikokooro* undertook to train young fishermen.
41. The iron and steel industry in Buhaya in ancient times is discussed by P. Schmidt, 'An Interim Report on Pre-History Research in West Lake' and in 'Pre-History of Iron Age Africa with a Focus on North Western Tanzania' (Kagera Region Archives).
42. Rugomora Mahe tried to build one high tower which collapsed, killing many workers, and the attempt was abandoned. Cf. Iris Berger, op. cit., p.36.
43. The rings are called *milinga* and the thinner type are *nyelele*.
44. Useful notes on East African trade before the sixteenth century are provided by D. A. Wilson, *East African History*, op. cit., pp.10–11 and 20–1.
45. The common agricultural implements were the hoe, banana sickle (orwabyo), banana knife (omuolo) and spade (ekiosho). For ornaments, there were bells for dancers and dogs and copper rings. Examples of weapons were spears and arrows.
46. For a captivating and concise account of the slave trade, *see* Zoe Marsh, op. cit., Chapter 5, pp.74–7. *Also see* D. A. Wilson, *East African History, 1000–1970*, op. cit., pp.22–5, and H. Mapunda, *Historia ya Mapambano ya Mwafrika* (Tanzania Publishing House, 1976), pp.79–94. Useful accounts are also to be found in J. H. Speke, *Journal of the Discovery of the Source of the Nile*, op. cit.

47. Other important departments were those of food (omuyondo) and animal care (omukondo), divinity (endagu), metalwork (emuhesi) and barkcloth beating (omukomagi). For an illustrated account, *see* H. Rehse, *Kiziba*, op. cit., pp.10–13.
48. Many books have been written in the vernacular providing reading material for primary school pupils. For an account of the traditional stories or fables, *see* Sir Harry Johnston, *The Uganda Protectorate*, op. cit., Vol. II, pp.601–3.
49. Why the Bahaya, and indeed the other Bantu-based communities of Central Africa, did not develop some form of writing remains one of the intriguing mysteries of African history. All the more so given that there were ample writing materials, including boards and papyrus which was woven into page-like basketwork. Besides, there had been migrations from the Nile Valley where writing had developed several millennia before. Furthermore, the cavemen had written (drawn) on the walls long before the arrival of the Bantu communities in Buhaya, for example at Nsongezi.
50. Canon Ignace Bonabaisi defines Nyarubanja as a composite plantation containing two, three or four plantations. Cf. his *Ikany-Nagambo*, op. cit.
51. In medieval parlance, Nyarubanja corresponds best to the *demesne* rather than to feudality in general or to the *manor*. It was the demesne which comprised land directly belonging to the landlord who, at will, could demand that the tenants work on it. A comprehensive analysis of the manorial system is provided by E. Lipson, *The Economic History of England*, Vol. I (London: A & C Black Ltd., 1929), pp.1–76.
52. Jacques J. Maquet, 'A Research Definition of African Feudality', in *Journal of African History*, Vol. III, No. 2 (1962), p.309.
53. Ibid.
54. Jack Goody, 'Feudalism in Africa', in *Journal of African History*, Vol. IV, 1 (1963), pp.1–18.
55. Marc Bloch, 'La Société Féodale', *Les Classes et le Gouvernement des Hommes* (Paris: Editions Albin Michel, 1940), pp.241–52.
56. For a full picture of medieval feudalism, *see* M. M. Postan (ed.), *The Cambridge Economic History of Europe*, Vol. I (Cambridge: University Press, 1971), *See also* Carl Stephenson, *Medieval History, Europe from the Second to the Sixteenth Century* (New York & Evanston: Harper & Row), pp.205–6.
57. For the general features of feudalism, *see* E. Lipson, *The Economic History of England*, Vol. I, op. cit.
58. Taken from M. M. Postan (ed.), *The Cambridge Economic History of Europe*, Vol. I, op. cit., p.235.
59. Jacques J. Maquet, 'A Research Definition of African Feudality', in *Journal of African History*, op. cit., p.309.
60. Lucy Mair, *Primitive Government* (Aylesbury: Hazel Watson & Vincy Ltd., 1964), p.166.
61. Hans Cory and M. M. Hartnoll, *Customary Law of the Haya Tribe*, op. cit., pp.123–4.
62. Priscilla Copeland Reining, 'Haya Land Tenure: Land Holding and Tenancy', in *Anthropological Quarterly*, Vol. XXV, No.2 (1962), pp.58–73.
63. A. O. Anacleti and D. K. Nagala, 'The Cattle Complex in the Ancient West Lake Kingdoms', in *La Civilisation Ancienne des Peuples des Grands Lacs*, op. cit., pp.148–59.
64. D. N. McMaster, 'Change of Regional Balance in Bukoba District of Tanganyika', op. cit., pp.79–93.
65. J. F. Mbwiliza, 'The Hoe and the Stick: a Political Economy of the Heru Kingdom c. 1750–1900' in *La Civilisation Ancienne des Peuples des Grands Lacs*, op. cit. pp.100–14.
66. A legal basis for nyarubanja rights is presented by Hans Cory and M. M. Hartnoll, *Customary Law of the Haya Tribe*, op. cit., pp.127–60. *See also* D. S. Ngalo, *Nyarubanja na Sheria* (Nairobi: East African Literature Bureau, 1976).
67. Lucy Mair, *Primitive Government*, op. cit., p.169.
68. The issue of sentimental attachment to a locality is of fundamental importance in understanding both the Bahaya and the African form of feudality. It provides the

missing link in the available analyses on this subject. Cf. E. Colson in L. H. Gann and P. Duignan, op. cit., pp.32–7.

69. It is believed that Bantu clans forged ahead with the metalwork technology they brought with them from the Bight of Benin.

70. For current legislation, *see* D. S. Ngalo, *Nyarubanja na Sheria*, op. cit., pp.65–96.

71. R. J. Unstead, *Kings and Serfs: A Pictorial History 1086–1200*, Vol. II (Aylesbury: Hazel Watson & Viney Ltd.), p.6.

72. A comparison of the tribal feudal systems is presented by E. B. Dobson, in *Journal of African Administration*, Vol. II, No.2 (1952), where he describes feudalism in 10 tribes, i.e. the Bahaya, Sukuma, Nyamwezi, Gogo, Arusha, Sambaa, Kuria, Kerewe, Hangaza and Azigua.

73. By the Tanganyika Law of 1961, chieftainships were abolished though communities were free to continue to revere their traditional rulers.

CHAPTER V

THE COFFEE REVOLUTION DURING THE OMUJUNGU PERIOD: 1890–1960

Introduction

The beginning of the European colonial era, referred to as the OMUJUNGU (European) period (1890–1960), coincided with the intensive cultivation of coffee, the impact of which rivalled that of the banana in the nineteenth century. Although other influences played a part, the establishment of the coffee industry was the result of three main factors, namely the colonial administration, the native political structure and the agricultural system of the time. The way these factors interacted to establish the coffee industry in Buhaya constitutes the major focus of this chapter. In providing the background to these elements, it will be necessary, in certain cases, to describe historical and political events at length. In this connection, the colonial administration is examined with reference to its impact on the indigenous people and their institutions. Similarly, a brief description of the coffee plant and its culture is provided as a background to the revolutionizing process of Buhaya. Emphasis, however, is to be placed on the important effects of the coffee industry on the social, cultural and monetary sectors.

Although the colonial era is divided up between the German and the British administrations, the two were similar in many respects except, of course, for the language. Therefore, a brief and essential description is provided for both administrations. It should be pointed out that a number of governmental measures introduced at the territorial level significantly affected Buhaya; these will be discussed as we go along.

The approach adopted in this chapter is essentially descriptive so as to maintain the interest of the general reader. As regards the cut-off dates for the Omujungu era, 1890–1960, its beginning coincides with the year when Emin Pasha, the first German administrator hoisted the German flag on Buhaya soil. 1960 is the year when Tanganyika Territory reached Responsible Government status. From the point of view of historical continuity, however, the period could really be extended at both ends.

The Early German Administration

It took more than five years from the moment that Mangungo, chief of Msovero in Usagara, affixed his thumb to a document presented by Dr Karl Peters of the German Colonizing Society (GCS) in November 1884, for the

German flag to be hoisted on Buhaya soil on 1 November 1890. The contract which Mangungo is believed to have signed in ignorance was a stepping-stone in the German colonization of the land west of Zanzibar.[1] That the administration took so long to reach Bukoba can be explained not only by the transport problems of the time (there were hardly any roads, steamer services or railways) but also by the flimsy nature of the treaty's legality; the treaty was not adopted by the German government until 1886. Before then, the German administrators in Bukoba were answerable to Dr Karl Peters and the GCS.

However, the white man was a familiar sight long before Emin Pasha (significantly nicknamed Bwana Basha = Mr Bad Omen) pitched his tent at Nyamukazi Beach, hardly a kilometre from the present town centre of Bukoba. One simply has to go back to 1861, when John Hanning Speke and his entourage arrived at Bweranyange, the palace of the famous Rumanyika Orugundu.[3] Henry Morton Stanley touched the shore of Buhaya in 1875 on his first trip around Lake Victoria.[3] He visited Bweranyange for the first time on 25 February 1876 and reached the west shore of Lake Victoria on 1 March 1876.[4]

In July 1880, Father P. Girault, of the White Fathers' Mission, landed at Mubembe village, on the southern tip of Kemondo Bay. On his abortive trip from Kibuga, the capital of Buganda, Dr Karl Peters landed at Nyamukazi beach in Bukoba town, in April 1890, as a stopover to Bukumbi and, further on, to the Indian Ocean. Both Emin Pasha and Stanley left Lake Albert for the eastward journey on 10 April 1889 and the caravan is believed to have crossed the Kagera, stopped at Bweranyange in August 1889, and at Bukumbi, the White Fathers' Mission station at the southern end of Lake Victoria on 28 August 1889, before heading for Zanzibar.[5] It was during this journey that Emin Pasha set foot on Buhaya soil for the first time and he was very likely fascinated by the country.

Long before the appearance of the European, the Arabs had penetrated and had established their centres in several parts of Buhaya. Their aim had been to carry on trade, including the slave trade, and Bweranyange had become their major centre for the collection of slaves from the surrounding areas and as a stopping point for caravans from Bunyoro, Buganda, Ankole, etc., on their way to Kaze, Unyanyembe or Tabora and onward to the Zanzibar international market. Besides the slave trade, Arab penetration linked the coast to the interior in terms of culture and the exchange of goods such as textiles, beads and metal items. This Arab presence in the interior facilitated the work of European explorers by showing them routes and giving them contacts with the African leaders of the time.[6]

The Arrival of Emin Pasha

By the time he took command of the Buhaya region, Mehemed Emin Pasha, whose real name was EDUARD SCHNITZER, was 50 years old. He was born in the town of Opole (Oppeln),[7] Poland, which was then under

Prussian rule and, after practising medicine in the Turkish army in 1865, he joined Charles George Gordon in Egypt in 1875 from where, in 1878, he took charge of Equatoria Province (Sudan) in the service of the British government. It was there that H. M. Stanley was sent to rescue him in 1887 and they travelled together towards Zanzibar where they arrived in November 1889. When he was administering Equatoria (Sudan) on behalf of the British general, Charles George Gordon, Emin Pasha was dangerously encircled by the Mahdi's army during the period 1885–8.[8] To rescue him, so to speak, Stanley was commissioned to travel to Equatoria. Stanley had to sail up the Congo River, commencing on 18 March 1887, and he managed to reach Lake Albert on 18 December 1887.[9] He reported that he had to comb the Ituri forest before rescuing Emin Pasha who, together with his encircled soldiers, had been expecting to die for lack of supplies.[10]

Emin Pasha had to travel back from Zanzibar to Bukoba to take up his commission as administrator on behalf of the German East African Company (GEAC). He effectively assumed duties as Reichskommissar on 1 November 1890.[11] When Karl Peters met him for the first time at Mpwapwa on 19 June 1890, he described Emin Pasha as follows:

> A gentleman under the middle height, wearing a simple blue uniform and helmet. A black beard framed in a face whose deep wrinkles told of a long mental strain.[12]

Emin's experience in other parts of Africa, however, enabled him to move quickly in handling the tribe by laying down various projects which had far-reaching effects on the region, such as the introduction of coffee production and road building. Whatever his shortcomings, the Bahaya people have taken his image to be that of the Germans in general, rough and tough but efficaciously hardworking. Unfortunately, time was too short for this image of both Emin Pasha and the German rulers to be changed.

Emin Pasha's unique position in Buhaya history is not solely due to his being the first German administrator but also partly to his personality and experience. True, some of his measures reflected the characteristic German harshness tainted with his trauma in Equatoria (Sudan), with his chequered life and mercenary adventurism. At heart, however, he was profoundly determined and dedicated to his principles, amongst which was his determination to eliminate the slave-trade and civilize the African.[13]

The economic base which Emin laid in Buhaya is perhaps what gives him such prominence in the chronicles of the region. Mention has already been made of his personal efforts to launch the coffee industry and to prove that 'good coffee grows here' and of his dedication to its success. Besides the coffee plant, he introduced strawberries, various flowers, sugar-cane, potatoes, peas, oil palm and wheat. After only two months in the area, he was able to write 'this morning I planted some fifty coffee trees ... oil palms are to follow'.[14]

Besides, it was Emin and Karl Peters who decided on the site of Bukoba for a regional capital, as the latter had called at the place on his way back from Kibuga. On arrival at the site, Emin confirmed Karl Peters' proposal. More importantly, he himself prepared a layout of the town and went ahead and constructed the buildings, roads and bridges. Within two weeks, he was able to write 'the bridges are finished ... we are busily at work making bricks, bricklaying and carpentering to our hearts' delight...'[15] His planning and developmental interests, however, were not confined to the capital for he devised roads to connect the kingdoms with the headquarters.

As a philanthropist-cum-politician, Pasha also laid a strong foundation of understanding between the Bahaya and the Germans. He appreciated good relations with the natives and, writing to his sister, he stated:

> I am on very good terms with the surrounding negro chiefs and tribes.[16]

His success in befriending Mukotani, the king of Kyamutwara, if it had lasted, would have had considerable influence on the history of Kyamutwara, if not Buhaya. He decided to make Bukoba the major administrative centre for Buhaya, Rwanda and Burundi. In a way, he had an esteem for the Bahaya native political system which he was ready to use in administering the territory. He also maintained good relations with the missionaries of all denominations. His human side was best displayed by the attachment he had to his servants and his guards, the Nubian soldiers and their families. This sentiment might have facilitated the acceptance of the German economic programmes. By working along with his people and setting the example, he greatly increased his credibility.

Emin Pasha, who stayed for 104 days or about three months, left early in 1891 to return to Equatoria and was succeeded by Mr Langheld (1891–92), then Dr F. Stuhlmann (nicknamed Bwana Muzuri) and others, as will be discussed subsequently.[17] As 'residents', meaning heads of administration in the Bukoba region, they had full powers to decide on any issue almost independently of the German government. However, they were under instructions to act through the Bakama. It should be noted, however, that the majority of the administrators, including Emin Pasha, had a military background which reflected not only the Germans' opinion of Buhaya but also might explain the harshness with which the Bahaya associated German rule.

The Germans and the Bakama [18]

At the time of Emin Pasha's arrival in Bukoba, the ruling Bakama in each chiefdom were as shown below:

Bugabo	Kahyoza ka Nkwere
Ihangiro	Nyarubamba eya Ntare
Karagwe	Kaketo
Kihanja	Kahigi ka Rugomora

Kiziba	Mutatembwa wa Ruhangarazi
Kyamutwara	Mukotani eya Kaitaba
Maruku	Bwogi (Omuhinda)
Missenyi	Rwekiika

With the establishment of German rule, the Bakama had to undergo a radical and abrupt change in their traditional method of governing the kingdoms. The Bakama tried their best to resist this change. The Germans, however, left no doubt of their readiness to resort to force when dealing with any dissidence to European rule and it was on this basis that the above-named Bakama had to cope with the newly installed administration of Emin Pasha.

Of the eight Bakama, Mukotani of Kyamutwara was certainly the most influential, not only because the Germans had established their regional headquarters hardly six miles from his palace, but also because, from the military point of view, he was the most powerful. A tall, handsome man, his face revealed an alert and intelligent character which could not hide an air of self-importance.[19] A capable ruler, his actions were characterized by foresight, caution and decisiveness. In 1890, he had just ascended a shaky throne and his prime objective was to consolidate his power by military expansion. In this connection, he had successfully waged war with Bugabo and would not have lost the opportunity to attack Kihanja, in the south.

Mukotani's hate and suspicion of white men could not be easily concealed though he used diplomatic tactics in dealing with them. Thus, on Saturday, 5 April 1890, he negotiated with and satisfied Karl Peters of the German Colonizing Service about the apparently trivial demands of King Mwanga of Buganda, who wanted to be recognized as the supreme ruler of Buhaya.[20] On hearing the demands of Mwanga, Mukotani conceded, knowing very well that it would be difficult to enforce such arrangements. More importantly, however, Mukotani had to handle Emin Pasha and other German administrators. Happily, the two personalities had realized in their relations how much they needed each other, as was demonstrated by Mukotani's act in hastening to send gifts to Emin shortly after the latter's arrival at Bukoba. Although Emin Pasha's initial impression of the Mukama was that of 'this tall dirty Negro', it did not take long for Emin to discover how to get along with him.

The arrival of the Germans helped Mukotani to consolidate his position as the Mukama of Kyamutwara.[21] However, it also implied an end to his expansionist ambitions, as the Europeans would not allow him to make wanton attacks on neighbouring kingdoms. This frustration exacerbated his hatred for the white man, which he was careful not to display to the administrators but which he could not hide when dealing with the missionaries, whom he despised as 'women'. In 1892, he attacked a White Fathers' Mission station at Nyanga near Kashozi and, had it not been for the intervention of the German administrator, Herr Langheld, who was backed by Kahyoza of Bugabo and Baganda soldiers, the missionaries would have been wiped out. Having lost the war to the Germans, Mukotani fled to Uganda where he lived in exile. As already indicated in Table IV–2, he was succeeded by Bwahama who, in turn, was succeeded by Muntu Emanzi ya Ilimamoshe, who remained on the throne until 1916. Those Bakama who succeeded Mukotani had learnt a lesson and so tried to avoid open dissidence with the colonial administrators.

Kahyoza ka Nkwere of Bugabo played another major role in the Bahaya–German interaction. Of an average height, dark complexion and long hair, Kahyoza was dandyish and fond of pomp and gaiety.[22] A fellow Bankango clansman of Mukotani, the two were arch-enemies, a feud which was deeply exploited by the Germans to help them rule these kingdoms. Quick to act, Kahyoza dealt effectively with Karl Peters' threats regarding the supremacy of King Mwanga and did not hesitate to curry the favour of Emin Pasha and the missionaries; consequently, he was able to preserve the Kingdom of Bugabo.[23]

Nyarubamba, the king of Ihangiro, was suspicious of the Europeans and yet he avoided clashes with them. Though showing open hostility to the missionaries, he gave a state reception for Lieutenant Langheld, in January 1891, when the latter was on his way from Mpwapwa to Bukoba to relieve Emin of his duties. On the whole, Nyarubamba was a person who preferred to play it safe and thus he succeeded in getting along with the European administrators.

Kahigi Rugomora of Kihanja was a contrast to Mukotani. He had built a huge rampart around his palace at Bulembo, Kihanja Plateau, and, for fear of Mukotani, he placed himself at the mercy of the Germans who, exploiting this timidity, coaxed him into shifting his palace to Kanazi, about 15 miles from Bukoba town. It is alleged that the Germans sought the move to Kanazi so as to provide them with a buffer against the aggressive Mukotani. In appreciation for his submissiveness, Kahigi was made the paramount chief of the land between Bugabo and Ihangiro, through which he earned the name 'Rubamba', meaning one who has united the kingdoms. Furthermore, the threat posed by Mukotani was permanently dealt with since he had regained the 'Greater Kyamutwara'. Being a colonial pinion of the Germans, however, cost him his life when the British took over.

Perhaps after Rumanyika of Karagwe, Mutatembwa of Kiziba was the next best known Mukama outside Buhaya before the time of the Germans. A tall, lanky individual, Mutatembwa had a commanding personality, characterized by a long face framed by a pointed beard. The awe associated with his name greatly contrasted with the inviting and congenial expression of his large, round, alert eyes. As a gifted speaker, he was known to have engaged his court for hours in serious discussion or in story-telling, though he was a good listener too and a wise, firm administrator by any standards. In 1870, he ascended the throne as the 17th Babiito Mukama of Kiziba, succeeding his father, Ruhangarazi II. He retained Bwanjai, his birthplace, as the capital of the kingdom.[24]

His reign of 33 years during one of the most crucial periods in Kiziba has made Mutatembwa one of the outstanding Bakama of all time. It is reported that, at the time of his death, he left behind 84 children and some 70 wives. Among his sons, Rweshabura, the eldest, and Karutasigwa, the ultimate successor to the throne, were the widest known. His reign can be described as strong, wise and progressive. In his old age, however, Kiziba was torn by rivalry among his sons, and this led to a bitter civil war from 1888–1900 during which many people died and thousands fled the country.[25]

During the fighting, the faction led by Rweshabura, known as Balekezi, succeeded in pushing the army of his brother, Bachumita, to the north-eastern corner of the kingdom and managed to imprison his father, Mutatembwa. The cruelty with which Rweshabura dealt with his enemies and others alike made it necessary for the Germans to intervene and help Mutatembwa regain his throne. When he died in 1903, Mutatembwa was succeeded by Karutasigwa, who was crowned Mutahangarwa and who retained the throne till his death in 1916. As shown in Table V–4, subsequent bakama of Kiziba were Mboneko II (1916–27), Mutakubwa (1927–37) and Nestori Lutinwa (1937–61).

Briefly, Mutatembwa's reign can be divided into four periods. First comes the period prior to the arrival of the Europeans, characterized by a highly centralized government which was endeavouring to repel attacks from neighbouring kingdoms, particularly Buganda.[26] Second was the period of the early missionaries, who were repulsed for fear that they would take over his kingdom. Third was the arrival of the Germans, who were forced to avoid him because he suspected their intentions about usurping his kingdom, though after assessing their might, he collaborated with them and even sought their military assistance to fight against Rweshabura. Last were the civil war years, which saw him humiliated and forced to abandon his Bwanjai palace for Kanyigo.

His successor was Mutahangarwa, stouter and shorter than his father. His reign witnessed the laying of the foundations for educational and economic development in Kiziba. However, he had come to the throne when the Germans had already established their rule; in fact, they helped him to acquire the crown and he continued to require their assistance in containing the rivalry of his brother, Rweshabura. Typical of the time, his reign was an extension of the colonial administration.

Mention has already been made of the situation in Karagwe. The succession of the famous Rumanyika went to his son, Kalemera II (Kayenje), who ruled Karagwe for only two years (1883–5) and was succeeded by his son, Nyamukuba, who became Ndagara II. Ndagara II was a minor and so, as it was necessary to have a regent, Kakoko, his uncle, undertook to administer the country though he turned out to be a murderous tyrant who killed many people including near relatives.[27] Ndagara II died shortly after assuming full powers and left behind a 5-year-old son, Ntare II (Kanyorozi). The regency this time was contested by many relatives from whom Kaketo, his uncle, emerged the winner.[28] When the latter tried to repeat the wanton tyranny of the previous regent, he was checked by the Germans who had then established their influence in Karagwe, and who used the opportunity to strengthen their position.

They therefore established a triumvirate of regents comprising Kaketo, Bakahuga, the previous chief minister of Ndagara I, and Kiobya of the Bahunga clan from Kihanja. With the support of the Germans, however, Kiobya became the most influential of the three regents and stayed on as the chief minister even after the king had assumed full powers in 1908. Kaketo was exiled from the country and Ntare II, having been charged with treason, was publicly executed by a firing squad in 1915. Consequently, for the third time in a generation, Karagwe required a regency and the British brought in the Baganda administrators this time. The monarchy was resumed in 1925 when Daud Rumanyika was crowned king and retained the throne until 1939 when he was deposed and replaced by B. I. Ruhinda, who continued to rule the kingdom until the time of independence.

To deal with the disturbances which were triggered off fundamentally by their rule, the Germans resorted to guns, recruited soldiers from outside the tribe and incited rivalry among the chiefs. Despite punitive measures, frequent resistance against European rule occurred in Kiziba, Kyamutwara and Karagwe; these were isolated incidents, but they reflected a feeling of opposition to foreign rule.[29] Consequently, native rulers were deposed, exiled or given other severe punishment.

Other Social Aspects

The role of the Catholic Church in the history of Buhaya was apparently not restricted to evangelization, for at the dawn of the European era it had taken on clear political overtones. With the backing of the German administration, the missionaries would influence the popularity of the Mukama or vice versa. Mukotani's invasion of the mission station at Nyanga in 1892 and the consequent reprisal by Administrator Herr Hermann is but one case in point.

The missionaries' experience in Uganda in setting one king against another taught a lesson to all parties involved, underscoring the need for being more prudent in the case of Buhaya. However, the absence of strong rivalries among the religious factions in the area and the unwavering command of the Germans might have combined to forestall the experience of King Mwanga of Buganda.[30]

The activities of the Catholic Church were spearheaded by the White Fathers (PERES BLANCS as they were known originally). Founded in 1874 by Charles Martial Allemand Lavigerie (1825–92), the Bayonne-born, unorthodox Sorbonne-educated priest-professor who became Cardinal in charge of Algeria, the White Fathers' Society was aimed at abolishing the slave-trade and at spreading the Gospel.[31] Within five years of the society's formation, the White Fathers had reached Uganda and, by 17 June 1879, had pitched their tent at Rubaga Hill, Kampala. About a year later, in July 1880,

Fr. P. Girault had landed at Mubembe Bay, about six kilometres south of Bukoba town, although it took the White Fathers many years before they could establish missions to convert the Bahaya to Christianity. Thus their first effective mission was established 12 years later at Kashozi, and it had meant fighting a war.

Other Christian denominations which were active from the early days of European domination were the Anglicans, particularly after the visit of Bishop Tucker to Bukoba in December 1890. The Bethel Mission also established a centre in Bukoba town from as early as 1907.[32] However, Protestant missionaries had long before been active in many parts of Tanganyika and many European explorers such as David Livingstone and Krapf had come to Africa primarily to undertake missionary work.[33]

The result of the religious conversion activities in Buhaya is presented in Table V–1, which shows the proportion of the various affiliations about half a century after missionary work started in the region. The figures shown correspond to more recent data produced by Goran Hyden which show the following percentages: Catholics (56.73), Protestants (26.92), Muslims (12.50), traditional religions (3.85).[34]

TABLE V–1 *COMPARISON OF RELIGIOUS AFFILIATION IN BUHAYA*

DENOMINATION	NUMBER OF FOLLOWERS	%
1. Catholics	168,920	45.26
2. Protestants	61,473	16.47
3. Muslims	37,068	9.93
4. Traditional Religions and others	105,756	28.34
TOTAL	373,217	100.00

Source: Bukoba Diocese Statistics for 1967/68, which excludes Karagwe District.

The Later Period of German Administration

During the ten years following Emin's departure, Bukoba had ten administrators who held the title of *stationschef*, which was equivalent to that of provincial commissioner. The average stay of the stationschef was one year. Of the ten, only Lieutenant Franz Richter (nicknamed Bwana Korongo) remained four years, from 1892 to 1902. The other exception was Major Willibald von Stuemer whose administration lasted from 1902 to 1916. The names of other stationschef are shown in Table V–2, which indicates that there were twelve administrations in all, three of which involved the same people, Lieutenant Wilhelm Langheld, Lieutenant Karl Hermann and Major von Stuemer.

If Emin opened the German chapter in Buhaya, Major von Stuemer developed it to the end. Stuemer (or Bwana Stima, as he was locally known), took command of Bukoba as stationschef in 1902, replacing Lieutenant Franz Richter. Of Prussian extraction, Stuemer had a long military career, mainly in the foot artillery. Described as short but robust, he had an un-German-like appearance with a congenial personality, perhaps the major quality explaining his long stay in Bukoba. The French missionaries had nicknamed him 'un joli compagnọn', the native version of which was 'Bonjoli kompanyo', because of his agreeable character.[35] His other qualities included a rich administrative

TABLE V–2 *GERMAN HEAD ADMINISTRATORS IN BUHAYA*

	NAME	NICKNAME	PERIOD	TITLE
1.	HEMEDI EMIN PASHA	BWANA BASHA	Nov., 1890 to March, 1891	Reichskommissar
2.	Lieutenant WILHELM LANGHELD	BWANA MUZURI	1891–1892	Stationschef
3.	Lieutenant KARL HERMANN	BWANA KARUMANI	1892–1894	Stationschef
4.	Lieutenant WILHELM LANGHELD	BWANA MUZURI	1894–1895	Stationschef
5.	Lieutenant BERNARD VON KALBEN	BWANA KAMA	1895–1896	Stationschef
6.	Lieutenant KARL HERMANN	BWANA KARUMANI	1896–	Stationschef
7.	Lieutenant GASTON SCHLOBACH		1896–1897	Stationschef
8.	Lieutenant ADOLF VON WULFFEN		1897–1898	Stationschef
9.	Lieutenant FRANZ RICHTER	BWANA KORONGO	1898–1902	Stationschef
10.	Lieutenant WILLIBALD VON STUEMER	BWANA STIMA or BONJOLI KOMPANYO	1902–1905	Stationschef
11.	Major WILLIBALD VON STUEMER	BWANA STIMA or BONJOLI KOMPANYO	1905–1916	Resident
12.	Major GODOVIUS	BWANA LAZIMA	1916	Resident

background, resourcefulness, energy and the capacity to handle the intrigues of the Bakama.

His work falls into two sections, the first one relating to the mandates from the territorial headquarters and the other relating to the administration of Buhaya. During civilian rule, the Germans could hardly have found a more suitable and capable person, for Stuemer was quick to master the political philosophy of the Bahaya and his resourcefulness enabled the Germans to boast of fast development in a region which was very remote from the sea coast. In the political arena, Stuemer aimed at establishing the progressive leadership of chiefs who were loyal to the Germans. This objective was achieved by deposing and substituting the Bakama whenever it suited colonial expedience. He stressed the education of the princes aspiring to the throne so as to facilitate communication with the chiefdoms. In the economic sector, Stuemer emphasized the cultivation of coffee, by more planting and the expansion of the area available for plantations. As a result, coffee output doubled in the 1905–10 period. As shown in Table V–8, the output for 1912 was 681 tons, which was about three times the figure for 1905. It is also reported that Stuemer tried to find markets for coffee (most of it was still being exported through Uganda and Kenya by private middlemen). In addition, he introduced measures for distributing land to peasants, who had been deprived of their property through feudalism, and steps were taken to regulate malpractices exercised under the century-old feudal system called *nyarubanja.*

On the whole, Stuemer had no difficulty in carrying out the directives of the headquarters at Dar es Salaam since most of the measures were left to his initiative. During the war, however, he was less fortunate. Bukoba was conquered by the British after hardly a day's fighting and the territorial command under General Paul von Lettow-Vorbeck could not forgive him for this shameful defeat. Stuemer had also angered the General by delaying a rescue mission to the German forces which, in September 1914, had attacked Kenya and had managed to occupy the small town of Kisii located south of Kisumu. The British defence was able to repulse the attack though it was felt that, had the Germans had some reinforcement, they might easily have advanced north-eastwards. Apparently, Stuemer had hesitated to send troops across Lake Victoria for fear that the British might cross the Kagera River and attack Bukoba town. Unable to get the reinforcements expected, the Kisii expedition had to retreat to Mwanza town by means of their ship, also called the *Mwanza.*[36]

While trying to avoid going into details of World War I military operations, even those which took place in Buhaya, a brief reference should be made to General Paul von Lettow-Vorbeck, the Saarland-born soldier who added a special dimension to the fighting in German East Africa. Since frequent mention will be made of his name, it might be noted that during the war he managed to establish a temporary capital at Tabora, where he relied on his own resourcefulness to manufacture the equipment needed by his army. He even went to the extent of establishing a mint and produced a currency which circulated for a couple of years.[37] Soldiers who served under him recall that he had a captivating personality and many followed him willingly on his escape to Nyasaland and Rhodesia.[38] He is described as 'a great man for improvisation ... (who) directed the making of salt from sea-water; he had sugar distilled from honey ... and bandages made from bark'.[39]

This section cannot be considered complete without a brief mention of Governor Freiherr Albrecht von Rechenberg, whose administration laid the

TABLE V–3 *GERMAN GOVERNORS IN TANGANYIKA*

PERIOD	NAME	TITLE
1. 1885–1889	DR KARL PETERS	MANAGER, GERMAN EAST AFRICAN COMPANY (DEUTSCHE OSTAFRIKA GESELLSCHAFT)
2. 1889–1891	MAJOR HERMANN VON WISSMANN	REICHSKOMMISSAR FÜR OSTAFRIKA
3. 1891–1893	FREIHERR JULIUS VON SODEN	GOVERNOR
4. 1893–1895	COLONEL FRIEDRICH VON SCHELE	GOVERNOR
5. 1895–1896	MAJOR HERMANN VON WISSMANN	GOVERNOR
6. 1897–1901	GENERAL EDUARD VON LIEBERT	GOVERNOR
7. 1901–1905	COUNT ADOLF VON GÖTZEN	GOVERNOR
8. 1906–1911	FREIHERR ALBRECHT VON RECHENBERG	GOVERNOR (First Civilian Governor)
9. 1912–1916	HEINRICH SCHNEE	GOVERNOR

Sources: Various publications including Laura S. Kurtz, *Historical Dictionary of Tanzania* (Metuchen, N. J. & London. The Scarecrow Press inc., 1978)

foundation for some important aspects of economic policy.[40] Born of a staunch Catholic and diplomatic family in Madrid in 1861, he specialized in East European affairs with particular emphasis on Russia. Through his linguistic flair, he could also speak Swahili, Arabic and Gujerati. His experience as a provincial magistrate in Tanga in 1893 and in Zanzibar in 1896 greatly influenced his appointment as governor. He arrived in Dar es Salaam in 1906 with a basic mandate to reconstruct the colony after the Maji Maji rebellion which had taken place during the administration of his predecessor, Count Adolf von Götzen.[41]

His impact on the economy of the territory was felt in all sectors, though principally in agriculture, transport, commerce and labour. On the agricultural front, he established measures for developing native or peasant production which was strongly opposed by European settlers. In transport, Rechenberg will always be associated with his personal effort to have the Central Railway Line constructed. As regards commerce, he favoured the middlemen though he was not opposed to the development of indigenous entrepreneurship. In the labour field, he devised laws which would govern the transportation and remuneration of plantation workers, so badly paid in

European farms. Overall, his administration was marked by the systematic enactment of the policy with which the German period is largely associated in Tanganyika.[42]

During the initial years, Rechenberg had only a peripheral interest in the up-country population like Buhaya but he gradually came to appreciate the inland tribes, particularly when they proved ideal for revenue collection. In the light of this, he included Buhaya in the itinerary of Reichs Colonial Minister Dernberg, who visited Buhaya in 1907 and so received an overall impression of the colonial administration.[43]

Fighting During World War I

If the German period began dramatically with the arrival of a gang of gun-wielding strangers led by Karl Peters and Emin Pasha, it ended in an equally dramatic defeat caused by the British. The departure of the Germans from Bukoba was signalled by the boom of cannon fire at dawn one June morning in 1916. The amphibious thrust of the British, whose guns were heard throughout the eight kingdoms of Buhaya, sent the Germans fleeing to Bihalamuro, 110 miles south, where they established a temporary capital.

The amphibious expedition of the British Army on Bukoba was operated from Uganda, the location of the headquarters of the East African command under General Sir Charles Crewe.

The first major British attack on Bukoba town took place at dawn on 30 October 1914 with shelling concentrated on the wireless tower situated on the northern bank of the Kanoni River.[44] The second major attack on the town occurred again at dawn on 22 June 1915, when a combined land and sea operation under General Stewart succeeded in reaching Kahororo village and began to shell the town simultaneously from the hills and the ships, which were approaching from the north-east. Shortly after disembarking, the British unit found itself engaged in fierce fighting at Rwonga Hill, near Kahororo, and indeed tested the strength of the German Army, which was under the command of Lieutenant Godovius (Bwana Lazima) and the direction of Lieutenant V. Brandes (Ruhosho), on the very day that Captain Stuemer was summoned to return from the Kagera River front, where he had been trying to repulse invading troops from Uganda. Fighting continued the following day when the Germans were forced to abandon Bukoba and move to Kishogo and Kamachumu further west. But on 24 June at 12.30 hours the British Army, without giving any explanation, evacuated the town.

According to the account of Major von Lettow-Vorbeck, the second expedition to Bukoba comprised 800 Europeans, 400 askaris (native soldiers) and 300 Indians.[45] It was equipped with three cannons, eight armoured cars and a fleet of armed steamers. At the end of the fighting, he counted 150 dead on the British side, as opposed to a loss, on the German side, of only two Europeans, five askaris and seven others. According to H. Cory, however, the number of German soldiers killed at Bukoba, Kyaka and Biharamulo numbered 276 out of the total of 400. The death toll on 24 June, for example, included four Germans and seven British.

From the beginning of the war up to the British occupation of Bukoba, many incidents of fighting occurred along the border between Buhaya and Uganda. It was not until June 1916, however, that Bukoba had to prepare for a fresh wave of invasions. By then, the Belgian Army was pushing forwards from the Congo towards Lake Victoria while the British Army in Uganda was moving southwards. Owing to the importance of the Belgian attack as a factor in the defeat of the Germans in Buhaya, a few paragraphs will be devoted to describing the Belgian action during the month of July 1916.

The Belgians in Buhaya

The presence of the Belgians in Buhaya had been noticed for many years before the war, though hitherto it had been associated with the administration of the Congo state. Their arrival in July 1916, however, received special attention from the local people, particularly those who had developed great loyalty to the Germans. After the Belgians defeated the Germans at Kimwani, however, the attitude of the Bahaya to them changed to that of admiration, as evidenced by a good number of the local children being named 'Mubiligi', i.e. 'the Belgian'.

After expelling the Germans from Rwanda and Burundi, the Belgian objective was to occupy the region between the Great Lakes and Tabora, located in the centre of German East Africa. As part of the general strategy of the allied nations, however, the British were to attack Bukoba from the north while the Belgians were advancing from the west; the two armies were to unite to invade Tabora, the stronghold of the German Army. To reach their target, the Belgian forces had to attack German posts, including those located in Buhaya.[46]

The Belgian command was centred at Stanleyville (Kisangani) under the general surveillance of Commander-in-Chief Major-General Tombeur.[47] The command comprised two brigades known as the North and the South. The North Brigade was commanded by Colonel Molitor who had two regiments under him, namely the 3rd Regiment under Major Bataille and the 4th Regiment under Major Rouling. The South Brigade was under the command of Lieutenant-Colonel Olsen, of Danish nationality. In all, it was estimated that, at the beginning of 1916, the Belgian force numbered 10,000 soldiers and 60,000 porters, not counting reserves and other security forces. Thanks to the Atlantic coastline of the colony, the army in the Congo was well supplied from Europe and there was no disruption by blockades of the ocean routes.

The British forces in East Africa were under the command of General Jan Christian Smuts for the Kenyan sector and Sir Charles Crewe in Uganda, as already mentioned. Under Smuts was Major-General Sir Jacob Louis van Deventer, who captured the town of Moshi. Other troops under him were led by Major-General Coen Brits, Major-General A. R. Hoskins, Brigadier General S. H. Sheppard and Brigadier General Hannington. In all, the British East African Army was estimated at some 42,000 troops, not counting the naval and airforce units. The force had a special advantage in having access to the sea, on which it depended for supplies from Britain and the rest of the Empire. The Ugandan Railway also proved to be a major advantage in supplying the units in Uganda and the interior of Kenya. In addition, the British Army benefited from the reinforcement of the Rhodesian and South African forces.

For an effective operation against the Germans, however, the Belgians and the British had to co-ordinate their action closely as well as working to complement their respective resources efficiently. In this context, the British supplied modern equipment to the Belgians while the latter tried to mobilize the colonial resources, without which the Germans could not have easily been dislodged from the region of the Great Lakes. Their logistics and communication systems also had to be co-ordinated.

As for the German side, the territorial command was under Major-General von Lettow-Vorbeck, whose army of 12,000 troops had to fight a combined allied force of about 300,000 soldiers.[48] In the early period of the war, the movements of the army also depended on the orders of the Governor in Dar es Salaam.[49] The initial target of the German offensive was to capture the Ugandan Railway line and thereby weaken the British advance from the north. However, since the British had mounted an effective blockade of the ocean routes from the early years of the war, Lettow-Vorbeck's supply lines from Europe had been cut and he was forced to resort to guerrilla-type tactics, a field in which he proved exceptionally competent, since he did not actually surrender until 1919.

The Entry of the Belgians into Buhaya

The initial entry of the Belgian Army into Buhaya took place on 18 June 1916 when Colonel Molitor, leading the 3rd Regiment under the command of Major Bataille, crossed the Kagera River. Owing to its rocky and marshy course, the river permitted easy crossing at three points only: Kageye, Migera and Rusumo. Indeed, the Germans had already identified Rusumo as a place to construct a railway bridge to link Kigali and Tabora and it was there that the 3rd Regiment crossed to enter the German colony. By the time the Belgian Army reached Rusumo, however, the Germans had already crossed to the eastern bank and had taken strategic positions so as to check the Belgian advance. After some fighting and manoeuvres, the Belgians managed to cross and push their way forwards to Biharamulo, which they captured on 24 June before advancing to seize Namirembe and Busira Yombo on the shores of Lake Victoria by 27 June. By occupying Namirembe, the Belgians had headed off the German Army from retreating to Tabora. Being chased by the British forces approaching from Uganda, the Germans had no choice but to confront the Belgian lines to the south of Buhaya. To reinforce the Belgian front on the Birharamulo–Namirembe line, the 4th Regiment under Major Rouling, marching from Burundi, had to cross the Ruvuvu River at Ruanilo and advance eastwards towards Lake Victoria. This crossing, which took place between 16 and 19 June, proved to be very perilous because of heavy attack by the German Army. Despite this handicap, which was aggravated by a shortage of artillery, Major Rouling was able to reach Biharamulo and Namirembe as planned.

Meanwhile, the rearguard of the German Army, which had been fighting in Bukoba, was frantically trying to advance southwards when it discovered that the Belgians had already blocked its way. On 2 July, the German units under Captain Godovius encountered Major Rouling's troops at Kashozi-Bakaya, located about 12 miles east of Biharamulo and 12 miles south of Namirembe.[50]

The historic battle was signalled by gunshot at midday on 2 July 1916 and, after sporadic shooting for some hours, calm returned until the following day when gunfire resumed again at midday. The climax of the battle occurred when Rouling came face to face with Godovius. The two soldiers staged a duel and in the process, Rouling was shot five times; one shot immobilized his right arm, another his left and the third went through his head. Godovius was seriously wounded and was captured by the Belgians. However, even when the commanders had fallen, fierce fighting raged on. No sooner had Captain Hubert assumed command of the Belgian side than he died of bullet wounds. At 15.25 hours, a Belgian reinforcement arrived under Lieutenant Campé with Lieutenants Benghem and Bauwerlinck. The three commanders were killed in succession. At that moment, when all appeared desperate on the Belgian side, something like a miracle occurred for, at 16.20 hours, signs of tiredness began to show on the German front and the soldiers began to retreat, disband and run away, although the remnants were able to proceed to Tabora.

So ended 3 July 1916 with the defeat of the Germans at the greatest battle ever fought by the Belgians in Buhaya.[51] That day marked not only the death of many people but also the end of the German era, during which the natives had been increasingly made to believe that the Germans were invincible and omnipotent.

With Namirembe and Biharamulo secured, the Belgian Army under Molitor embarked on the second phase of the advance towards Tabora. From Biharamulo, their next target was Maria-Hilf (Ushirombo), which was occupied on 14 and 15 July 1916 after eight days of fighting at a nearby place called Djobahika. Collaborating closely with the British command of Sir Charles Crewe which had captured Mwanza, the Belgian Army was able to advance steadily towards Tabora. However, it had to fight a fierce battle there at Itaga on 2 September before Tabora surrendered on 19 September. The Belgian Army then pushed eastwards with the British troops advancing from the north and east.

Evaluation of the German Period

The arrival of Emin Pasha in Buhaya signified an unprecedented change in the history of the region. Here was a foreign non-African rule superimposed upon the centuries-old dynasties. Even the tribal religion, hitherto unchallenged and omnipotent in the wilderness, had to face real competition from European and Asian forms of worship. Banana and cattle, until then the backbone of economic life, were supplanted by the coffee bush and the money it was generating. The very philosophy of personal and tribal life was transformed to reflect monetary pursuits, classroom education and interaction with people from other parts of Africa, Europe and Asia. All these changes took place within a few decades, if not years, which precipitated a rare cultural experience. By the year 1900, attire had changed from bark cloth, skin, raffia or even 'nature's garb', to factory-made clothes of some kind. A road network had been built linking Bukoba town to the outer stations up-country and a steamer service linked the region with Mwanza and Bagamoyo on the Indian Ocean coast.[52] Many people had embraced Christianity and schools and dispensaries had been opened at several places including Kashozi, some 10 kilometres north of Bukoba. Even by the standards of that time, if the social change was not complete, it was at least dramatically real.[53]

In the social field, a new class of people was emerging, following the acquisition of classroom education and European techniques enabling one to earn money and influence without having to depend upon social class. Religious movements were also gathering momentum while political and economic liberty were facilitating the fast growth of the monetary system.

One can discern four major elements which influenced the Bahaya, namely the traditional political structure, the Germans, the missionaries and the monetary sector. These four elements have remained fundamental to the social development of the Bahaya tribe in the twentieth century. The impact on the socio-cultural base of the tribe attributable to the European culture can be appreciated if examined from various angles, including the cultural and political revolution, economic changes and social developments. The revolution needs to be considered against the background of the Enfura period of the nineteenth century, characterized by strong centralized and despotic dynasties which were all-powerful and supreme, claiming even the divine right of kings. Providing an administration base to the king was the aristocratic social stratum whose members, though constituting a minority, derived most of the benefits which accrued from the feudalistic system. The majority of the population, mainly of Bantu stock, had been gradually driven into serfdom by means of the manipulation of cattle ownership and political corruption.[54]

With the imposition of the German administration, the Bakama supremacy was automatically curtailed, since orders ceased to originate in the palace (kikale) and came instead from Bukoba, Mwanza, Dar es Salaam and Berlin, according to the hierarchy of the colonial system.

The quick defeat of the Germans and the arrival of the British were equally awesome. The Germans had given the impression of omnipotence and were thus described as 'abadaki abarugile omwa imara', that is 'the Germans whose home is the land of all power'. That the Germans could be defeated by anybody, not to mention the soft-spoken British, was a fact many Bahaya could not come to terms with.[55] Even in accepting British rule, the

Bahaya were trying to bide their time in the hope that the Germans would return after a while.

The Period of British Rule — The Arrival of Baines

Reminiscent of the arrival of the Germans was the official opening of the British Administration at Bukoba on 28 July 1916, some 35 years after the inauguration of German rule. Major D. L. Baines, arriving from Uganda, found

TABLE V–4 *BAKAMA DURING THE BRITISH ADMINISTRATION*

CHIEFDOM	NAME	PERIOD OF REIGN	REMARKS
1. BUGABO	RUGACHWA	1910–1927	DIED
	GABRIEL RUTALEMWA	1927–1937	DEPOSED
	GALIKANI RWEGELERA	1937–IND	
2. IHANGIRO	MUHILE RUHINDA	1911–1936	DIED
	PETRO MUGUNDA	1936–1952	DEPOSED
	SYLVESTER NTARE	1952–IND	
3. KARAGWE	NTARE (VII) KANYOROZI	1908–1916	ONLY TITULAR
	KIOBYA	1903–1916	IMPOSED BY THE GERMANS
	DAUD RUMANYIKA II	1916–1940	DEPOSED
	RUHINDA	1940–IND	
4. KIHANJA	KAHIGI KA RUGOMORA	1890–1916	DIED 1916
	ALFRED KALEMERA	1943–1943	DIED
	HENRICO BWOGI	1943–IND	
5. KIZIBA	MUTAHANGARWA	1903–1916	DIED
	EDWARD MBONEKO II	1916–1927	DIED
	WILLIAM MUTAKUBWA	1927–1937	DEPOSED
	NESTORI LUTINWA	1937–IND	
6. KYAMUTWARA	MUNTU	1901–1916	DEPOSED
	EDWARD LWAIJUMBA	1916–1939	DIED
	GABRIEL RUGABANDANA	1939–IND	
7. MARUKU	DAVID RUGOMORA	1916–IND	
8. MISSENYI	RWEKIIKA	1902–1919	FIRST EFFECTIVE MUKAMA OF MISSENYI
	PAULO RWAMUJONGO	1919–1955	
	SERAPIO KYAMUKUMA	IND	

IND = Time of Independence

a ransacked, shelled town and his first task was reconstruction. A career civil servant, Baines had been working in the provincial administration of Uganda where he had acquired useful experience for dealing with Buhaya. His tall, commanding stature and rough approach, however, made him look more like a German than his predecessor, Stuemer. He even made frequent use of lashing and outdid the Germans by dealing harshly with the Bakama whom he reshuffled like cards.[56] Thus, within a few months of his arrival, he had changed five of the seven Bakama: Alfred Kalemera (Kihanja) succeeded Kahigi, Mboneko (Kiziba) succeeded Mutahangarwa, while Daud Rumanyika (Karagwe), David Rugomora (Maruku) and Lwaijumba (Kyamutwara) were all reinstated. His first preoccupation was therefore to come into contact with the Bakama and his first meeting with them took place within a week of his arrival. At the meeting, which was held on 29 July 1916, Baines wasted no time in getting across the message that the British had replaced the Germans and that he was in no way less serious or determined to administer Buhaya than the latter.

The Bakama who were in place during the British administration are shown in Table V–4, which also indicates those who were deposed and those who were in power at the time of independence.

In the economic field, Baines directed his efforts to the intensification of coffee production and resorted to cruel and forceful methods with the dual objective of demonstrating the power of the newly-arrived authority and promoting economic development. Notwithstanding the methods used, coffee output had increased by 1919 by two-thirds over the 1916 level.[57] Force was also generously applied to further the production of food crops, so badly required in the region which had been cut off from the Indian Ocean supply lines.

The reforms attributed to Baines included the clarification of the regulations governing the powers of the Bakama, particularly with regard to the relations between the chiefs and the administrative office and between the chiefs and subchiefs. The appointment of subchiefs had to be approved by the British administration. Secondly, the feudal system, nyarubanja, was further controlled by making it illegal to evict a tenant without due consideration of the circumstances affecting the ownership of the property. Thirdly, the power of the Bakama to levy tax arbitrarily was also curbed and the amount to be collected or retained was defined. Fourthly, the custom of taking girls to be slaves of the Bakama was outlawed forthwith in November 1916. Before that, tradition had permitted the Bakama to summon any girl to their palaces to become a maidservant.

To a large measure, the firm grip of Baines's administration over Buhaya was facilitated by the Baganda, who had been engaged to ensure that the colonial instructions were carried out at village level. This was due to their ability to communicate with the local people, since the two tribal languages are similar. At the same time, their loyalty to the British made them an apt instrument for a foreign power aiming to occupy the region.[58] As administrators, they were installed at various levels in the chiefdom; in some cases they were in charge of several chiefdoms and in others they occupied the post of subchief. Their responsibilities included supervising tax collection, judging cases and administering civil penalties. On the pretext that they were better able to understand orders than the Bakama, the British administrators preferred dealing directly with them, thus bypassing the Bakama.[59] Consequently, some of the Baganda became as powerful as chiefs and even demanded traditional tributes and recognition. To the British, however, the availability of Baganda executives greatly facilitated the new colonial administration and its effective takeover and enabled it to concentrate on economic development.

British Territorial Policy

Because the Germans were defeated quickly, Buhaya was able to limit the destructive effects of the war and to enjoy an early start to the period of British administration. This depended to a large extent on the policy originating in the capital, Dar es Salaam. Central to the territorial policy was Sir Horace Byatt, who occupied the post of Administrator from 1916 to 1920 before being designated Governor. It is to him that Tanganyika owes its name. It later changed to Tanganyika Territory, and later still to Tanganyika Trusteeship after World War II.

On assuming office as Administrator in 1916, Sir Horace was mainly concerned with restoring the conditions which would enable economic development to be resumed. At the time he took command, the country was in a state of war, for Major-General von Lettow-Vorbeck was still winning battles in Central Tanganyika. Thus, his immediate task was to fight a war and establish British control in a country which for more than three decades had been under German rule. Byatt, however, put to good account his long experience in Somaliland where he had worked in the colonial service. On his arrival in Tanganyika in 1916, he was 41 years old. He was later appointed Governor of Trinidad and Tobago, immediately after leaving Tanganyika in 1924, where he remained until 1929; he died in 1933.

The British had inherited, through the Treaty of Versailles, a Tanganyika which was dilapidated by war. Thousands of people had died on the battle fields and the survivors were plagued with disease, famine and epidemics. The influenza epidemic of 1918–19 and the famine of 1920 are still well-remembered for the rampant social disruption which followed from so many deaths. Though very far removed from Sarajevo and the Balkans, which were starting points of the war, Tanganyika was among the worst victims of World War I.

Sir Horace's term was marked by a cautious and smooth transition from German administration, as he was committed to strengthening indirect rule by upholding the system of 'akidas' or chieftainships established by the Germans. However, his most unforgettable work lay in the rehabilitation and reconstruction of the economy during the war and post-war period.

His successor, Sir Donald Charles Cameron, assumed office as Governor in 1925, after Mr John Scott had acted for him during the interval following the departure of Sir Horace. Born a West Indian Creole in 1872, Sir Donald came to Tanganyika after serving in Nigeria for 17 years in various capacities, including that of Chief Secretary. A tall man with a rather uninviting appearance, Cameron introduced fundamental reforms in the territory. Decisive and efficient, he created a Legislative Council comprising 14 officials and 10 unofficial members nominated by the Governor.[60]

Other political measures established included the formation of 17 provinces from the 22 which had been established by the Germans, the reorganization of the ministries and the stimulation of development among the African population without abandoning the principle of indirect rule. It was in this area of indirect rule that Sir Donald made a practical application of the theory propounded by Lord Lugard. He was quoted as saying that 'indirect rule is a fiction' if it did not help the government to reach the natives. On another occasion he stated:

> It is our duty to do everything in our power to develop the native on lines which will not westernize him and turn him into a bad imitation of a European ... we want to make him a good African... We must not ... destroy the African atmosphere, the African mind, the whole foundation of his race, and we shall certainly do this if we sweep away all his tribal organizations.[61]

The above quotations suggest that while Sir Donald was pragmatic, he was committed to a clear principle of elevating the overall standard of the African people without destroying their indigenous culture. After commissioning an investigation of the political situation in the territory, he rearranged the provinces, established native administrations at the district and lower levels and instituted native courts. The task of forming tribes, however, proved to be more difficult than expected since some of the units established under the akidas involved breaking up natural groupings while, in other cases, the process entailed the creation of a unit out of disparate tribes.[62]

In the field of economics, he laid down commercial policy with respect to the two East African dependencies, namely Uganda and Kenya. In this respect, he was opposed to very close economic ties with the neighbouring territories because he felt that Tanganyika was less developed and therefore likely to be exploited by them. Besides, he felt that the settlers' policy in Uganda and Kenya would be detrimental to the interests of the natives.[63] Overall, his policy was considered to be revolutionary within the context of British colonial policy. On leaving Tanganyika in 1929, he became Governor of Nigeria for the period 1931–35.

Other governors who ruled Tanganyika during the British period are shown in Table V–5. In all, ten governors administered the territory from 1916 to 1961 with the term of Sir Edward Twining being the longest under a single governor.

TABLE V–5 *BRITISH GOVERNORS IN TANGANYIKA*

PERIOD		NAME	TITLE
1.	1916–20	SIR HORACE BYATT	ADMINISTRATOR
	1920–24	SIR HORACE BYATT	GOVERNOR
	1924–24	JOHN SCOTT	ACTING GOVERNOR
2.	1924–31	SIR DONALD CHARLES CAMERON	GOVERNOR
3.	1931–33	SIR STUART SYMES	GOVERNOR
4.	1934–38	SIR HAROLD McMICHAEL	GOVERNOR
5.	1938–42	SIR MARK AITCHISON YOUNG	GOVERNOR
6.	1942–45	SIR WILFRED JACKSON	GOVERNOR
7.	1945–49	SIR WILLIAM BATTERSKILL	GOVERNOR
8.	1949–58	SIR EDWARD TWINING	GOVERNOR
9.	1958–61	SIR RICHARD TURNBULL	GOVERNOR

Among the other major policy measures prevalent under British rule, besides seeking to strengthen the British base, was the application of indirect rule, as mentioned above. Where the tribal units were adequately large and organizationally coherent, a paramount chief was designated. But where tribes were too small to form viable political units, amalgamation was undertaken and the tribes were placed under one leader.[64] Another measure was the passing of the National Authority Ordinance in 1923, by which some of the settlers' land was reallocated to the natives. By the same act, the Masai Reserves were created to cater for their pastoral interests. Mention has already been made of the establishment of the Legislative Council. Note should also be taken of the commencement of nationalist movements, in particular of the African Union and the Tanganyika African Union, which was officially established in 1929 with the support of Sir Donald Cameron. In the light of the political path of the country, the formation of nationalist movements constituted a fundamental development. In 1922, the government passed legislation to abolish all forms of slavery in the territory.[65]

In the monetary sector, the major innovation was the introduction of the British shilling as the standard monetary unit to replace the German rupee. This process was complicated by the lingering war as well as by the expectation of many that the Germans would be returning to power after some time. Consequently, it is said that the German money was buried in the ground and some of it continues to be unearthed today in the process of cultivation.[66]

On taking over, the British emphasized cultivation of food crops in order to compensate for shortages experienced during the war, alongside the measures established to develop cash crops. In the field of commercial policy, the government tried to link the territory to the two other colonies in East Africa, namely Uganda and Kenya. From the point of view of the settlers and Asian communities, this link was a matter of great concern and featured widely in the politics of the time. The 1918 Convention of St Germain-en-Laye upheld the open-door policy (for Tanganyika) which had been enshrined in the Congo Basin Treaties of 1885 and 1890.

In general, the measures undertaken by the administration derived largely from British colonial policy as well as from directives issued by the League of Nations. While colonial policy applied to all dependencies, the League of Nations had laid down terms under which a mandated territory ought to be governed by the trustee nation or mandatory. Thus, the League of Nations had stipulated in Article 3, among other things, that:

> The Mandatory shall be responsible for the peace, order and good government of the territory and shall undertake to promote to the utmost the material and moral well-being and the social progress of its inhabitants. The Mandatory shall have full powers of legislation and administration.

In taking over the administration from the Germans, the British acted with considerable expedition and efficiency. One factor explaining this was the early penetration of the territory while attention was still on fighting the war and not so much on the nationality of the new colonial power. By the end of the war, the British had already established themselves administratively and politically in Tanganyika. The second factor was the proximity of Kenya and Uganda, from whence originated both the experience and the supply of material and personnel needed to run the newly conquered territory. The common language, Swahili, should also be cited as having contributed to facilitate the work of the new administration.

The British colonial period can be divided into a number of chronological phases, the first one being the reconstruction phase which commenced in earnest in 1920 and culminated at the end of Byatt's administration. Then came the economy-building period characterized by Cameron's term. This was followed by the Great Depression of the early 1930s when Tanganyika experienced a general decline in commerce and investment. From 1933 to 1938, there was a general price increase in export commodities and the territory was able to enjoy a short-lived prosperity.

A general picture of the economy is provided in Table V–7, which shows the level of imports and exports of the whole territory. The general impression given by the table is that of slow growth, as the import figure for 1937 shows only a slight increase over that of 1928. In fact, imports declined between 1929 and 1938 and this trend probably continued until the war years. Given the likelihood of a fast increasing population and an expanding market, the period might be described as one of stagnation. The major reason for this was the hesitation of the British government, which feared Hitler's threat to recapture the colonies lost by Germany in the previous war. The significant items exported were sisal, which contributed in 1938 to about 40% of the value of exports, coffee 10%, cotton 10%, and hides and skins 5%. On the import side, the major items were cotton piece-goods, artificial silk, boots and shoes.

The experience of Buhaya during the period 1920–45 was largely a reflection of what was taking place in other parts of the country, particularly with regard to the development of the coffee industry. The efforts of the British administration to maintain the rate of growth of production doubled the level of coffee exports in 1926 as compared to the figure for 1913. The 1920s were marked by a significant rise in prices which fell again during the Great Depression. In the years 1933–38, however, coffee prices soared again to record levels, resulting in an unprecedented increase in the consumption of imported items such as shoes, gramophones and bicycles. The boom of the

TABLE V–6 *BRITISH PROVINCIAL COMMISSIONERS IN BUKOBA*

	NAME	PERIOD	MAJOR GOVERNMENT MEASURES
1.	Major D. L. Baines (Bengesi)	1916–1923	Transitional measures following German rule. Re-emphasized coffee production. Laid down basic social and administrative reforms effected by the British.
2.	Major McMillan (Machumilane)	1920–1921	Acting for Major Baines.
3.	F. W. Brett	1924–1926	
4.	A. H. White	1926–1930	Period coinciding with that of Sir Donald Cameron's governorship.
5.	E. C. Richards	1930–1930	Acting.
6.	A. H. White	1931–	Period of Great Depression.

It should be noted that between 1916 and 1931, Bukoba was administered by the British under a separate Provincial Commissioner. In 1931, Bukoba was joined to Mwanza Province.

post-Depression period, however, was cut short by World War II, which was marked by economic disturbances and shortages.

Politically, during this period, Buhaya was drawn more into the orbit of Tanganyika. It may also be recalled that, during the German administration, the region had been accorded a special status corresponding to that of a sub-state. By recognizing the principle of indirect rule, both Baines and Sir

Horace had followed in the footsteps of the Germans.[67] As if they were anticipating the action of Governor Cameron, Baines and successive administrators tried to deal directly with the people, thus bypassing the Bakama. Some names of British Provincial Commissioners are shown in Table V–6.

The Coffee Revolution

Mere contact with the white man would not have produced such a profound change among the Bahaya had it not been accompanied by an economic transformation based on the coffee culture. Though there are reasons to believe that coffee had been grown in Buhaya for many centuries, its systematic commercial production is only associated with European colonization.[68]

The German administration gave priority to the coffee industry and it is said that Emin Pasha, whose stay at Bukoba lasted hardly three months, personally distributed coffee seeds and seedlings and launched a planting campaign of which he had gained experience when in Equatoria (Sudan). Equatoria is adjacent to the region where coffee is believed to have originated.[69] Using the tribal political structure, the Bukama, German officers, and local leaders embarked on coffee planting throughout the region. Measures to reinforce the campaign included heavy fines, lashing (hamsa-ishirini or 25 lashes, as it was generally known) and, of course, positive incentives in the form of free seeds or seedlings and an assured market.

TABLE V–7 *TANGANYIKA FOREIGN TRADE (1925–28)*

YEAR	EXPORTS in £ millions	INDEX 1925 = 100	IMPORTS in £ millions	INDEX 1925 = 100
1925	2.901	100.0	2.760	100.0
1926	3.026	104.3	3.051	105.2
1927	3.295	113.6	3.529	127.8
1928	3.874	135.5	3.563	129.1
1929	3.723	128.3	4.021	145.7
1930	2.636	90.8	3.721	134.8
1931	1.645	56.7	2.250	81.5
1932	2.190	75.5	2.039	73.9
1933	2.543	87.6	1.764	63.9
1934	2.645	91.2	2.132	77.2
1935	3.445	118.7	2.711	98.2
1936	4.516	155.7	3.067	111.1
1937	4.969	171.3	3.582	129.8
1938	3.708	127.8	3.105	112.5

Source: C. Leubuscher, *Tanganyika Territory* (London: Oxford University Press, 1949), p.205. (Indices calculated by the author)

The success of the coffee planting campaign, however, cannot be attributed solely to the bulldozing and high-handed methods of the Germans, for the hardworking habits of the Bahaya had an important contribution to make as well. The serf, or non-aristocratic clans, viewing the campaign as an emancipation process from the feudalistic bonds of the banana/engaju system, hardly needed to be pushed. But even the monetary revenues were enough of an incentive for, within a few years, a monetary/business class had begun to emerge, attracted by the liberty derived from money. Thus those who were enterprising turned their resources to opening up large farms or to the coffee sale business.[70] By and large, the campaign was encouraged by the social set-up and general competitive conditions.

Geographical factors also played no minor role in the fast development of the coffee culture. The 80-inches average annual rainfall coupled with the red fertile soil was incontestably a necessary factor. Unfortunately, the hilly nature of the country rendered it virtually impossible to mechanize farming or even operate large-scale acreages. This shortcoming, however, was made up for by the small peasant holding system whereby a farmer would look after a limited number of coffee trees on a relatively small area managed by a household. The individualized farm system helped to eliminate managerial expenses while ensuring horticultural attention to each plant. The fact that coffee could exist with bananas on the same farm greatly facilitated the rate of planting and reduced the problem which would have arisen if fresh land had to be opened up.

The above factors combined to explain the relatively fast rate at which the coffee culture developed in Buhaya. However, how the industry itself brought about the revolution is discussed in the following paragraphs.

The Coffee Tree

Most of the coffee species are believed to have originated in the Ethiopian province of Kaffa where it was grown before the thirteenth century BC.[71] There is evidence, however, to show that robusta coffee was grown by the Baganda and the Bahaya, for chewing and ceremonial purposes, from as early as the seventeenth century AD Buhaya was famous for coffee production long before the arrival of the Europeans. The explorer, Speke, and others went to the extent of saying that coffee was indigenous to the region.[72] Even Emin Pasha, shortly after his arrival, once exclaimed 'good coffee grows here'.[73]

Earlier on, in August 1858, Speke had received information on coffee grown in Karagwe and beyond. He described the region as:

> A country where coffee grows abundantly, and is called *Muanyé*. He described the shrub as standing between two and three feet high, having the stem nearly naked, but much branched above; it grows in large plantations, and forms the principal article of food. The people do not boil and drink it as we do, but eat the berry raw, with its husk on. The Arabs are very fond of eating these berries raw, and have often given us

some. They bring them down from Uganda, where, for a pennyworth of beads, a man can have his fill.[74]

The Arabica species, on the other hand, is believed to have been introduced by the missionaries who brought the seeds from the Reunion Islands (situated east of Madagascar) and planted them first in Morogoro in 1883, then at Kilema, Moshi, in 1885 and subsequently in Buhaya in the late 1880s.

Systematic cultivation of coffee in Buhaya, however, commenced with the German administration. Happily, the geography of the region encouraged the cultivation of both varieties, robusta and arabica. Robusta, which is characterized by large dark green glabrous leaves, with a sombre red cherry, does well in all parts of the region and has a high resistance to many diseases. Arabica, which had a brighter red but larger cherry and lighter green leaves, is more fastidious as to soil conditions and prefers the high altitudes and lower temperatures of the plateaux of Ihangiro and Karagwe.[75] Ideal regions must

TABLE V–8 *COFFEE PRODUCTION IN BUHAYA*

YEAR	TONS	INDEX 1905=100	YEAR	TONS	INDEX 1905=100
1900	(127.2)	54.3	1920	1269	542.3
1901	(141.3)	60.9	1921	2594	1108.5
1902	(157.0)	67.1	1922	2738	1170.1
1903	(174.5)	74.6	1923	2563	1095.3
1904	(193.0)	65.5	1924	3535	1510.7
1905	234	100.0	1925	4150	1773.5
1906	215	91.8	1926	4637	1981.7
1907	182	77.7	1927	3943	1685.0
1908	284	121.4	1928	7826	3444.4
1909	280	119.7	1929	6794	2903.4
1910	493	210.6	1930	7368	3148.7
1911	554	236.7	1931	6586	2942.7
1912	681	291.0	1932	7111	3038.8
1913	403	172.2	1933	7922	3385.5
1914	(869.5)	371.6	1934	10210	4363.2
1915	(982.5)	419.8	1935	10882	4650.4
1916	1110.3)	474.0	1936	8810	3764.9
1917	1228	524.8	1937	9540	4076.9
1918	1138	484.6	1938	8727	3729.5
1919	2042	872.6	1039	10861	4641.4

Sources: R. A. Austen, *Northwestern Tanzania under German and British Rule* (Yale University Press, 1968), pp. 270–1. Figures in brackets estimated.

also fall within the 20° zone on either side of the equator, to which coffee cultivation is normally confined. Other conditions include an altitude of up to 1,800 metres above sea-level where temperatures average 70°F (17°C) and annual rainfall ranges from 40 to 70 inches. A coffee bush, which may attain a height of 9 to 10 metres in a natural state, begins to produce berries in its third to fifth year and might remain in production for 100 years.

On the assumption that extensive planting commenced in 1880, there ought to have been sizeable production for local consumption or export some five years later. Statistics on coffee production during the German period, however, are hard to come by, mainly because of poor records and the interruption caused by the First World War.[76] Another reason was that the coffee trade was monopolized by Indian and Arab middlemen who preferred to buy and sell coffee produce secretly in order to avoid taxation and were therefore reluctant to divulge export statistics. Evidence of early coffee exports from Buhaya comes from Sir J. F. Cunningham who, having visited the region in the 1890s, reported from Uganda that the Bahaya's 'coffee is a well-known article in Uganda'.[77] However, the visible results of the coffee planting campaign were too conspicuous to be hidden, for coffee trees could be seen everywhere, and the incomes derived thereby were fully reflected in the fast-growing monetary sector.

A rough picture of the level of coffee production is presented in Table V–8, the figures for which were obtained principally from Ralph A. Austen, though the statistics quoted by other writers tend to corroborate these.[78] The data for the periods 1900–05 and 1914–17 have been improvised. The overall picture is that of a steadily growing coffee industry reflecting mature bushes and an expansion of planting. The big increase in the 1919 figure over that of 1913 is attributed to the vigour with which the newly arrived British administration pushed the industry. The 1920s witnessed a high growth which was sustained into the 1930s, culminating in a peak of 10,882 tons in 1935. During the period 1935–39, annual production tended to level off.

Predictably, the sector to be first affected by the coffee culture was agriculture. Areas hitherto planted with bananas alone were now used to grow coffee bushes, which rivalled the banana in economic importance, thus claiming a good share of the Bahaya's love for the banana trees. Farming time had to be re-allocated accordingly. The coffee tree demanded separate attention and time at the different stages between planting and harvesting. Thus the berries had to be picked, dried, husked, sorted and marketed at certain specific times of the year. To sustain a good yield necessitated careful pruning, weeding, mulching, manuring and the combating of diseases.[79] Fortunately, the fact that both banana and coffee trees could thrive on the same farm helped to maintain the century old pattern of the people's habitation and occupation. The expansion of the farms was insignificant even after taking into account the cultivation of communally-owned, open land known as *rweya*, which, in many cases, proved agriculturally unsuitable as it happened to be marginal land.

As the monetary sector grew with increased incomes, the Bahaya's daily and annual work schedule was modified to reflect the economic switch from bananas to coffee. Thus, in the first quarter of the year, coffee shambas (gardens) are usually weeded and mulched. April to July is the time for plucking the coffee berries and getting them dried, husked and marketed. From September to the end of the year, work on the coffee farm mainly involves planting, weeding and pruning, while berries are picked in the minor harvest season.[80]

Commercial activities during the Omujungu era were largely based on coffee. Most traders dealt in coffee by purchasing from peasants and supplying exporters. With the profits thus earned, they stocked retail items, the sale of which yielded income in the off-season period. Being a major source of monetary income, the quantity harvested significantly influenced the level of economic activity during the season.

The German administration had embarked on a policy of encouraging European settlers in Tanganyika just as it had done in Kenya. The aim was to inject a settler's element into the economy which would catalyse agricultural production. Accordingly, a law was passed in 1886 by which Tanganyika became a crown colony like Kenya, an exception being made for areas claimed by chiefs, native communities and landholders. The areas most affected by the measure were in the Arusha–Moshi–Tanga section where European settlers had opened up farms, forcing the natives to emigrate to other regions.[81] However, the settlers spread to almost all parts of Tanganyika.

Buhaya was also affected by this settlers' programme and European farms were opened at Kamwana, Rwamurumba, Kibimbili, Nshamba, Muhutwe and other places where coffee production was to be undertaken with the help of cheap local labour. The experiment turned out to be a fiasco for several reasons, including the inadequacy of land for large-scale farms. Apparently, by the turn of the century, the best land had been planted with bananas and signs of over-population congestion and land shortage were already visible in Buhaya.[82] The settlers, therefore, had to confine themselves to the ravines which could not sustain crops for successive years. More serious, however, was couch-grass weed, known locally as *rumbugu*, which penetrated several feet below the ground and which could only be eradicated with personal attention involving horticultural care and peasant production. Thirdly, as both banana and coffee plants required individual attention, they could best be produced under the peasant system which did not requite supervision and was both less costly and more efficient under such circumstances. Long before World War I even, the settlers found it advisable to abandon their farms and turn their hands to petty industries or the middlemen's trade or, in certain cases, to become general peasants. For these reasons, coffee production in Buhaya has remained in the hands of small farmers. From the fiscal point of view, coffee continued to be a source of revenue for the German administration and the local authorities. As it was a major source of monetary income, the public sector felt an obligation to develop the coffee industry.

The further away one moved from agriculture, the more nebulous the impact of coffee tended to be, though something should be said about the industrial sector during the period. Strangely enough, the coffee industry was unable to attract or generate a variety of related industrial establishments. The only sizeable unit located at Bukoba was the Shariff Jiwa Coffee Curing Company plant, which catered for the husking and cleaning of all the produce of the region before it was exported. Other small curing plants established elsewhere did not prove successful, as exemplified by the abortive efforts of Mr Klemens Kiiza who tried to erect a coffee factory at Buganguzi, some 40 miles south-west of Bukoba town.[83] Not even small-scale industrial units took root, with the exception of those for individual tailors, mechanics and coffee huskers. The beneficial effect of the neglect of large-scale industries, however, was to enable the medieval type of artisinal production to survive and continue to supply a wide market of agricultural implements, carved tools and diverse forms of artefacts.[84]

The transport sector showed signs of transformation right from the early days of German administration. Thus, roads were constructed joining the villages and the administrative capital of Bukoba. The latter was connected with Mwanza by a regular steamer service from as early as 1894 and this proved to be a vital link with the rest of Tanganyika.

The Coffee Revolution During World War I and After

The coffee revolution dominated everyday Bahaya life from the arrival of the Germans onwards. Politically, the Omujungu period can be divided into two parts, namely the German administration and the British administration, both periods being neatly separated by World War I. From the economic point of view, the switch to the British involved, at the very least, a change of approach, currency and, certainly, of administrative language. While the economic and administrative pattern remained virtually unchanged, the jostle caused by wartime disturbances had affected all aspects of life, including the fledgeling coffee revolution, as will be briefly discussed in the subsequent paragraphs.

Buhaya had its fair share of devastation from the war. As pointed out, the town of Bukoba was shelled by British steamers early in the war, though the resultant social disruption inflicted as much suffering as the cannon fire. The village administration system facilitated conscription, which took away many a young man who never returned home and whose whereabouts have never been traced.[85] The village headman was called upon to deliver a certain number of men to the German recruiters who would then distribute them among various services. Many were employed as porters though some earned medals for actual combat.

Economic disruption was as noticeable as social disturbances. Coffee lost its market as there was no system for buying or transporting the produce to the places of curing or to export sales points. Consequently, monetary income dropped drastically, pulling down the general standard of living which, low as it still was, tended to slip back to the levels of traditional society. Thanks to the system of indirect rule, law and order remained in force during the war.

Once the administration of the Germans became threatened, power returned to the Bakama who ensured that order was maintained. It was also luck in disguise that the Germans were easily defeated and that the British takeover maintained emphasis on coffee production.

Measures established by the British to rehabilitate the coffee industry have already been summarized in the preceding paragraphs in connection with the administration of Major D. L. Baines. It should be added, however, that most of the reconstruction efforts in the post-war period were launched at the territorial level and that Buhaya, as a constituent region, was affected thereby. Thus, within three years of Baines's arrival in the area, coffee output had more than doubled from the 1913 level. The overall performance of the coffee industry after the war is indicated in Table V–8, production figures continuing to rise until the pre-World War II peak of 10,882 tons in 1935.

Compared with Tanganyika and the rest of the world with regard to coffee production, Buhaya enjoyed an upward trend during the period between the two World Wars. Table V–9 demonstrates this trend, showing that the increase in coffee production in Buhaya corresponded well with that of the rest of Tanganyika, though it somewhat contrasted with that of the world which was undergoing considerable stagnation, if not decline, during the same period. By then, the production of Buhaya contributed significantly to the total output of Tanganyika, the percentage contribution ranging between 55 and 76%

From the point of view of price, there was a rising trend during the period 1925–30, followed by a sharp decline which was succeeded by a quick recovery in the period 1932–36. The years immediately preceding the Second World War were characterized by depressed prices.

Particular note should be made of the economic stagnation already referred to which characterized the 1930s and which applied not only to Buhaya but to the rest of the world as well. Though it is believed that the immediate cause was the Great Depression, it is also alleged that part of the blame lies in the fear of Hitler's military build-up, including his direct threat to recapture the pre-World War I German colonies.[86] The fear assumed the form of a reduced flow of investment to the territory and a slow pace of project implementation. The fact that this was a real fear is demonstrated by the contrast in the speed with which the British resumed investment and reconstruction activities after 1945.

By the end of the Second World War, the coffee revolution had influenced all aspects of Bahaya life, including education, culture, social systems and even the philosophy of life. Monetary incomes provided an additional incentive for sending children to school. Allegiance to the family, clan and even the tribe had been shaken to the roots as both social and physical mobility increased. Feudalism recoiled before the vast opportunities offered by paid labour and the liberty to purchase according to one's wealth. Women's rights were uplifted with the freedom to own property and travel at will. In short, many norms of the tribes were continually being changed, not by legislation but by practice. The economic revolution continued to flourish

TABLE V–9 *COMPARISON OF COFFEE PRODUCTION DURING THE PERIOD 1928–1939*

Year	World Production (1000 tons)	Index 1928= 100	Tanganyika Production (1000 tons)	Index 1928= 100	Buhaya Production (1000 tons)	Index 1928= 100
1928	2383	100.0	10.4	100.0	7.2	100.0
1929	2336	100.4	8.9	85.6	6.8	93.2
1930	2383	100.0	11.5	110.6	7.4	101.1
1931	2060	86.4	9.3	89.4	6.6	90.3
1932	2388	100.2	11.4	109.6	7.1	97.5
1933	2572	107.9	12.7	122.1	7.9	108.7
1934	2481	104.1	14.8	142.3	10.2	140.1
1935	2052	86.1	18.6	178.8	10.8	149.4
1936	2547	106.8	12.1	116.3	8.8	120.9
1937	2420	101.5	13.6	130.8	9.5	130.9
1938	2088	87.6	13.7	131.7	8.7	119.7
1939	2070	86.6	18.6	159.6	10.8	149.0

Sources: (1) FAO Statistical Yearbook, Vol. 21 p.253. (2) Ralph A. Austen, *Northwestern Tanzania Under German and British Rule* (Yale University Press, 1968) pp.271-2

in the years after World War II when it became quite pronounced as a feature of the economy.

Conclusion

This chapter has attempted to correlate three somewhat disparate variables, namely the German and the British administrations and the coffee industry in Buhaya. To state the relationship simply, German colonial rule established the coffee industry on a commercial basis while the British provided the impetus for its growth. Coffee production, in turn, enhanced the objectives of colonial rule by satisfying an economic need in the metropolitan country to which it was exported. Secondly, coffee was an important agent for the social transformation of the tribal way of life, which also formed a basic, express objective of the colonizing powers. With the incomes derived from coffee, the indigenous people were able to buy manufactured articles produced in Europe, such as clothes, shoes and foodstuffs, which were taken by the colonizing powers as indications of development. Furthermore, coffee linked the local community to the cosmopolitan economic complexes whose widely fluctuating conditions began to be felt in Buhaya.

In short, during the Omujungu era, the region experienced a period of dynamically changing development, characterized by the superimposition of a totally foreign, high-technology culture on a predominantly traditional society. The development process, which involved the fitting of a peasant agriculture into a European type of economy, brought innovative features but also a number of problems and contradictions. This chapter has briefly described this experience from an economic angle.

From the political point of view, the period 1890–1960 was dominated by colonization and all its transformational implications. To the natives, the nationality of the colonizing powers did not make much difference since any colonial administration represented a cultural and political invasion and domination. A strict comparison between the German and the British administrations would not reveal many marked contrasts. Thus, the foundation laid by the Germans was developed by the British, although, in each administration, a few personalities emerged to shape the events of the time. By way of illustration, the German period was influenced by Emin Pasha, whose philanthropic and adventurous personality set the stage for German–Bahaya relations. Major von Stuemer, who administered Buhaya for more than 40% of the whole German era, contributed most of the changes that the Germans claimed to have introduced in the region. The leading characters on the Bahaya side then included Mukotani, Mutatembwa, Kahigi ka Rugomora and Kahyoza ka Nkwere among the Bakama. However, there is no doubt that the whole tribe was fully involved in the drama.

Similarly, the British period had its major actors, opening with Major Baines at the district level and Sir Horace Byatt at the territorial level. The limelight of the British era, however, was stolen by the revolutionary and pragmatic Sir Donald Cameron, who gave Tanganyika the best of what the colonizing nation bestowed on the territory. He established the Legislative Council, built the Tabora–Mwanza railway, launched various development projects and, above all, nurtured the embryo of the nationalist movement.

The Omujungu period, however, was significantly affected by the two World Wars. For the first time, Tanganyikans were involved in international fighting, the causes or objectives of which were not of direct interest to them. The remoteness of the causes and the directly interested parties, however, did not diminish the ravages and suffering endured by the people during those wars.

Dominating the Omujungu period was the coffee culture and the Bahaya community, both important factors of social and economic changes. Coercion had been used to establish coffee agriculture but, once it took root, the production momentum was self-propelling and, in the process, accelerated social transformation. As coffee production outstripped the banana culture, the revenue derived thereby tipped the balance of the social structure in favour of the non-aristocratic majority, who had been reduced to serfdom in the nineteenth century. Thus the colonial period witnessed continuing social transformation, with the old dynastic and aristocratic feudal complexes dying out to be replaced by democratic or egalitarian structures which culminated in political independence in 1961.

1. A concise description of Chief Mangungo's treaties is provided by Zoe Marsh and W. Kingsnorth, op. cit., pp.61–100.
2. John Hanning Speke, *What Led to the Discovery of the Source of the Nile* (Edinburgh and London: William Blackwood and Sons, 1854), p.161. Speke, accompanied by J. Grant, arrived in Karagwe on 17 November 1861.
3. Stanley encountered Ntare II (Ihangiro), Kaitaba (Kyamutwara) and Kahyoza (Bugabo).
4. Henry Morton Stanley called the Buhaya coast 'Usongora' which should have been Buzongora, a derogatory reference to the region around the Kagera River. Cf. *The Exploration and Discoveries of Henry Morton Stanley* (London: William Kimberlay, 46, Wilton Place, London, 1961), Part III, pp.81–116.
5. From Stanley's diary at the Musée Royal de l'Afrique Centrale, Tervuren, Belgium.
6. J. H. Speke testified to the accuracy of the information given by one Arab at Bukumbi. Cf. *What Led to the Discovery of the Source of the Nile*, op. cit., pp.198–200.
7. The town of Opole (Oppeln) is situated about 260 kilometres south-west of Warsaw and its bearing is 50.40 N and 17.56 E.
8. From Stanley's diary at the Musée Royal de l'Afrique Centrale, Tervuren, Belgium.
9. Karl Peters, *New Light on Dark Africa*, op. cit., p.465.
10. The objective of Stanley's mission to rescue Emin Pasha remains one of the most bizarre episodes in tropical African history. The mystery of the issue is further aggravated since Emin was assassinated in 1892 at Kanena, now in the Central African Republic, before clarifying the matter, though he had been sceptical of the mission; cf. G. Schweitzer, *Emin Pasha, His Life and Work*, Vol. II (Westminster: Archibald Constable & Co., 1890), p.132.
11. J. Werlen, *Edini Omuli Buhaya* (Bunena: Rumuli Press), p.2.
12. Karl Peters, *New Light on Dark Africa*, op. cit., p.536.
13. Most of this information was obtained from G. Schweitzer, *Emin Pasha*, op. cit., pp.130–3.
14. Ibid., pp.103–33.
15. Ibid., p.132.
16. Ibid., p.141.
17. Cf. Table V–2.
18. A general description of the approach of the Germans towards the Bakama is presented by Ralph A. Austen in *Northwestern Tanzania under German and British Rule* (New Haven: Yale University Press, 1968), pp.112–18.
19. *See* Fr. J. Werlen, *Edini Omuli Buhaya*, op. cit., p.4.
20. On his return journey from Buganda, Karl Peters had promised he would stop in Buhaya and compel Mutatembwa of Kiziba and other Bakama to recognize the sovereignty of Mwanga. Cf. Karl Peters, *New Light on Dark Africa*, op. cit., pp.460–6.
21. Mukotani was the first effective Bankango Mukama in Kyamutwara. His father, Kaitaba, had reached the status of a regent when his nephew, Kajurunga, was facing a civil war. At the time of the Germans' arrival, his power was still challenged by Kinyonyi of Kihanja (Bulembo) who, being of a Bahinda clan, was opposed to the Bankango starting a new dynasty.
22. Description of Fr. J. Werlen, *Edini Omuli Buhaya*, op. cit., p.6
23. Karl Peters landed in the northern part of Bugabo on 4 April 1890, and mistakenly called the country Tabaliro; cf. Karl Peters, *New Light on Dark Africa*, op. cit., p.460. Bugabo was named differently by H. M. Stanley who called it Usongora, a derogatory name used by the Baganda for the whole region they called Buzongora. In fact, there is a country in the west of Uganda called Buzongora. *See also* Fr. Werlen, ibid., p.5. Even in formal discussion, it was common to refer to Buhaya as Buzongora, e.g. 'one day, he went to trade in Buzongora, but he was killed in a fight by the Baziba at Kanyigo in Mutatembwa's country': quoted from Apolo Kaggwa's *Basekabaka Be Buganda*, translated by M. S. M. Kiwanuka (Nairobi: East African Publishing House, 1971), p.100.

24. For basic records on Mutatembwa, *see* H. Rehse, *Kiziba Land und Leute*, op. cit. *See also* A. G. M. Ishumi, 'The Kingdom of Kiziba', in *Journal of World History*, Vol. XIII, 4 (1971), pp.726–8.
25. Among those who fled the country was the author's grandfather (on the mother's side), Nshubo. A Baganga by clan, born in Bwanjai, Nshubo grew to be a famous diviner of Mutatembwa. During the civil war, he and his household had to escape to Ihangiro where he settled in Itongo village.
26. Kiziba had been a part of the Kitara kingdom for many dynasties. This political relationship had been perpetuated by the Babiito ruling clan, which was the same as that in Bunyoro and Buganda but which differed from that in other parts of Buhaya where the ruling dynasties were of the Bahinda or Bankango clans.
27. The left-handed Kakoko, who acted as regent of his younger brother, is said to have been a sadistic tyrant who killed 17 near relatives of his and took out the eyes of some of his subjects including those of his brother-in-law.
28. The contestants for the regency were Kaketo, brother of Nyamukuba, Bakahuga, then chief minister, Rwahimba, Ndagara's nephew, the latter's brother, Kemandwa, and Mukwano, a distant cousin of Kaketo. The struggle led to political chaos during which many died or fled Karagwe.
29. For a general discussion of the reaction of the African societies against colonial rule, *see*, M. H. Y. Kaniki, *Tanzania under Colonial Rule* (London: Longman's Group Ltd., 1979), pp.86–127.
30. A concise presentation of the missionary political experience in Uganda is given by Zoe Marsh and G. W. Kingsnorth, *A History of East Africa*, op. cit., Chapter 6, pp.78–104.
31. A comprehensive survey of missionary activities in the territory before 1914 is provided by Anthony Smith in 'The Missionary Contribution to Education (Tanganyika) to 1914', *Tanganyika Notes and Records*, No. 60 (March 1963), pp.91–119.
32. Bukoba was a stopover station because the sect was allowed to establish a mission on Lake Kivu. Cf. C. T. Hellberg, 'The German Evangelical Mission and the North-Western Boundaries of Tanganyika', *Tanganyika Notes and Records*, Nos. 58 and 59 (1961), pp.207–10.
33. Ibid.
34. The sample is taken from five villages drawn from different chiefdoms. In all, 104 cases are sampled and grouped according to religious affiliations. Percentages are the author's. Cf. Goran Hyden, *Political Development in Rural Tanzania* (Nairobi: East African Publishing House, 1974), p.146.
35. Version of Benedicto (Kikoba) Rwamarungu of Mafumbo, Kihanja.
36. Cf. B. T. Yonge, 'The Stranding of Sybil', in *Tanganyika Notes and Records*, No.75 (1974), p.29.
37. Normally, coins for the colony were minted at the Berlin and Hamburg mints. During the war, coins were made at Tabora in denominations of 15 rupees, 20 heller and 5 heller. Cf. P. J. du Toit, 'Notes on the Coinage of German East Africa', in *Tanganyika Notes and Records*, No. 21 (July 1951).
38. Part of Lettow's account was told by Kalisti Kyamwanza of Ijumbi who claimed to have been the general's porter for years and travelled with him to Nyasaland. *See also* Paul von Lettow-Vorbeck, My *Reminiscences of East Africa* (London: Hurst and Blackett, 1920).
39. R. F. Eberlie, 'The German Achievement in East Africa', in *Tanganyika Notes and Records*, No. 55 (September 1960), p.208.
40. For a concise description of Rechenberg's background, *see* John Iliffe, *Tanganyika Under German Rule, 1905–1912* (Nairobi: East African Publishing House, 1973), pp.49–81.
41. For more about the Maji Maji rebellion, *see* G. C. K. Gwassa, 'The German Intervention and African Resistance in Tanzania', in *A History of Tanzania*, by I. N. Kimambo and A. J. Temu (eds.) (Nairobi: East African Publishing House, 1969),

pp.85–122. *See also* M. H. Y. Kaniki (ed.), *Tanzania Under Colonial Rule* (London: Longman Group Ltd., 1980), pp.116–19.

42. For texts of the legislation in question *see*, *Extracts from German Ordinances and Decrees of German East Africa*, by General Headquarters East African Forces (Nairobi: The Standard F. P. Works, 1916).

43. *See* J. Iliffe, op. cit., pp.78–9.

44. The shelling boats emerged from off Makongo village and quickly sailed back to the north before the Germans could return fire.

45. General P. von Lettow-Vorbeck, *La Guerre de Brousse* (Paris: Payot, 1933), *See also* H. Cory, *History of Bukoba District*, op. cit., p.183.

46. For a contemporary account of the collaboration between the British and the Belgians in East Africa during the World War I, *see* Charles Steinon, *La Campagne Anglo-Belge de l'Afrique Orientale Allemande* (Paris: Berger-Levrault, 1918).

47. His full name was Charles Marie Ernest Tombeur, Baron of Tabora. He was born in Liege in 1867 and died in Brussels in 1947. With a brilliant record of military education and experience, he rose to the post of Vice-Governor-General in 1915. He was conferred the title Baron of Tabora to commemorate his victory on 19 September 1916.

48. This is an estimate of von Lettow-Vorbeck. G. W. Hatchell estimated that the German forces comprised 3,000 Europeans and 11,000 askaris; *see* his article 'The British Occupation of the South-Western Area of Tanganyika', *Tanganyika Notes and Records*, No. 51 (December, 1958), pp.131–55. C. Steinon estimated 26,000 soldiers of whom 12% were Europeans; cf. his *La Campagne Anglo-Belge*, op. cit., p.23. According to General Smuts, the strength of the German Army was 16,000 troops including 2,000 Europeans.

49. The Civil Governor during the war was Dr Henrich Schnee who had to shift his capital from place to place to avoid the British forces.

50. The battle is sometimes referred to as the Battle of Kato.

51. Casualty figures vary widely according to different accounts. Hans Cory says that only three Germans and three Belgians died. According to Charles Stienon, however, at least five commanders died. Von Lettow-Vorbeck only notes that the Germans sustained considerable losses. However, no account is given of the African dead. Mikaili Kampoli Kamalampaka, who was on the scene on 2 July 1916, talks of hundreds dead. Local people also say the number totalled thousands.

52. The Germans had two ships for regular services, namely the *Mwanza* and the *Heinrich Otto*, the latter being the smaller of the two. For more about the boats on Lake Victoria during the period, *see* B. T. Yonge, 'The Stranding of Sybil', in *Tanzania Notes and Records*, No. 75 (1974), pp.29–35.

53. A synthesized evaluation of the German period is presented by R. F. Eberlie, 'The German Achievement in East Africa', op. cit., pp.181–214.

54. This issue is discussed under the Bahaya feudal system called Nyarubanja, *see* Chapter IV.

55. The anticipation of the return of the Germans lingered on for many decades and was shared by many tribes or groups in many parts of Tanganyika. It is said that the last hope was abandoned in 1945.

56. It was rumoured that Baines was so harsh to Kahigi ka Rugomora, the pawn of the German rulers, that the Mukama committed suicide in 1916. Baines, who left no special account of his Bukoba experience, died in Gloucestershire, UK, in 1955. His wife survived until March 1983.

57. The sudden jump in the output figure is said to have been due to better care of the plants and more efficient harvesting, which had been neglected during the war. Production rose from 681 tons in 1912 to 2,042 in 1919.

58. For more about this, *see* A. D. Roberts, 'Baganda', *Journal of African History*, Vol. III, No. 2 (1962), pp.435–50.

59. A concrete case of a Muganda administrator is Kamili of Ijumbi, Ihangiro. Born in

Masaka (Uganda), he had served in the British Army in Eastern Kenya. His jurisdiction extended over 10,000 people and his wisdom and personality made him a powerful ruler, rivalling Mukama Ruhinda. On expiry of his term, however, he settled down on his property, ceasing his administrative activity, but his son continued to take an active role in civic functions.

60. As Sir Donald put it, the Legislative Council was intended to *ventilate* the views of the government and the general public in the territory.

61. John Iliffe, *A Modern History of Tanganyika* (Cambridge: Cambridge University Press, 1974), pp.20–1.

62. For a detailed account of how Sir Donald manipulated the chieftaincy in order to facilitate the establishment of British rule, *see* J. D. Graham, 'Establishing Chiefs and Tribes in Cameron's Tanganyika', in *Tanganyika Notes and Records*, Nos. 77 and 78, pp.1–10.

63. For more about inter-territorial commercial policy, *see* C. M. Tibazarwa, *Economic Impact on Tanzania of East African Common Market* (to be published by Nairobi: East Africa Literature Bureau).

64. Many areas experienced the amalgamation process because the traditional units had been too small. Even in the case of a homogeneous tribe like the Bahaya, there were eight separate kingdoms which did not make political sense. As explained elsewhere in that particular case, the British created a ruling council of the Bakama. *See also* J. D. Graham, 'Establishing Chiefs and Tribes in Cameron's Tanganyika', in *Tanganyika Notes and Records*, op. cit.

65. While the slave-trade had been abolished, slavery still existed in many forms. In Buhaya, for example, until the arrival of K. L. Baines, the Bakama used to take girls away from their homes and make them slaves by decree.

66. More about German currency is to be found in an article by K. M. Phatak, 'A Note on the German Two-Rupee Coin and the Maria Theresa Dollar', in *Tanganyika Notes and Records*, No. 57 (September, 1961), pp.177–80. *See also* P. J. du Toit, 'Notes on the Coinage of German East Africa', *Tanganyika Notes and Records*, op. cit.

67. Useful notes on Baines's concept of indirect rule are provided by Hans Cory and M. M. Hartnoll, op. cit., pp.274–5.

68. Traditionally, coffee beans were cooked while green and chewed as a mouth freshener by the Bahaya. Though a monopoly of the chiefs, it featured in the trade with Arabs during the nineteenth century.

69. The question of the place of origin of coffee is discussed in the subsequent paragraphs.

70. An enlightening account of the socio-economic changes in Buhaya during the colonial period is given by K. E. Svendsen and Merete Teisen, *Self-Reliant Tanzania* (Dar es Salaam: Tanzania Publishing House, 1969), pp.46–62.

71. A historical and commercial account of the coffee industry is presented in *The Courier*, No. 59, January/February 1980 (Brussels: African Caribbean and Pacific Group — Commission of the European Communities), pp.46–71.

72. While at Bweranyange in Karagwe, J. H. Speke was informed that the area to the east of Karagwe up to Lake Victoria (or Lake Rumanyika, as described then) was 'Uhaya' which is famous for 'ivory and coffee production', cf. J. H. Speke, *Journal of the Discovery of the Source of the Nile*, op. cit., p.261. D. N. McMaster also tends to think that coffee has grown in Buhaya from time immemorial; *see* his article 'Change of Regional Balance in the Bukoba District of Tanganyika', in *Tanganyika Notes and Records*, op. cit., p.91.

73. G. Schweitzer, *Emin Pasha*, op. cit., p.128.

74. J. H. Speke, *What Led to the Discovery of the Source of the Nile*, op. cit., p.348.

75. For a scientific description of the soils of Buhaya, *see* Coffee Research Station Lyamungu and Coffee Services Tanganyika, *Research Report 1965* (Tanganyika Coffee Board, June 1968), p.35.

76. A general idea of the early days of the coffee industry in Buhaya is presented by T. Jervis (one time district agricultural officer in Bukoba) in 'A History of Robusta Coffee in

Bukoba', in *Tanganyika Notes and Records*, No. 8 of 1939, pp.47–58.

77. J. F. Cunningham, *Uganda and Its People*, op. cit., p.286.
78. J. P. Moffet quotes 215 tons for 1906 while Goran Hyden gives 234 tons for 1905 and 493 tons for 1910. Cf. J. P. Moffet (ed.), *Tanganyika. A Review of Its Resources and Their Development* (Dar es Salaam: Government Printer). *See also* Goran Hyden, *Political Development in Rural Tanzania*, op. cit., p.99.
79. A general survey of coffee diseases is to be found in *The Courier*, No. 59, January/February 1980, op. cit., pp.58–61.
80. In certain years, there are two harvests from one plant: a major one in June and a minor one in December/January.
81. Zoe Marsh and G. W. Kingsnorth, *A History of East Africa*, op. cit., pp.146–52.
82. A scientific analysis of the land problems in Buhaya is provided by D. N. McMaster, 'Change of Regional Balance in Bukoba District of Tanganyika', op. cit., pp.79–93.
83. Knud Erik Svendsen and Merete Teisen, *Self-Reliant Tanzania*, op. cit., p.54. More about the industrial initiative of Mr Klemens Kiiza will appear in the next chapter.
84. Examples of the various implements are: the omuoro, a banana tree cutting long-handled knife; the orwabyo, a banana leaf sickle; the ekiosho, a banana stamp spade; the eichumu, a spear; the ekyoma kyembwa, a dog bell.
85. During the war, Morogoro was supposed to have been the headquarters of the Germans where recruits underwent training. All conscripts, whether dead or alive, were assumed to have gone there. Hence the popular saying of 'those who died at Morogoro', implying those who went there and whose whereabouts could not be traced.
86. For additional information on this issue, *see* C. M. Tibazarwa, *Economic Impact on Tanzania of the East African Common Market* (in the process of being published by the East African Literature Bureau, Nairobi), Chapter II.

CHAPTER VI

THE EZONI ERA: 1948–1960

Introduction

Many Bahaya tend to share the viewpoint that the zenith of the coffee based prosperity in the region was reached in the 1950s. This chapter, while not aiming to refute the general opinion, sets out to analyse the salient features of the economic structure of Buhaya during that period.

By the 1950s, the commercial production of coffee, which was introduced at the beginning of German rule in Buhaya, continued to develop steadily, as witness the increasing number of plants and expanding bushes. Coffee based incomes were becoming indispensable to that portion of the population which had acquired a taste for foreign produced commodities. Returns from coffee sales, however, had become subject to frequent and wide price fluctuations or even utter market disruption, as had been the case during World Wars I and II. By the early 1940s, however, the level of coffee production had become more predictable since the rate of planting and the growth of bushes had somewhat stabilized. Two events occurred immediately after World War II which significantly affected the coffee industry and the overall economy during the period 1948–60, hereafter referred to as the EZONI ERA. More than anything else, the establishment of the co-operative marketing system and the commodity price boom of the Korean War period combined to give a special character not only to the coffee industry but also to the Bahaya economy as a whole during the 1950s.

The Meaning of 'Ezoni'

Before proceeding further, it seems necessary to explain the origin of the term 'ezoni'. To establish marketing units for coffee, the region was divided into sub-regions, each responsible for collecting the beans and delivering them to a central place for cleaning and grading. Each of these units was called a *zone*; hence the word 'ezoni' which could easily be assimilated into the local language. Though the zone system was later abandoned in favour of the co-operative marketing system, the term 'ezoni' survived although it connoted something slightly different, namely the coffee marketing complex together with the economic prosperity it conferred on Buhaya during the period. Thus, the term came to be associated with the improved system of marketing coffee, the place of collecting and weighing the produce, the farmers' meetings and the overall socio-cultural complex associated with the marketing.

The Marketing Revolution

Commercial coffee planting, dating back to the beginning of the German administration, had added an element of duality into the Bahaya agricultural economy, based on banana and coffee. The farming habits of the people had changed to accommodate the cultivation of coffee as it became necessary to allocate the time of the farmer to both crops. More importantly, the revenue derived from coffee was bound to affect people's lives because it influenced consumer habits and tastes.

The drastic economic change which took place after World War II was brought about largely by improved marketing, by which the same crop was collected and sold in a more efficient way. In consequence, a spectacular rise in incomes was effected, as if a new crop had been introduced or as if a totally new technology in the agricultural sector had been adopted.

The revolutionizing effects of the marketing function derived from its capacity to reduce the cost of processing the product for sale and to maximize farmers' earnings. It is fair to assume that, even if production levels were to remain the same, increased incomes would be realized simply through better marketing techniques alone.[1] In the case of post-war Buhaya, the coffee marketing function was characterized by several features, the most outstanding being the improved collection of produce, better transportation and curing arrangements and participation by farmers in all stages of marketing up to the level of international auctioning. Equally significant, however, was the increase in farmers' revenues from coffee.

Collection of coffee from farms constituted a basic improvement. Hitherto, no systematic way of purchasing dried coffee beans had been used. Consequently, peasants were not encouraged to give proper attention to the husbandry of the crop and had little choice but to dispose of it through middlemen, who paid low prices to farmers and later bid for higher prices in export markets. In the absence of a centralized purchasing system, grading could not be undertaken properly and therefore the whole industry realized lower earnings than would otherwise have been the case. Lack of proper storage and transport facilities might also have added to the poor quality of the produce, thereby leading to low prices on the international markets.

Transportation constitutes a significant element of coffee production; it involves moving the crop from farms to drying beds,[2] delivering it to primary societies' sales stores, moving it to curing works and finally to auction markets. However, given the system of production prevalent in Buhaya, the handling of beans from the farm to drying places is undertaken by individual peasants. The curing usually takes place at the same plant or factory where grading and bagging is done. Being a beverage, coffee must be stored very carefully since moisture or disagreeable smells can damage the quality and consequently lower the grade of the crop.[3] For the same reasons, at all stages of marketing, transportation to the auctions has to be conducted with care.

Coffee curing involves husking, or the removal of the dry outer cover and parchment, taking off dust particles and grading the beans.[4] In addition, the curing function involves packing the coffee, weighing it and preparing it for shipment to international markets.

Selling coffee at international auctions became a feature of the revolutionized marketing system because, hitherto, only middlemen had had direct contact with outside buyers. Once co-operatives were established, farmers obtained both a say and an interest in the overall marketing system right from the farm to the auction floor. This involvement in production is believed to have boosted both the psychological and economic morale of the peasant farmer.[5] The stimulation of his interest in the industry was a basic revolutionary element of the economy during the Ezoni era. Ownership of the coffee industry was in the hands of farmers who also controlled the Union of the Co-operative Societies, which was the administrative centre for coffee marketing for the whole region. The directly interested farmers strove to improve the quality of the beans and to reduce the cost of transportation and storage, with a view to maximizing returns on sales, in the hope that the saving realized thereby would accrue to them.

The marketing reform benefited not only the farmer but also the industry as a whole and the government as well. It eliminated the middlemen who used to retain much of the proceeds from coffee exports and completely disregarded farmers. By introducing the co-operative marketing system, the price paid to farmers substantially increased, simply because of the restructuring of income distribution. The government also benefited from the centralized marketing system, which facilitated the levying of taxes on sales. However, unlike personal profit, government revenue is not a total loss to the farmer, for it is, at least in part, spent on essential public services including law, order and public goods. Overall, establishing a coffee marketing system led to gains in economic welfare, as was demonstrated by increased incomes for a good part of the population.

The Coffee Co-operative Marketing System —
The Development of Coffee Marketing Co-operatives

As early as 1932, the Co-operative Societies Ordinance had been passed by the Government of Tanganyika to facilitate the registration of societies and the marketing operations of the European farmers mainly in the Kilimanjaro and Tanga regions where societies were established forthwith.[6]

In 1935, the Export Ordinance was enacted, placing emphasis on the quality of coffee and other commodities. During the following year, the government passed yet another act, the Coffee Industry (Registration and Improvement) Ordinance 1936, by which grading of coffee was more strictly controlled.[7]

The first co-operative to be registered was the Kilimanjaro Native Co-operative Union on 1 January 1933. Other registered co-operatives were the Bugufi (Ngara) Coffee Co-operative Society, in 1936, and the Rungwe (Mwakaleli) Coffee Growers Association, in 1949.

In Buhaya, legislation on co-operatives was introduced more than 18 years after the passing of the Co-operative Societies Ordinance of 1932. Possibly, this delay was due to government neglect since coffee production in Buhaya was largely in the hands of African peasants.[8] Surprisingly though, the government was fully aware of the exploitation from which African peasants were suffering at the hands of Arab and Indian traders. The latter, posing as owners of large farms managed by African labourers, were able to explain how they amassed wealth so quickly from coffee sales.[9]

The establishment of co-operatives in Buhaya was apparently precipitated by the contract made by the British government to sell 4,000 tons annually to certain overseas purchasers, one of them being South Africa, for the 5-year period 1947–52. The implementation of the contract was placed in the hands of the British Government Ministry of Food, which created the Bukoba Native Coffee Board (BNCB) to organize production so as to honour the contract.[10] More about the various institutions involved in coffee marketing is provided later on, though note should be taken that the improved marketing system took hold as a result of the promotion by the British Ministry of Food of the establishment of the BNCB.

The Institutions of the Buhaya Co-operative System

As the co-operative marketing movement gathered momentum, various institutions were set up to deal with purchasing, the retail trade and information and examination services, among others. Of the various institutions, only four are of direct relevance to coffee production, namely

- **(A)** The Bukoba Native Coffee Board acting on behalf of the British Ministry of Food;
- **(B)** The Coffee Marketing Zones;
- **(C)** The Primary Coffee Co-operative Societies;
- **(D)** The Bukoba Native Co-operative Union (BNCU).

A. *The Bukoba Native Coffee Board and the British Ministry of Food*

As pointed out already, the establishment of the Bukoba Native Coffee Board was primarily intended to facilitate the execution of the British Ministry of Food contract. In drawing up the contract, the Ministry had not consulted the farmers or the Bahaya authorities with respect to price levels or the mode of delivery of the coffee. As can be expected, both the stipulated price levels and quantities were low enough to ensure the honouring of the contract. Thus, the contracted tonnage of 4,000 was about half the average annual production for the region, while the average price per pound weight in 1947 was only one shilling.[11] There were two prices for exported coffee: one for the stipulated 4,000 tons and the other for the uncontracted quantities. The proceeds from sales of contracted and non-contracted amounts were then combined to determine the price payable to the farmer.

To facilitate the collection of produce from the peasants, the Coffee Board organized Buhaya into zones, each of which was to designate a purchasing point for the coffee within an area. In the meantime, a campaign was mounted to get farmers to organize co-operatives. For each zonal purchasing station, one Indian trader was appointed to purchase the produce and deliver it to the coffee curing factory at Bukoba. The Board succeeded in introducing the above mentioned two-tier payment system whereby a farmer would receive an initial payment on delivery of the coffee at the primary society's purchasing point, while the second component of the price would be paid as a residual after auctioning had taken place and marketing cost had been deducted. The peasants very much appreciated this system of staggered payments and have retained it to date. Moreover, by regulating the marketing system, the Coffee Board was able to eliminate exploitation by the middlemen. To encourage the establishment and growth of the co-operative movement, the Coffee Board made available a stand-by credit of 500,000 shillings to help the co-operative societies, each of which would receive a 12,000 shillings grant as initial capital for purchasing coffee.[12]

B. *The Zone System*

As pointed out earlier, the zones were established by the Bukoba National Coffee Board in order to facilitate the purchase of coffee from farmers and so ensure the fulfilment of the quotas stipulated in the British Ministry of Food contract. The zone system was short-lived for it was superseded by the co-operative system, described in the following paragraphs.

C. *The Primary Co-operative Societies*

The primary co-operative constituted a basic organizational marketing unit which, on average, comprised three or four villages with a total population of some 2,000 to 5,000 people. A single co-operative would handle between 100 and 200 tons of coffee a year.

In 1950, there was already a total membership of 45 primary societies comprising 31,642 farmers representing more than 39% of the estimated coffee growers in the region.[13] By 1952, society membership had reached 43,926. The growth of the membership of co-operative societies is illustrated by Table VI–1. To be formally established, each society would be registered

TABLE VI–1 *GROWTH OF PRIMARY SOCIETIES IN BUHAYA*

Date	Number of Primary Societies	Membership of Farmers	Average Membership per Society
September 1950	45	33,000	733.3
December 1950	50	40,000	800.0
December 1952	51	43,926	861.3

Sources: J. P. Moffet, *Tanganyika: A Review of its Resources and Their Development* (Dar es Salaam: Government Printer, 1955), pp.774–5. *Engoma Ya Buhaya*, Vol. III, No.11, November 1950, p.70.

independently under the National Co-operative Society Ordinance, Cap. 390.

Major functions of a primary society included collecting the produce and transporting it to the curing factory from where the union of co-operatives would assume marketing responsibility. To the farmer, the society was an instrument for ensuring optimum earnings from coffee sold. Moreover, it was a means of communication between farmers and other marketing units and conducted such activities as the distribution of insecticides and seedlings, the making of proposals on improving yields and the dissemination of other information to farmers.

The administration of a co-operative society was placed in the hands of a democratically elected committee (or Halmashauri) which was backed by a secretariat of three or four people including an accountant. The Bukoba Native Co-operative Union was expected to assist the primary societies by training the secretarial staff and auditing the accounts.

D. *The Bukoba Native Co-operative Union (the BNCU, and later the BCU)*

The Union, as it was generally referred to, was registered in December 1950; its main objective was to collect coffee from primary societies and to process and ship it to international auctions. The responsibility of the BNCU also extended to ensuring that prices offered at auction sales were the highest possible and that marketing costs were kept to the minimum. Other functions of the BNCU included the supervision of coffee curing and grading and, finally, transportation to Mombasa for auctioning. In addition, the Union undertook various social and infrastructural programmes, including educational programmes for its staff and those of the primary societies, pilot projects on cultivation of various types of coffee and experimentation under different agricultural conditions.

The central position of the BNCU in the marketing of coffee can be seen in Chart VI–1, which appeared in a local paper called *Engoma Ya Buhaya* in a 1950 issue. The diagram shows how the Union functioned as a link between primary societies and export markets. At the Union level, the secretariat was under a general manager.[14]

Above all, the chart shows that the farmers were vital to the functioning of the structure. Not only did they produce coffee but they were also crucial to the decision-making processes in the industry.

Next in importance were the primary coffee societies which were at the foundation of the marketing system; closely linked to the co-operatives was the zonal system which enabled the produce to be efficiently collected, stored and transported. The next stage was the factory for coffee curing. To co-ordinate the activities of the industry for the whole region, the Union linked Buhaya with external markets, mainly Mombasa, where the produce was auctioned. Lastly, there was the British Ministry of Food, which had concluded a contract under which coffee was sold during the period 1947–52 and which provided an impetus for the co-operative movement in Buhaya.

CHART VI–1 *THE COFFEE MARKETING SYSTEM*

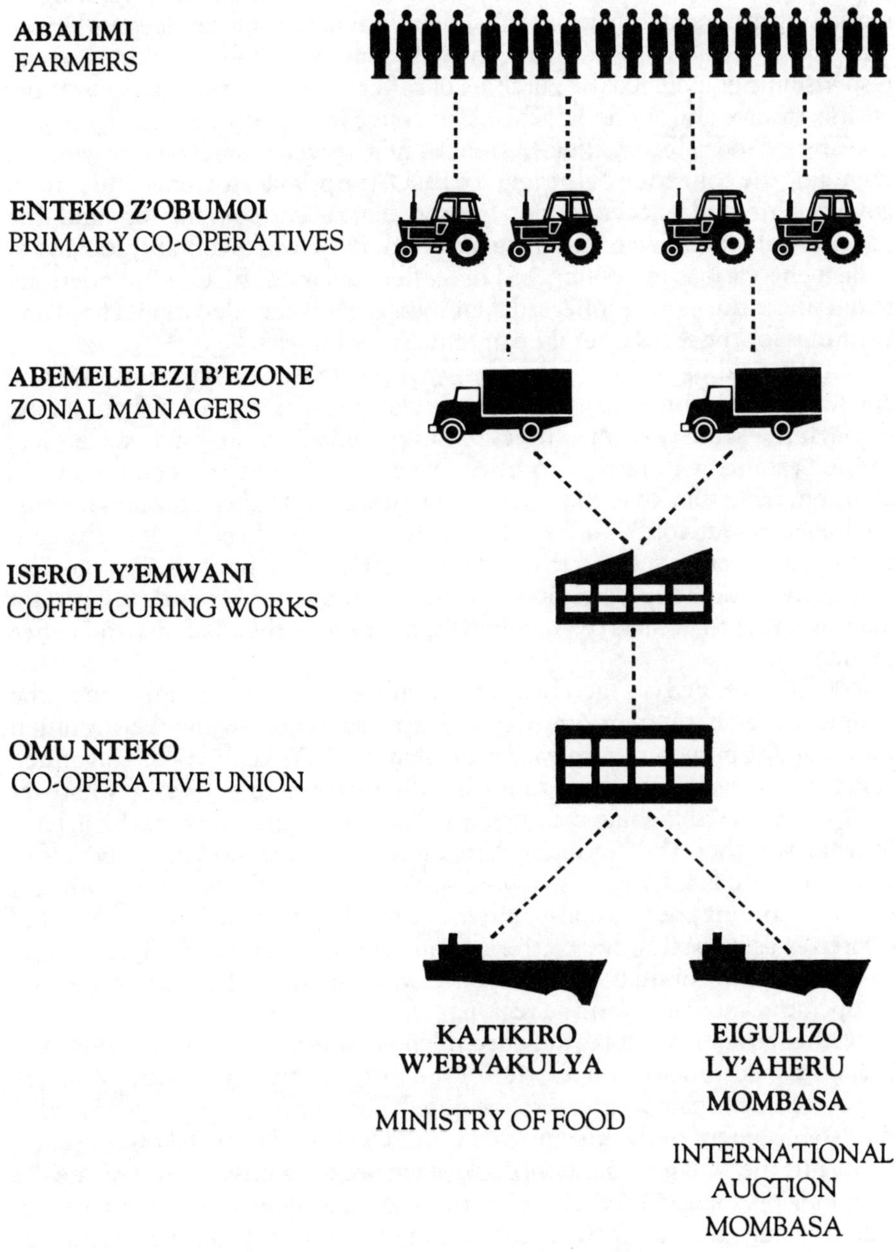

Source: *Engoma Ya Buhaya*, Vol. III, No. 1, January 1950.

Among other important functions, the Bukoba Native Co-operative Union (BNCU) took over the activities of the Bukoba Native Coffee Board in 1954, from the stage of the collection of the produce to the auction level. In all, the major activities of the BCU can be categorized as relating to marketing, financial organization, agricultural extension services and social functions. Mention has already been made of marketing undertakings, whose responsibilities included the purchase of coffee from peasants, transportation, curing, storage and auction of the clean coffee in export markets.

The second category of BCU's functions involved financial management, including the collection of the levy for BCU, the primary societies and central government and the collection of the marketing commission and the educational fund. Given its central position, BCU was favourably located to collect the various levies imposed on coffee revenues. BCU also undertook to distribute the money collected, mainly as regards the educational fund and the funds for the Agricultural Loan scheme for farmers.

In the field of extension services, BCU established coffee nurseries and encouraged the farmers to undertake the planting of new trees. What is more, through the primary co-operatives, BCU provided various advisory services to the peasants with respect to insecticides, care for the trees and so on. In addition, BCU took over the coffee research station located at Maruku, some 8 kilometres south of Bukoba town. Mention should also be made of the cash crop diversification scheme that led to the establishment of the Bukoba Tea Company, which ran tea estates. Furthermore, a scheme was developed for loaning cattle to farmers to enable them to improve their banana and coffee production.

BCU extended its activities to business ventures, mainly from the moment when it was transformed from a primary commodity marketing union into a multi-purpose co-operative movement.[15] As such, BCU organized consumer co-operative shops to enable the peasants to buy easily whatever their coffee-based income could afford. The Union also took up the agency of what was then the National Agricultural Products Board, on behalf of which it purchased and distributed agricultural products for export and internal consumption. It also moved into the distribution of beer and cigarettes as a local agent of the national firms. Through its initiative, a co-operative insurance business unit was established to cater for the co-operative movement in the region.

Other business ventures included the purchase of Lake Hotel in 1960 and the construction of the Coffee Tree Inn during the same year. A motor-vehicle repair shop was also acquired. Later on, the Union spearheaded the establishment of the instant coffee factory located near Bukoba harbour.

While the activities mentioned above are not exhaustive, they indicate the wide-ranging influence of BCU on the economy during the Ezoni period. Unfortunately, such a general account cannot go into a detailed evaluation of the effectiveness of BCU's activities. It suffices to mention, however, that the economic features of the period were greatly associated with the role of BCU.

The Economics of the Ezoni Era

The significance of the marketing variable in the development of Buhaya during the period was reflected in rising personal monetary earnings and an improved income distribution. Higher incomes resulting from economies of scale were realized from the rationalization of the marketing function with respect to transportation, storage, curing and auctioning. The change in income distribution was due to the already mentioned economies of scale as well as the elimination of exploiting middlemen, who used to cream off the greater part of the proceeds for private expenditure in areas which were of no relevance to the coffee industry. Thus, marketing had an impact on the whole industry including its various sectors. The effects of the coffee marketing system are therefore considered in the following paragraphs, which highlight the pricing mechanism, agriculture and transportation of the produce and the manufacturing sector.

The Coffee Pricing System

Among the innovative features of the pricing structure was a two-tier payment system, introduced by the Bukoba Native Coffee Board, as has already been discussed. The system appealed to the farmers because it enabled them to sell the harvest promptly and to receive the first instalment to cover urgent expenses. The second payment, known as arrears, was received months later and was considered as savings or a bonus, arriving at the time of year when most needed.

With the predictability of his income, as a result of the marketing structure, the farmer was in a better position to plan his annual social and economic activities. In addition, he was better able to benefit from jointly organized activities such as advisory and extension services. Other services which were conducive to economies of scale when jointly run were the coffee nurseries, the application of insecticides, crop husbandry and transport.

Secondly, the new pricing system enabled farmers to participate in the revenues realized from final sales (auction) of the coffee as well as in the cost of marketing.[16] Thus, since farmers would be notified early in the season about the initial price, they were able to estimate their annual earnings. Mention should also be made of the occasional distribution of residual amounts which were realized through cost reductions in marketing operations and more efficient management of the system. By being involved in the process of marketing their produce, farmers had the feeling that they were indirectly participating in the determination of the price of their coffee. The sense of being involved in the marketing of the commodity made the farmers receptive to various suggested improvements made by governmental bodies and marketing organizations.

The estimated impact of the coffee industry on the monetary income of the Bahaya during the Ezoni era is indicated by simulated figures presented in Table VI–2. The price assumed is rather conservative, for it had actually increased more than four times over the period 1948–54 and therefore the

TABLE VI–2 *SIMULATED COFFEE PRODUCTION AND EARNINGS IN BUHAYA FOR THE PERIOD 1948–1960*

Year	Estimated Coffee Production in Tons (a)	Estimated Earnings in Shillings (b)	Population (c)	Per Capita Earnings in Shillings (d)
1948	5700	6,894,720	293,583	23.48
1949	6200	7,499,520	299,860	25.01
1950	7000	8,467,200	306,157	27.65
1951	7960	9,628,416	312,586	30.80
1952	7980	9,652,608	319,150	30.24
1953	8000	9,676,800	325,852	29.69
1954	8100	9,797,760	332,695	29.44
1955	8300	10,039,680	339,682	29.55
1956	8400	10,160,640	346,815	29.29
1957	8500	10,281,600	367,796	27.95
1958	8600	10,402,560	377,161	27.58
1959	8800	10,644,480	386,590	27.53
1960	8900	10,753,344	396,254	27.13

(a) Estimates are based on actual figures for 1946, 1960, 1961 and 1962.
(b) The estimated produce in (a) was multiplied times the price per Fair grade average price of (shillings) 1209.60 per ton, cf. *Engoma Ya Buhaya*, Vol. III, No. 1, January 1950.
(c) Population from the 1949 census figure at a 2.1% increase rate for 1950–57 and a 2.5% rate for 1957–67, adopted by the International Bank for Reconstruction and Development. Cf. IBRD/IDA Report No. AE–7, *The Economic Development of Tanzania*, Vol. I, March 1970, Appendix 1.
(d) Cf. IBRD/IDA Report No. AE–7, *The Economic Development of Tanzania*, Vol. I, March 1970, Appendix 1.

total and per capita earnings were much higher in the period 1951–56 than those shown in the table.[17] Viewed from the household point of view, the increase in coffee earnings led to an accumulation of income, to an improvement in residential housing, diet and attire and to the ability to acquire modern items such as bicycles and radios.

The Industrial Sector

Coffee harvesting can give rise to various agro-based industries, such as pulping, entailing the removal of the juicy external flesh from the seed; husking, namely the removal of the translucent parchment from the seed; hulling, involving the removal of the dry cover from the bean; and, lastly, the curing process, which involves the removal of dust from the beans and grading. However, there are other coffee-based industrial processes such as roasting, the production of instant coffee, the grinding and packaging of roasted beans and the brewing of liquor. The Ezoni period, unfortunately, witnessed little success in the establishment of industrial units for the production of coffee derivatives. Mention has already been made of the unsuccessful attempt to erect coffee hulleries. For the greater part of the period, curing works were undertaken by the Shariff Jiwa factory. Otherwise, there was no significant breakthrough in establishing industries of any size for processing coffee or for facilitating its marketing. However, some of the features of industrial development in Buhaya during the period deserve at least a brief comment, namely the import-substitution industries, coffee hulling, coffee curing, small-scale and cottage industries and, later, the growth of Bahaya industrial entrepreneurship.

Despite incomplete data on consumer items, adequate indications exist to show that there was a substantial increase in the consumption of such imported items as corrugated iron sheets, bicycles, beer, cigarettes and textiles. Regrettably, no industrial units were established to manufacture, assemble or even package those items on which the coffee generated income was largely spent. Failure to take advantage of the period to establish an industrial base, even if it were to involve a few import-substitution units, constituted one of the lamentable features of the Ezoṇi era.

While playing a supervisory and nurturing role to the co-operative movement, the Bukoba Native Coffee Board, acting on behalf of the British Ministry of Food, provided a grant to the various zones for the erection of coffee hulleries. In this connection, elaborate industrial buildings were constructed at Kagondo (Kyamutwara), Gera (Kiziba), Makonge (Maruku), Kanazi (Kihanja), Luhanga (Kihanja), Kaigara (Ihangiro) and Kibengwe (Bugabo). The building complexes, however, were never used as hulleries and the fact that they remained unutilized for so long proved that even the seemingly perfect British administrators were capable of making costly errors of common sense. Allegedly, the project planners failed to take into account the supply of coffee beans from the peasant farmers as well as the need for a power source to run the engines, some of which had been promptly installed. Hearsay had it that the buildings were so poorly constructed that they would never have stood a month's shock of the vibrations of the mills. In all, if the hulleries project in Buhaya was not much publicized, it was probably because its failure was overshadowed by a contemporary and equally disastrous project known as the Kongwa Groundnut Scheme.[18]

To sum up, among the factors which led to the failure of the coffee hullery project were, firstly, the lack of any reliable sources of power to run the plants, for it had been discovered belatedly that thermal power units would have been uneconomic.[19] Secondly, a steady flow of coffee berries to the mills could not be guaranteed, given that harvesting from peasant holdings was not easy to synchronize. Thirdly, transport was likely to have been uneconomic as it would have involved a double trip, namely delivery to the hulleries and then further transportation to the curing mill in Bukoba town. Fourthly, the construction of the buildings was not sound enough to withstand the engine vibrations.

Since curing is an essential process for the effective selling of coffee on international markets, facilities were established in Buhaya in the early years of the coffee industry. Before the 1950s, the produce was sent to the Shariff Jiwa Coffee Curing Plant, located on the northern outskirts of the Bukoba town. In 1955, when the need to expand curing facilities had been felt, the BNCU endeavoured to form a joint venture with the Shariff Jiwa Company but the latter declined. BNCU therefore turned to Bukoba Coffee Curing Works Ltd., whose factory was located near the harbour, and formed the Bukoba Coffee Curing Company (BUKOP). The latter eventually bought out the Shariff Jiwa factory, whose premises were used as a godown and whose plant provided spare parts for the BUKOP engines.

The period witnessed considerable developments in the service oriented industries. Thus, many tailoring shops sprang up in the villages to cater for the stimulated demand for clothes and fashions. However, no apparent effort was put into forming sizeable tailoring organizations or firms, nor was there any noticeable success, even when such efforts were made.

Similarly, motor vehicle and bicycle repair services developed significantly, hand in hand with the booming market in the transport sector.

The building industry was stimulated by the switch of the tribe from round grass-huts (mshonge) to more modern mud- or stone-wall square houses. Activities which were highly boosted by the industry included brick-making, stone quarrying, lumbering and carpentry. Flowing from these activities was the spectacular increase in the number of modern huts which mushroomed during a relatively short span of time in the early 1950s. On the whole, the industrial pattern remained on a small or artisinal scale, oriented towards providing a service to the consumer-led economy. It appears that any momentum which existed to favour intensification of these industries was not sustained and they began to decline as soon as the high consumption spell levelled off. Also worth mentioning was the failure to develop industries based on the banana fruit, which is found in abundance in the area. A noticeable exception was the production of banana wine, distilled in a rather primitive manner to convert it into a liquor which was consumed on an alarming scale in the region.

Efforts to establish industries by indigenous people were best exemplified by the coffee hullery project undertaken by Mr Klemens Kiiza, who was mentioned above. Of average height and with a dark, prominent aquiline face, Kiiza was born an aristocrat in Kiziba, served at King Mutatembwa's court as a young man and was later educated at Catholic mission schools. He was first employed as a clerk by the missionaries and subsequently by the district office. An engaging and tireless speaker, he was capable of arousing political feeling although his natural bent tended to be more in the business world.

In 1920, he founded a trading company called the Bukoba Buhaya Union and, as early as 1928, he purchased a coffee hulling plant which he intended to erect at Buganguzi, some 40 miles to the south-west of Bukoba. Partly owing to the Great Depression, his project proved unprofitable, as he was unable to obtain the necessary credit.

In a bid to obtain adequate coffee supplies for his factory, he established an association known as Native Growers. This did not help much either for he found himself stranded with an uncommissioned plant while interest and capital repayment obligations continued to mount up. More critically, he was refused a government licence to run his business. By 1946, it had become clear that his project would have to be abandoned and the plant was impounded and sold to the Indians.[20] Many tended to attribute his failure to sabotage by Indian traders and British administrators who feared his business-like shrewdness.

The Transport Sector

Since transport costs are a significant component of marketing operations, attempts to reduce them should have constituted a priority preoccupation of the coffee industry. An achievement worth mentioning in the transport sector during the Ezoni period was the construction of a 12-mile tarmac surface from Bukoba harbour to Maiga River, near Kemondo Bay, which, having taken ten years to build at the rate of about two yards a day, has recently been scaled off leaving the old mud surface. Less was done for the bridges; neither those within the township area nor the ones in the interior were substantially modified after they were first built during the German times. Bridges across the Ngono River at Kamishango, Kyabakoba and Kalebe were in a weaker structural state at the end of the Ezoni period than at the beginning.[21] Similarly, the Kyaka ferry, linking Bukoba and Uganda, was replaced by a permanent bridge only after Tanzania had attained independence. No improvements were added to Bukoba harbour, which was in a state of decay during the 1960s.

The period witnessed the digging of numerous but poor quality feeder roads to link villages and facilitate movements of bicycles, motor cycles and coffee carrying vehicles. As for the major roads, they were constructed and maintained by the Buhaya Council. That maintenance was generally poor is well reflected in the low priority placed on the transport sector by the government at that time, as is shown in Table VI–3, which indicates that only 5.11% of the budget for 1949 was allocated to roads and bridges. The percentage had only risen slightly by 1950 to 5.89%. Typical of the colonial budget is the fact that emphasis was laid on administration, which claimed 60% of the total amount; nothing was allocated to manufacturing, while agriculture, the backbone of the region, received only about 1% of the budget.

If Bukoba town was not securely linked with its hinterland, at least it had good connections with Mwanza and the other Lake Victoria ports of Kisumu (Kenya) and Luzira (Uganda). The major Lake Victoria steamers, namely the SS *Busoga*, SS *Rusinga*, SS *Kavirondo* and SS *Nyanza*, used to call at Bukoba at least once a week. With the exception of the *Kavirondo*, which was a tug used for cattle and bulky cargo, the other three steamers transported both passengers and cargo. The reliability of the steamer service was an important factor in the economic development of the region during the 1950s for it

TABLE VI–3 *SECTORIAL ALLOCATION OF THE ANNUAL BUDGET OF THE BUHAYA COUNCIL*

SECTOR	1949 Amount in shs.	%	1950 Amount in shs.	%
1. Administration	447,960	67.63	471,980	60.39
2. Health	96,860	14.62	93,400	11.95
3. Education	46,900	7.08	58,780	7.52
4. Agriculture	10,360	1.56	6,500	0.83
5. Forestry	4,000	0.61	4,000	0.51
6. Veterinary	3,380	0.51	4,060	0.52
7. Roads and Bridges	33,880	5.11	46,020	5.89
8. Water	1,000	0.15	1,000	0.14
9. Other	18,000	2.73	85,740	12.25
TOTAL	662,400	100.00	781,520	100.00

Source: *Engoma Ya Buhaya*, Vol. III, No. 1, January 1950, p. 9. Calculations by the author.

ensured the carrying of coffee to auction markets and the arrival of consumer goods manufactured overseas or in other parts of East Africa.

Commerce

Commercial activities at the wholesale import level were conducted mainly by Indian traders, though the retail trade was fast passing into the hands of the Bahaya. Importers could secure goods from all over East Africa, which by then formed a single customs area.[22] The import trade was largely in the hands of Indians who, besides having easy access to capital, had external connections based on the close-knit and widely-spread Indian community. Concern about the cartel-like monopolization of trade by the Indians was expressed by many, including members of the British administration. As Leubuscher observed in 1933 in relation to Africans who tried to penetrate the Indian trade monopoly:

> Those who tried to work at the wholesale level were usually thwarted and many found themselves bankrupt.[23]

The view was prophetic since, indeed, the half dozen Bahaya who tried to attain the Indian level of success during the Ezoni period went bankrupt before long. Reference was made to the monopolization of the coffee export business by Indian traders prior to the establishment of the co-operatives. When the latter assumed the coffee marketing role, the Indians retreated to the wholesale business but maintained their commercial supremacy by continuing to attract farmers' earnings through their practice of stocking

TABLE VI–4 *RETAILERS IN ONE VILLAGE*

PERIOD	NO. OF RETAILERS
Before 1946	4
By 1954	14
By 1970	4

TABLE VI–5 *OTHER COMMERCIAL INDICATORS FOR A SAMPLE VILLAGE*

PERIOD	BICYLES	BATI HOUSES	BUTCHERIES	BEER STALLS
Before 1948	2% of homes	2% of homes	0	0
1948–1960	80% of homes	80% of homes	2	2
After 1960	10% of homes	95% of homes	0	0

Sources for Tables VI–4 and VI–5: Observation by the author over the years. The village concerned is Ijumbi in Ihangiro, about 40 miles south of Bukoba town. It covers about a square mile of uninterrupted plantation. In 1956, the count was 850 inhabitants in 155 houses (homes). The population had doubled by the census of 1979. As the village is situated far away from Bukoba town, the figures tend to be underestimated, thus allowing a margin for wider application.

consumer items which were in great demand at that time.

As for the retail trade, shops sprang up in many parts of the region, some with as little starting capital as 100 shillings or less and even retailing single matchsticks or cigarettes. Others, however, stocked their shops with clothes, European drinks and all sorts of fancy goods. The growth of the retail trade can be illustrated by the observations made at a typical village, as shown in Table VI–4 and Table VI–5.

A general picture of the consumption-dominated economy of the Ezoni era is given by Table VI–6. Out of the nine major items imported bicycles experienced the highest rise: 200% over the period 1939–52. During the period 1947–49, the index increased by 238, while the biggest jump of 1304% was in the 1951–52 period. Cement was next in demand with a 340% rise in the period 1948–50. Apparently all nine items gained more than 300% during the 1939–52 period.

While the picture provided applies to Tanganyika Territory as a whole, it indicates what transpired in Buhaya during these years. Mention has already been made of the unprecedented increase in the number of bicycles in the villages, the substitution of corrugated iron (bati) roofs for thatches and the introduction of tinned milk, cigarettes and other items shown in the table.

The Politics of the Ezoni Era — Political Developments

The political system during the Ezoni era was virtually the same as that during the early years of British administration. The final authority rested in

TABLE VI–6 *INDEX OF THE QUANTITY OF CONSUMER ITEMS IMPORTED FOR THE WHOLE OF TANGANYIKA*

	ITEM	UNIT	1939	1946	1947	1948	1949	1950	1951	1952
1.	Tobacco and cigarettes	million lbs.	100	116	116	133	200	233	216	400
2.	Condensed milk and cream	tons	100	49	112	221	352	377	551	290
3.	Cotton piece goods	sq. yards	100	57	61	82	129	108	83	115
4.	Rayon piece goods	sq. yards	100	18	27	54	145	318	845	590
5.	Petrol and oils	gallons	100	139	196	250	357	368	341	422
6.	Cement	tons	100	106	213	330	553	733	753	720
7.	C.I. Sheets	tons	100	41	52	129	152	188	417	247
8.	Bicycles	units	100	127	235	373	473	515	796	2100
9.	Tyres and tubes	cwt.	100	167	319	426	473	521	574	518

Source of import figures: J. P. Moffet, *Tanganyika: A Review of its Resources and Their Development* (Dar es Salaam: Government Printer, 1955), p. 736.

the hands of the British government in London, which acted through the Governor in Dar es Salaam down the line to the Provincial Commissioner in Mwanza and the District Commissioner at Bukoba. From there the Bakama would take over, exercising their power through the *Bami* or subchiefs and the *Bakungu* or village headmen. The power of the Bakama had been established by legislation passed in the 1920s, the Native Authority Ordinance, which confirmed the indirect rule system introduced by the Germans, whereby the colonial government acted through the traditional rulers or chiefs.

Deprived of their nineteenth century absolute and semi-divine powers, the Bakama tended to vent their frustration through high-handedness while executing the orders of their British colonial masters. Their arbitrariness, however, was kept in check by the authority of the *Lukiiko* or Council of the Bakama, which could call into question any measures taken by a Mukama in his domain. Eventually, the Lukiiko and the Bakama themselves became the voice of the British masters at the expense of justice and the economic development of the people. Such a level of resignation on the part of the Bakama was the result of intimidation and a cracking down on the dissident chiefs by the Europeans.[24] In short, the Bakama ceased to be a power to be reckoned with, for real authority rested in the hands of the District Commissioner.

Typifying the relationship between the British administration and the Bakama were the events which led to the ousting of Petro Mugunda, the Mukama who ruled Ihangiro from 1936 to 1952. Born in 1906, he attended Rubya Primary School from 1913 to 1917 before proceeding to Bukoba Central School. From 1926 to 1927, he was employed as a clerk at district headquarters before being appointed chief clerk at the main administrative office of the chiefdom of Ihangiro. He became subchief (Mwami) of Nshamba in 1932 and remained in that position until 1936 when he became Mukama on the death of his father, Mukama Muhile Ruhinda. Of average height, dark complexion and plumpish features, his circular eyes radiated a penetrating intellect which was coupled with a photographic memory for faces and events. He would call out by name a prostrating admirer and remind him of their previous encounter many years before. It was his command of detail and popular touch, however, which made him such a charismatic personality, long before he even assumed the throne. Luguma Lwa Nchwele Kinshwi Kya Kagazi, as he was popularly known, Mugunda quickly won the hearts of the people of Ihangiro. Unfortunately, as early on as 1936, the clouds of World War II had begun to gather and by 1940, shortages of essential commodities and outbreaks of famine and disease were troubling his kingdom, despite his efforts to launch rescue operations.[25] In 1941, Mugunda earned an award from the British government, the King's Medal, and in 1945 he made an official tour of Kenya Colony.

When nominated to the national Legislative Council to replace Chief Kidaha Makwaia of Shinyanga, he had no doubt won the confidence of his fellow Bakama and the colonial administrators alike. His performance in the national Legislative Assembly earned him national recognition and his name became widely known within Buhaya and other parts of Tanganyika. Among the important issues he took up in the Legislative Assembly were the coffee prices paid to the producer with respect to the contract of the British Food Ministry and the question of sending chiefs to the United Kingdom to learn more about administrative techniques.

As Mukama of Ihangiro, Mugunda organized a council of subchiefs and pushed for the introduction of development programmes aimed at inculcating work ethics among the local youth, fighting animal pests, constructing proper market places, maternity wards and a post office, creating educational programmes for Standard VI leavers and the adoption of other measures aimed at improving the general standard of living of his people. Though believed to be a direct descendant of the founder of the dynasty, Ruhinda Kibonabagabe, Mugunda was democratic and republican in outlook and endeavoured to arouse political awareness and participation among his people.

In the eyes of the British administrators, however, Mugunda was a naughty boy to be whipped into subjugation. Luckily, the two District Commissioners of Bukoba immediately after the War were old-timers and on their way to retirement. Thus, J. E. S. Griffiths, MBE, left Bukoba on 2 December 1949 to go into retirement. His successor as District Commissioner, Mr D. J. Powell, retired in June 1950. A much younger and more dynamic Oxbridge British administrator was appearing on the scene and he, more than anybody else, was to influence the politics of Buhaya in the early 1950s.

This important character on the British side was the District Commissioner, Mr C. C. (Tim) Harris, locally known as Kitemanio kya

Kalonge, later to be awarded an OBE. Born in Bristol in 1917, where he completed his secondary education at Clifton College, he attended Wadham College, Oxford, studying political science. His experience in Tanzania included being a DC in Iringa and Bukoba and a Provincial Commissioner in Dar es Salaam at the time of Independence. Of average height and a stout individual, Harris was known to be a tough but efficient administrator and, to his colleagues, a humorous equitable character. He took up the post of District Commissioner in Bukoba in June 1950, replacing Mr D. J. Powell. By then, the economy was recovering fast from the war shortages and consumer goods were filling the shops to an unprecedented level in the history of Buhaya. At the same time, Petro Mugunda was also rising as an undeniable star on the political stage of the region. The drama of the early 1950s was the question of how Harris would oust Mugunda.

Accusing him of mismanaging the kingdom, Harris forced Mugunda to abdicate in 1952 and replaced him with his brother, Sylvester (Rushoni) Ntare, a very handsome man but one with little administrative experience or capability. Until his death in the 1960s, Mugunda led a retired but highly respectable life at his Nshamba home. For the people of Ihangiro, Mugunda remains the last popular and powerful king and, for the Bahaya, he still represents the lingering image of a true Mukama.

The Lukiiko or the Council of the eight Bakama, which had been in existence since 1926, maintained its role during the period as the co-ordinating organ of native policy for the whole region of Buhaya. For the greater part of the Ezoni period, the Bakama were Nestori Lutinwa (Kiziba), Gabriel Lugabandana (Kyamutwara), David Rugomora (Maruku), B. I. Ruhinda (Karagwe), Galican Lwegelera (Bugabo), Paul Lwamujongo (Missenyi), H. Bwogi (Kihanja), Petro Mugunda and, later, Sylvester Ntare (Ihangiro).

Even when under constant constraint to comply with colonial orders, the Lukiiko was able to make plausible initiatives from time to time. Foremost, it succeeded in introducing a sense of unity among the Bahaya and in inculcating a concerted approach on the formulation and implementation of social and economic programmes. Until the formation of the Council of the Bakama, the only unifying factors among the Bahaya were language, common customs, intermarriage, frequent wars and ever-changing boundaries. The Council also engendered a spirit of competitiveness between the kingdoms in such fields as sports, education and administration, with a view to facilitating economic development. Furthermore, it enabled the Bakama's work to be effectively co-ordinated.

Keeping the authority of the Bakama under control, however, had a positive effect in further weakening the feudal system, which had reached stifling proportions at the dawn of the European era. Thus, by 1950, the non-aristocratic groups were moving up socially, exploiting the new educational and commercial opportunities open to them to rise to key positions of political and financial influence. With the democratizing and politicization impact engendered by the newly-found wealth of the Ezoni period, the nineteenth century social balance was overturned; whether irrevocably or not remains to be seen.

If the Lukiiko was able to play a uniting role in the region, it was mainly due to the vision and initiative of Mr Francisco Xavier Lwamugira. Born a Mushaga by clan in the tiny, densely populated village of Bwekera, Kiziba, in 1875, Lwamugira, like Klemens Kiiza, was trained as a page at King Mutatembwa's court where his father, Katabaro, had served as a great courtier and which his mother, Korushusho, had frequented, being the king's sister. Of average height and with wavy hair, Lwamugira combined a rare intellectual capability with a determination to defy any situation that might have tended to obscure his genius. At court, he had to study the history and administration of the tribe before qualifying for the post of king's bursar. Having taught himself to read and write Swahili, German and English, he was employed as a civil servant in the German administration from 1900 to 1916. In 1926, he was appointed secretary to the newly formed Lukiiko or Council of the Bakama, a post he held until retirement in 1946, only a few years before his death on 11 August 1950.[26] He was a leading Muhaya author on the affairs of the tribe with works ranging from customary law to historical treatises.[27] The greatest debt owed by Buhaya to Lwamugira, however, remains in respect of his contribution to the unification of the region by civil means. Had his Messianic word on unity been duly heeded, Buhaya's history would have taken a significantly different course. But many misunderstood his vision and the politics of petty chiefdoms were still too strong to allow a united Buhaya. One reason for the short-lived effect of the Ezoni boom might have been the political fragmentation of Buhaya, which led to a wastage of public funds through the duplication of services when efforts should have been concentrated on a few key development projects.[28]

The nationalist movement, which had clearly emerged in 1920, continued to gather momentum during the Ezoni era. One of the most important factions was the Kihanja Labour Association (KLA), which aimed at fighting the status of the aristocrats by emphasizing the need for hard work and the abolition of social privileges, particularly those based on the feudal system or nyarubanja. The KLA further demanded the abolition of the institution of Mukama or king, though it soon realized that the political climate was not yet ready for doing without Bakama. Overall, however, KLA remained a local movement, confining its interest to the chiefdom of Kihanja and the ruler/ruled confrontation.

Efforts aimed at the unification of Buhaya were reactivated later on in the 1950s by various factions, one of which advocated the establishment of a paramount chief or RUBAMBA system. While the Germans had experimented with this system in Buhaya, the British abandoned the practice altogether and established a council of chiefs instead.[29] The basic objective of having a paramount chief was to centralize the administration of the whole region and thereby rationalize the various development programmes. After all, the paramount chief system had been successfully introduced in Moshi, Sukumaland and other areas in Tanganyika.[30] The proposed Rubamba system, however, was fundamentally different as it was to be based on popular elections and on personal rather than aristocratic qualities.

Consequently, the movement was opposed by the royalists and the aristocrats who feared for their positions of influence.[31] Besides, the movement was short-lived because it was overtaken by the wave of agitation for independence which was experienced throughout the length and breadth of Tanganyika Territory.

When discussing the political arena, mention should also be made of Ali Migeyo who, in Buhaya, spearheaded the work of the Tanganyika African Association (TAA), which was the strongest political party for Africans at that time. Born in Maruku in 1896, Ali was a capable agitator, a gifted, sensational orator and a charismatic politician.[32] Despite his limited formal education, Ali could master the details of an issue and make a convincing argument to an audience. Riding on a wave of opposition to colonial measures calling for the uprooting of the old banana stumps (Bikonya), Migeyo was able to convince the Bahaya that the stumps campaign tended to eradicate the banana plantations. He argued that the removal of the stumps would result in weaker bananas and that the plants would ultimately disappear, enabling the European settlers to come in and occupy the land as they had done in Kenya.

Introduced almost simultaneously was another agricultural programme, aimed at ensuring that coffee farms were mulched so as to increase the yield per bush. Capitalizing on this newly-introduced measure, Ali fanned the doubting Bahaya into a resistance movement known as TWAMWANGA BWANA SHAMBA (we hate the agricultural officer).[33]

By and large, the political developments of the 1940s and 1950s featured economic and social movements such as the Kihanja Labour Association and the Twamwanga Bwana Shamba. Their objectives further illustrated the close link between politics and economics and are a clear example of how an improvement in economic welfare can generate greater nationalist consciousness. Towards the end of the 1950s, the movement towards political independence had become so strong that it swept away local and parochial factions such as the KLA. Under the capable leadership of the TAA and, later, the Tanganyika African National Union (TANU), local factions were being galvanized into a single force fighting for the independence of Tanganyika.

Conclusion

One obvious conclusion to be deducted from the above analysis is that the Ezoni era constituted a unique period in the history of Buhaya. Its major characteristics included a buoyant market for consumer goods, high coffee prices and higher incomes resulting from those prices. This uniqueness was accentuated by the preceding years of World War II, which had been characterized by shortages of basic consumer goods and the famine calamity of 1942–43, which claimed many lives. The post-war period stood in sharp contrast to those hard times and witnessed a phenomenal economic recovery marked by vigorous commercial activities.

One of the outstanding features of the Ezoni era was the influx of consumer goods imported from Dar es Salaam, Nairobi, Kampala and other East African towns. Even Britain had stepped up its drive to sell to the colonies as part of its design to accelerate its own economic recovery.[34] It was alleged that in 1954, Buhaya alone consumed more than half of all the beer marketed in Tanganyika. Other commodities purchased on a similarly extraordinary scale included cigarettes, bicycles and corrugated iron sheets. It might well have been the abundance of consumer items which bedazzled many into concluding that the Ezoni era was the *Pax Economica*, if not the zenith of the glory that used to be Buhaya.

Concomitant with the exuberant mood of the post-war years was the reorganization of coffee marketing in Buhaya and the accompanying price rise of the product. The reorganization was spearheaded by the Bukoba Native Coffee Board, whose main task was to collect the produce and organize its sale so as to honour the contract of the British Ministry of Food. To enable it to carry out its mandate, BNCB undertook a number of measures, including the establishment of co-operatives and hulleries. While the co-operative marketing system proved to be one of the important economic innovations of the decade, the construction of hulling factories turned out to be a most ill-conceived industrial project in the region, matched only in careless planning by the contemporary Kongwa Groundnut fiasco.

The *zones* system, by which the BNCB divided the region into subregional centres to facilitate the collection, purchase, storage and transportation of coffee, preceded the co-operative movement. However, the system relied heavily on Indian middlemen for the purchase and transportation of the crop. It was not until the establishment of the primary coffee marketing societies and the derivative Bukoba Native Co-operative Union that the foundation of economic changes for the 1950s was laid. While high prices might have been instrumental to the coffee boom of the period, the marketing system, more than anything else, was what made farmers realize increased incomes. Rationalizing the marketing function and eliminating middlemen increased the farmer's income many times over. Besides, coffee marketing was turning out to be a central socio-economic activity of the community, involving frequent meetings to discuss the growing of coffee, pricing, the use of insecticides and similar subjects.

Most instrumental to the prosperity of the Ezoni era, however, was the exceptional rise in the price of coffee and other commodities. Thus in 1954, the price of robusta was quoted as standing at an average of 4.36 shillings per pound (lb.) as compared to 1.95 shillings per lb. in 1950, the increase being in the order of 123%.[35]

If examined critically, however, the Ezoni boon was a brushfire-like consumer wave, fanned by pent-up post-war demand and high coffee prices but otherwise vanishing as rapidly as it had begun and leaving Buhaya in its centuries-old economic predicament. Thus, with the exception of the corrugated iron roofs, which artistically broke up the monotonous greenery of the countryside, there was little done by way of infrastructure investment in roads, bridges or industrial establishments. The agricultural sector hardly changed during the period; the banana remained the staple food and its cultivation, if it was modified at all, deteriorated, as people gave more attention to coffee and commercial undertakings. Strangely enough, coffee production even declined as peasants spent more time enjoying incomes derived from higher prices.[36]

Overall, the major criticism of the period was the failure to lay an emphasis on industrialization at a time when, generally, the cost of capital goods was rather low and credit for securing them easier to come by. Even the agricultural sector, at that time the basis of prosperity, was not substantially developed. The failure of the coffee hulleries project might have further discouraged the industrialization of the coffee industry and other sectors.[37]

The high trends of consumption during the Ezoni era, however, had a number of positive effects as well. Firstly, they encouraged a good portion of the population to move into the monetary sector, thereby sharpening their eagerness for development. Secondly, they enabled the Bahaya to improve their housing by abandoning the traditional grass huts for corrugated iron-roofed buildings. Thirdly, they encouraged the establishment of permanent structures for marketing coffee produce, especially that of the Bukoba Co-operative Union. Fourthly, the Ezoni period encouraged social improvements, particularly in the area of education. As in other regions of Tanzania, the co-operative movement increased the general awareness of the population, which culminated in independence.

In all, the Ezoni period was a product of four major elements. The first was the maturing of the decades-long efforts to establish the coffee industry. The second was the post-war market buoyancy, characterized by high coffee prices on the international markets and an influx of consumer goods. The third was the economic development, which reflected a higher level of social welfare and political awareness, immediately preceding the national struggle for independence. The fourth was the revolutionization of coffee marketing through the co-operatives and the BCU, which ensured a more effective distribution of the proceeds. These major factors, taken together and with others, gave the Ezoni period its main characteristics.

In general, the period might be seen as the culmination of the decades-long process of bombarding Buhaya with European, non-African culture. The process was apparently accelerated by the coffee industry, which transformed the overall life pattern of the tribe from an unsophisticated peasant structure to an agriculture-based, partially monetary economy. Historically, the Ezoni era was a watershed between the tides which led to national independence. Psychologically, the period made the Bahaya become more aware of their dependence on the other regions of Tanzania and other parts of the world, from where they purchased many commodities and without which they could not have fought for independence. Economically, the Ezoni era was characterized by an unprecedented level of consumption of externally produced goods. Indeed, Buhaya had become a classic example of a colonial economy appended to the metropolitan centres on which it was closely dependent for the supply of manufactured goods and to which it had to export primary commodities. It was largely owing to the influx of consumer goods that the period is considered by many Bahaya to have been the peak of economic prosperity of the region.

1. For a theoretical rendering of the marketing function, *see* Michael Rines (editor), *Marketing Handbook* (Gower Publishing Company Limited, 1981), pp.1–3.
2. The handling of hard coffees is simpler as it just involves drying the beans in the sun. For the milds, however, the red beans have to be taken to the pulperies where the juicy red skin is removed and the beans are fermented before being dried.
3. Common damage and faults encountered in handling coffee are discussed in the report of the Tanganyika Territory Department of Agriculture, *Coffee Crop, 1943–44: Report on Quality and Its Improvement* (Dar es Salaam: Government Printer, 1944), Pamphlet No. 37.
4. A summary of the curing process is presented in *The Courier*, No. 59, January/February 1980, pp.58–61.
5. The marketing process and how it could affect the peasant way of life is analysed in 'The Role of Marketing in the Development of Non-Market Sectors and Conditions Necessary for Success', by Mikhilesh Dholakia and Faut A. Firat, in *Marketing Systems for Developing Countries*, by Dov Izraeli and Frank Meissner (eds.), (John Wiley & Sons, 1976), pp.50–61.
6. For a general background to the co-operative movement, *see* T. R. Sadleir, *The Co-operative Movement in Tanganyika* (Dar es Salaam: Government Printer, 1961).
7. *See* Agricultural Report, 1936, p.68.
8. Lake Province, which included Bukoba, had a relatively small acreage under European farming with only 41,000 acres in 1938, compared to 641,000 acres in Tanga Region alone. Cf. Charlotte Leubuscher, op. cit., p.202. European farms had been established at the following locations: Kaboya (Kihanja), Katoke (Kihanja), Kishojo (Kihanja), Nshamba (Ihangiro), Karumyo (Ihangiro), Kibimbili (Kihanja), Kanyangereko (Maruku), Rwamurumba (Kyamutwara) and Kyanyabasa (Kihanja).
9. Traders and middlemen were trying to explain to the coffee buyers how coffee was produced. This claim of ownership of large farms was frequently repeated to the African farmers by the Indian traders, despite its being a blatant lie.
10. Some of the measures enacted by the Ministry of Food were explained by Mr H. Griffin Smith in his address at Bukoba on 28 September 1950. *See*, *Engoma Ya Buhaya*, Vol. III, No. 10, October 1950, pp.67–8.
11. Estimated total annual production for the region was of the order of 8,000 tons, while the price of first grade robusta at Mombasa had reached 4.36 shillings per lb. in 1947 for lots outside the contract.
12. This financing information was made public at a coffee marketing meeting on 11 January 1950 by Mr Powell, the DC, and Mr Elliott, the Co-operative Officer, *vide*, *Engoma Ya Buhaya*, Vol. III, No. 2, February 1950.
13. Cf. J. P. Moffet (ed.), *Tanganyika: A Review of its Resources and Their Development* (Dar es Salaam: Government Printer, 1955), p.774.

14. For more about the BNCU management, *see* Goran Hyden, *Political Development in Rural Tanzania*, op. cit., p.118. The Bukoba Co-Operative Union — BNCU — changed into the BCU when the Union assumed the functions of the Bukoba Native Coffee Board.
15. The subject of BCU activities was discussed with Mr Gervas Ishengoma, General Manager, Balimi, c/o PO Box 5, Bukoba, on 2 September 1983.
16. The importance of involving peasant farmers in the marketing process was discussed earlier. *See* Mikhilesh Dholakia and Fuat A. Firat in *Marketing Systems for Developing Countries* by Dov Israeli and Frank Meissner (eds.), (John Wiley & Sons, 1976), pp.50–61.
17. According to Mr Gervas Ishengoma, General Manager of Balimi, and Mr Mukamba, the statistician of the organization, average annual coffee production was about 12,000 tons. Arabica comprised about a quarter of the total quantity produced or marketed.
18. The Kongwa Groundnut Scheme had been designed to produce groundnuts in central Tanganyika by using the latest agronometrical technology, including artificial rain-making. As John Lonsdale put it, 'About £36 million were spent on the disastrous "groundnut scheme", not one ounce of cooking oil was produced...' Cf. *Africa South of the Sahara 1981–82* (London: Europa Publications Limited), p.1031.
19. This issue was discussed with Mr Burchard R. Baisi, who was associated for many years with the Bukoba coffee co-operative movement.
20. Some parts of the plant could not be extricated from concrete and can still be seen at the factory site in Buganguzi.
21. The toll bridges during the German period were the following:

Location	Subchiefdom	Chiefdom
1. Kyanyabasa	Minazi	Kihanja
2. Kalebe	Rwagati	Kihanja
3. Kyabakoba	Muhutwe	Kihanja
4. Kishara	Kizigo	Kihanja
5. Kaigembe	Bugandika	Kiziba
6. Nkenge	Kitobo	Kiziba
7. Kamishango (Ikondo)	Buleza	Ihangiro

22. East Africa had constituted a single customs area since 1885 when the Congo Basin Treaties were signed. For more about this, *see* C. M. Tibazarwa, op. cit., Chapter II. *See also* C. Leubuscher, *Tanganyika Territory*, op. cit.
24. To reduce opposition, the Germans deposed chiefs and the British resorted to the same tactics. Ntare, Mukama of Karagwe during the rule of the Germans, was not only deposed but was also publicly executed later on.
25. The famine of 1941/42 was called Ikambula Mabati and was believed to have been the worst in Buhaya for centuries.
26. A concise biography of Lwamugira is presented by I. K. Katoke and P. Rwehumbiza in *Modern Tanzanians* by John Iliffe (ed.), (Nairobi: East African Publishing House, 1973), pp.43–65.
27. Among the popular publications of Lwamugira was *Omwana Muhara*. Other works include *Amakuru ga Kiziba n'Abakama Bamwo* (The History of Kiziba and its Kings), (Bukoba, 1949).
28. An illustration of waste was the financing of study tours of the Bakama to Europe and other places. It had become the practice to compose the study tour teams by selecting candidates from several of the eight chiefdoms.

29. Mukama Kahigi ka Rugomora of Kihanja was declared paramount chief in 1895. Similarly, Mukama Mutahangarwa of Kiziba was made senior chief (obersultan) in 1905.
30. In Moshi, the paramount chief was known as *Mangi Mkuu.*
31. Proponents of the Rubamba movement used to air their views in a local newspaper called *Bukya na Gandi* (It Dawns with Fresh News), edited by E. Munseri of Kabanga Mirembe, Bukoba.
32. For a full account of the politician, *see* G. R. Mutahaba, *Portrait of a Nationalist: The Life of Ali Migeyo* (Nairobi: East African Publishing House, 1969).
33. The extension-service or agricultural officer symbolized the measures introduced by the European administrators, and thus found himself the scapegoat of the resistance. Goran Hyden refers to the movement as *Twayanga,* though the complete slogan was *Twamwanga Bwana Shamba,* cf. his work, *Political Development in Rural Tanzania,* op. cit., pp.115–16.
34. During the inter-war period, the British government tended to curtail its investment in Tanganyika Territory, for fear of Hitler's threats to recapture the pre-1918 German colonial possessions.
35. The prices are f.o.b. Mombasa for robusta first grade or f.a.q. from Uganda, which would be the most comparable with that from Bukoba in terms of type of coffee and transportation costs.
36. Falling production resulting from a big increase in peasant income is not a rare phenomenon as farmers tend to attach more importance to enjoying the income already earned than trying to increase it.
37. TANICA (Tanganyika Instant Coffee Company) was established subsequently as a result of the national independence momentum.

CHAPTER VII

CONCLUSION

Introduction

Although each chapter carries a summary of its own, it nevertheless appears necessary to highlight and synthesize the major issues which tend to emerge from this work. One set of conclusions relates to the economic forces which influenced the path of history followed by the tribe as it developed through the centuries and, to this effect, a summary of the economic revolutions is provided.

Another set of conclusions deals with the indebtedness of the tribe in respect of the cultural impact upon it of previous civilizations and external social forces. This indebtedness is discussed in such a way as to situate the tribe within the African and universal setting, to demonstrate how Bahaya culture was a product of many other cultures and also to show how it managed to grow as a society by preserving its cultural identity. The last set of conclusions focuses on the recent economic and social conditions of the tribe and attempts to project the direction of its short-term development.

Summary of the Major Economic Revolutions

Four major economic periods are discernible in the history of Buhaya. The first ended around 1500 but went back to time immemorial. The scanty data obtainable on this period, however, has meant that the entire lapse of time has had to be treated as one epoch divided into two: the Pre-Stone Age and Stone Age epochs. Then follows the period starting with AD 300, when Bantu culture is believed to have been established in the area; once again, shortage of reliable data has made it necessary to rely on non-written records. The later part of the Stone Age was dominated by the arrival of the Bantu stock, who may have come from the north as part of the migratory wave sweeping the continent at the time.

The discussion of the Bantu's arrival draws heavily on existing accounts of the various races of Africa.

In Buhaya, this period witnessed the settling of the original Bantu-stock clans who founded a culture which has survived to date. They also sowed the seed of the ethnic group which continues to form the majority of the region's population. From any angle, therefore, this period is the most important formative stage of Bahaya society, which was characterized by the clan system, comprised of kin who recognized one leader but co-operated with other clans for the purposes of defending the land and intermarriage. The social and economic implications of the clan system and how they affected later civilization was therefore examined.

Also dominating the period from the economic point of view was the cultivation of the small-sized grain called fingermillet (ELEUSINE CORACANA), which became the major occupation of the tribe whose way of life came to revolve around the production and consumption of the grain. Fingermillet provided the flour from which the meals of the household were made: liquid porridge was the normal breakfast and the bread-like dough made from its flour formed the main dish at most tables.

Superseding the fingermillet revolution was the banana-based culture, which was ushered in by the arrival of the people of the Nilo-Hamitic race who traced their source to the Nile Valley but migrated to search for good land where they could settle and graze cattle. As a perennial crop, the banana entailed a change in the social structure of the people who then had to have permanent farms. Besides, the banana plant was able to support a large population on a relatively small area and this led to the formation of the villages. Banana culture became the centre-piece of economic activity during the period and constituted the second major agricultural revolution.

To attain maximum productivity, the banana plant required manure obtained from the longhorn cattle called *Ankole* or *Sanga*. This cattle breed was able to produce large quantities of manure and therefore made it possible for a relatively small area to yield adequate quantities of fruit, thereby reducing the recurrence of famine and laying the foundation for cultural development.

The banana revolution was interrupted rather abruptly by the arrival of the Europeans who totally transformed the economy from a simple, purely peasant, closed economy into an appendage to a larger Tanganyika economy which was, in turn, peripheral to a metropolitan system.[1] While the importance of the economic transformation resulting from the European contact can hardly be overemphasized, it was the development of the coffee industry which, in Buhaya, helped to bring about the change at the rate at which it occurred. Thus, European colonization of the region was the starting point for the coffee industry and the factor which gave rise to an agricultural-based revolution. One of the basic features of the revolution was the planting of coffee trees on the same plots as bananas, thus converting the hitherto purely banana plantations into a mixed culture. Consequently, husbandry techniques had to be modified to suit the dual culture farm. It was through contributing to the monetary sector, however, that the coffee industry facilitated the revolutionization of the Buhaya economy.

For convenience, the account of the economic revolutions has been arranged in this book in chronological order and, to a certain extent, the revolutions coincide with the four major political epochs of Buhaya, these being the Stone Age period, the Bantu era, the Nilo-Hamitic invasion and the European colonization period. The revolutions which have been identified, though essentially agricultural in nature, affected all other sectors equally radically. Indeed, history tends to categorize its epochs in terms of the prevalent materials used in making tools, such as stone, bronze and iron. Conceivably, it is possible to choose some other criteria and perhaps make a more convincing case out of it. In oral history, for example, there has been a tendency to use the criteria of dynastic successions, conquests or major events. However, Buhaya being predominantly a farming area and being likely to remain so for many years to come, categorization of the historical development from the agricultural point of view constitutes a realistic approach.

Cultural Highlights

While assuming that the reader has drawn his own conclusions from the text, there are a few themes which need to be underscored. Firstly, the Bahaya as a tribe constitute merely a sociological genus within the context of Tanzanian and African society and, as such, whatever generalizations are made about the Bahaya historical experience can be applied to other tribes or communities in Africa or elsewhere. Therefore, much as this study has concentrated on only one tribe, its conclusions should have a broad application in Africa and elsewhere.

Secondly, the Bahaya civilization is heavily indebted to the prehistoric heritage which, universal as it was to origin and spread, continued to manifest itself uniquely in the tribal way of life until the dawn of the European era. The tendency for these prehistoric features to linger can be partly explained by the phenomenon that was general to Africa south of the Sahara, namely that the region tended to remain in the shadow of civilizations prevailing in other parts of the world. The actual cause of this phenomenon falls outside the scope of this work though it should be noted that Buhaya appears to have been insulated even from the surrounding communities by virtue of its geographical location. Illustrative of the prehistoric heritage is the wide use of stone tools such as querns as well as hunting and fishing techniques, the system of gathering food, the social system in force and the cave paintings found in many parts of Buhaya.

As expected, Buhaya borrowed significantly from other cultures and, in this connection, it should be recalled that the founders of the tribe are believed to have originated in areas around the Cameroon/Nigerian border. It is to that region, therefore, that the tribe owes its Bantu base and stock as well as its linguistic character. It is also to this source that the tribe owes its indigenous technology, principally in the sectors of husbandry, iron and copper.

As an interlacustrine tribe, the Bahaya have continued to be influenced by neighbouring groups such as the Baganda, Bunyoro, Banyankole, Burundi and Bazinza, to mention a few. The uniformity of the geography of the interlacustrine region, marked by heavy rainfall, cool highland temperatures and perpetual greenery, provides the essential factors for the interlacustrine character. Supplementing factors include intermarriage and migrations caused by political and economic upheavals.

A synthesized view of the character of the Bahaya tribe reveals how it evolved by enriching itself from other cultures and developing from within. However, much as the tribe borrowed from the cultures of the interlacustrine and other tribes, it nevertheless succeeded in preserving its identity as a basically Bantu community. Even the Nilo-Hamitic invasions and domination, which extended over 500 years, could not destroy the original tribal character but rather encouraged its adjustment and, ultimately, its enhancement. The Nilo-Hamitic culture thrived symbiotically on the Bantu social base upon which it constructed a dynastic political structure characterized by a feudal system called nyarubanja.

For a relatively brief period, the Bahaya culture was subjected to the European colonial experience. Despite its brevity and its recent occurrence, the period had a fundamental impact on the tribe. To evaluate the influence of European culture, historians will be hard put to compare the 70 years of European domination with 500 years of Nilo-Hamitic monarchies and 1,000 years of purely Bantu civilizations. Evidently, the European presence fundamentally affected the cultural base of the tribe by introducing a totally different form of religion, approach to life, attitudes and mores. Equally fundamental was the introduction of a new mode of education based on literacy and classroom teaching, which affected even the psychological roots of the tribe.

Economically, colonial domination introduced a monetary economy based on coffee and, to this effect, measures were taken to encourage the growing of cash crops, the marketing of all sorts of commodities and the provision of services, porterage in particular. With the money realized, the items purchased by households included clothes, soap, beads and salt. Consequently, commerce was stimulated because of the use of money as a medium of exchange and the commercial system of the pre-European period was replaced by a network of exporting facilities and import, wholesale and retail centres. The revolutionizing elements introduced by the European presence have continued unabated to date.

Prospect of a New Economic Revolution

This work has focused on the period before the independence of Tanzania in 1961 on the assumption that the subsequent period would need a different basis for analysis since it was dominated by political developments. Besides, this last period was considered too recent for a sound historical analysis to be made of it, given that the events are contemporary and therefore require a different approach. Moreover, there have been no noticeable significant changes in economic structure, since the region has continued to depend largely on the cultivation of bananas and coffee. All these assumptions, however, do not deny that the period has had extreme importance for the history of the tribe.

The general perspective of the region appears to be a continuation of the coffee/banana economic base for the foreseeable future. However, there are clear indications that the production of the two crops cannot continue to increase very fast owing to scarce land, poor production techniques and the swiftly expanding population. A pertinent question then is what are the prospects for the future of economic development in Buhaya? Of course, the formulation of an adequate answer to such a question would call for a totally different form of study, aimed at projecting alternative paths of economic development. Such a study, however, would have to take into account, *inter alia*, the following possibilities and realities.

First of all, coffee/banana production might be improved so as to ensure a higher growth rate. Such a measure would necessitate the use of more efficient techniques aimed at better husbandry, use of fertilizer or manure and the adoption of improved crop varieties. In all, this type of policy would necessitate careful planning and research.

A second alternative would be to introduce the cultivation of a different crop which could trigger off another form of revolution in the same way as the three crops mentioned did over the centuries of civilization of Buhaya. Indeed, experimentation has been carried out with various plants, such as rice, pepper and cinnamon, and there is room for the experiment to continue. The introduction of tea has already proved successful as an alternative cash crop. There is no reason why experimentation could not be undertaken with animal husbandry, which could be fitted into the existing economic constraints of land shortage.

Lastly, some kind of manufacturing industry could be established. Again, this would require careful planning and access to both natural and capital resources in the form of infrastructure and directly productive investments.

1. The phenomenon of the periphery-metropolitan relationship is illustrated by Benjamin Higgins, *Economic Development*, op. cit., pp.267–326.

BIBLIOGRAPHY

I — ARCHIVAL SOURCES

1. KAGERA REGIONAL ARCHIVES OFFICE
   Bukoba, Tanzania.
2. BIBLIOTHEQUE ROYALE ALBERT 1er
   Boulevard de l'Empereur 4
   1000 Bruxelles, Belgium.
3. FONDATION EGYPTOLOGIQUE REINE ELIZABETH BIBLIOTHEQUE
   Musées Royaux d'Art et d'Histoire
   Parc Cinquantenaire 3
   1040 Bruxelles, Belgium.
4. MUSÉE ROYAL DE L'AFRIQUE CENTRALE
   Steenweg op Leuven 13
   3080 Tervuren, Belgium.
5. RHODES HOUSE LIBRARY
   Oxford, United Kingdom.
6. SERVICE DE DOCUMENTATION EN AGRONOMIE TROPICALE ET EN DEVELOPPEMENT RURAL
   Rue de Facq 1
   1050 Bruxelles, Belgium.

II — OFFICIAL PUBLICATIONS

1. COLONIAL PAPER No.46: *Report by His Majesty's Government of the United Kingdom of Great Britain and Northern Ireland to the Council of the League of Nations on the Administration of Tanganyika Territory for the Year 1929*. London: His Majesty's Stationery Office, 1930.
2. Extracts from German Ordinances and Decrees of German East Africa. Nairobi: The Standard P. and P. Works, 1916.
3. Intelligence Notes on British and German East Africa. The Intelligence Department, British East Africa, March 1916.
4. *Report by His Britannic Majesty's Government to the Council of the League of Nations on the Administration of Tanganyika Territory for the Year 1927*. London: His Majesty's Stationery Office, 1928.
5. Tanganyika Territory: Native Administration Memoranda. No. 1: *Principles of Native Administration and Their Application*. Dar es Salaam: Government Printer, 1930.
6. Tanganyika Territory General Administration Memoranda (For Official Use Only). Dar es Salaam: Government Printer, 1930.

7. Tanganyika Territory Department of Agriculture: *Coffee Crop, 1943–44: Report on Quality and Its Improvement.* Dar es Salaam: Government Printer, 1944 (Pamphlet No. 37).
8. Report No. AE–7, *The Economic Development of Tanzania.* International Bank for Reconstruction and Development/International Development Assistance, March 1970.
9. *Economic Development of Tanganyika.* International Bank for Reconstruction and Development/International Development Assistance (ed). Baltimore: John Hopkins Press, 1961.

III — PUBLISHED SECONDARY WORKS

Anacleti, A.O. and Nagala, D.K. 'The Cattle Complex in the Ancient West Lake Kingdoms'. *La Civilisation Ancienne des Peuples des Grands Lacs.* Colloque de Bujumbura, Paris: Editions Karthala, 1979.

Armstrong, R.G. 'Glottochronology and African Linguistics'. *Journal of African History,* Vol. III, 2 (1962), 283–90.

Austen, R.A. *Northwestern Tanzania under German and British Rule: Colonial Policy and Tribal Politics, 1889–1939.* New Haven and London: Yale University Press, 1968.

Berger, I. *Religion and Resistance: East African Kingdoms in the Precolonial Period.* Tervuren: Musée Royal de l'Afrique Centrale, 1981.

Betbeder, P. 'The Kingdom of Buzinza'. *Journal of World History,* Vol. XIII, 4 (1971), 736–59.

Bloch, M. 'La Société Féodale'. *Les Classes et le Gouvernement des Hommes.* Paris: Editions Albin Michel, 1940.

Bonabaisi, Fr. I. *Ikany-Ngambo.* Limburg: Printing Press of the Pallottine Fathers, 1957.

Boulding, K.E. *Economic Analysis.* New York: Harper & Brothers, 1953.

Brooklyn Museum *Africa in Antiquity: the Arts of Ancient Nubia and the Sudan.* Vol. I.

Clark, D. 'The Spread of Food Production in Sub-Saharan Africa'. *Journal of World History,* Vol. III, 2 (1962), 211–18.

Clough, S.B. *European Economic History.* New York: McGraw Hill Book Company, 1968.

Cory, H. and Hartnoll, M.M. — *Customary Law of the Haya Tribe*. London: Cass Library of African Studies, 1945.

Cory, H. — 'The People of the Lake Victoria Region'. *Tanganyika Notes and Records*, No. 33 (July 1952), 22–7.

Cory, H. — *History of the Bukoba District*. Mwanza, 1960.

Courier, The — Brussels: African, Caribbean and Pacific Group — Commission of the European Communities. No. 54 (January/February 1980).

Cunningham, Sir J.F. — *Uganda and its People*. London: Hutchinson & Co., 1905.

Davidson, B. — 'Africa in Historical Perspective'. *Africa South of the Sahara*. London: Europa Publications Ltd., 1981, 3–18.

Day, C. — *Economic Development in Europe*. New York: Macmillan Company, 1942.

Dholakia, M. and Firat, F.A. — 'Market Sectors and Conditions Necessary for Success', *Marketing Systems for Developing Countries*. Dov Izraeli and Frank Meissner (editors). John Wiley & Sons, 1976.

Eberlie, R.F. — 'The German Achievement in East Africa'. *Tanganyika Notes and Records*, Vol. 55 (September 1960), 181–214.

Engoma ya Buhaya — Newspaper. Bukoba: Buhaya Council, 1950.

Goody, J. — 'Feudalism in Africa'. *Journal of African History*, Vol. IV, 1 (1963), 1–17.

Graham, J.D. — 'Establishing Chiefs and Tribes in Cameron's Tanganyika'. *Tanganyika Notes and Records*, Nos. 77 and 78 (1976), 1–10.

Gray, R. and Birmingham, D. (editors) — *Precolonial African Trade. Essays on Trade in Central* and Eastern Africa Before 1900. London: Oxford University Press, 1970.

Greenberg, J.H. — *Studies in African Linguistic Classification*. New Haven: The Compass Publishing House, 1955.

Greenberg, J.H. — *Africa as a Linguistic Area*. Chicago: University of Chicago Press, 1963.

Greenberg, J.H. — 'Linguistic Evidence Regarding Bantu Origins'. *Journal of African History*, Vol. XIII, 2 (1972), 189–216.

Greenberg, J.H. — *The Languages of Africa*. Bloomington: Indiana University, 1966.

Guthrie, M. — 'Some Developments in Prehistory of the Bantu Languages'. *Journal of African History*, Vol. III, 2 (1962), 273–82.

Higgins, B. *Economic Development*. New York: W.W. Norton & Co., 1968.

Hyden, G. *Political Development in Rural Tanzania*. Nairobi: East African Publishing House, 1974.

Iliffe, J. *A Modern History of Tanganyika*. London: Cambridge University Press, 1979.

Iliffe, J. *Tanganyika under German Rule 1905–1912*. Nairobi: East African Publishing House, 1973.

Ishumi, A.G. 'The Kingdom of Kiziba'. *Journal of World History*, Vol. XII, 4 (1971), 714–35.

Jervis, T. 'A History of Robusta Coffee in Bukoba'. *Tanganyika Notes and Records*, No. 8 (1939), 47–58.

Johnston, Sir Harry *Uganda Protectorate*. London: Hutchinson & Co., 1902.

Jones, G.I. 'European and African Tradition on the Rio Real'. *Journal of African History*, Vol. XVIII, 3 (1963), 391–402.

Kaijage, J.F. 'Kyamutwara'. *Journal of World History*, Vol. XIII, 3 (1971), 542–74.

Kaniki, M.H.Y. *Tanzania Under Colonial Rule*. London: Longman's Group Ltd., 1979.

Karugire, S.R. *A Political History of Uganda*. Nairobi–London: Heinemann, 1980.

Katoke, I. 'The History of the Precolonial States of North-Western Tanzania: Introduction'. *Journal of World History*, XIII, 3 (1971), 115–41.

Katoke, I. *The Karagwe Kingdom: A History of the Abanyambo of North-West Tanzania*. Nairobi: East African Publishing House, 1975.

Kibira, J.M. *Church, Clan and the World*. Uppsala: Almquist & Wicksell, 1974.

Kurtz, L.S. *Historical Dictionary of Tanzania*. Methuen, N.J. & London: The Scarecrow Press Inc., 1978.

Langlands, B.W. 'Uganda: Physical and Social Geography'. *Africa South of the Sahara, 1981–82*, 1–77.

Leakey, L.S.B. *Stone Age Africa: An Outline of Prehistory in Africa*. London: Oxford University Press, 1949.

Lettow-Vorbeck, P. von *My Reminiscences of East Africa*. London: Hurst and Blackett, 1920.

Leubuscher, C. *Tanganyika Territory*. London: Oxford University Press, 1949.

Lipson, E. — *The Economic History of England*. London: A. & C. Black Ltd., 1929.

Mair, Lucy — *Primitive Government*. Aylesbury: Hazel Watson & Vincy Ltd., 1964.

Mapunda, H. — *Historia ya Mapambano ya Mwafrika*. Dar es Salaam: Tanzania Publishing House, 1976.

Mbwiliza, J.F. — 'The Hoe and the Stick: a Political Economy in Heru Kingdom c 1750–1900'. *Journal of World History*, Vol. XII, 3 (1971), 100–13.

McCall, D.F. — *Africa in Time Perspective: A Discussion of Historical Reconstruction from Unwritten Sources*. New York: Oxford University Press, 1969.

McMaster, D.N. — 'Change of Regional Balance in Bukoba District of Tanganyika'. *Tanganyika Notes and Records*, Vol. 56 (March 1961), 79–92.

Maquet, J.J. — 'A Research Definition of African Feudality'. *Journal of African History*, Vol. III, 2 (1961), 307–10.

Marsh, J. and Kingsnorth, G.W. — *A History of East Africa*. London: Cambridge University Press, 1972.

Moffett, J.P. (Editor) — *Tanganyika: A Review of its Resources and Their Development*. Dar es Salaam: Government Printer, 1955.

Mturi, A.A. — 'Ancient Civilisation of the People of the Great Lakes, the Linguistic and Archaeological Evidence: An Overview'. *La Civilisation Ancienne des Peuples des Grands Lacs*. Colloque de Bujumbura, Paris: Editions Karthala, 1979.

Mupapi, Padre W. — *Amakuru G' Abaihuzi Ba Buhaya*. Bunena: Rumuli Press.

Murdock, G.P. — *Africa: Its People and their Cultural History*. New York: McGraw Hill, 1959.

Musso, M. — *Mukwava Na Kabila Lake*. Arusha: East African Publications Ltd., 1968.

Mutahaba, G.R. — *Portrait of a Nationalist: The Life of Ali Migeyo*. Nairobi: East African Publishing House, 1969.

Ngalo, D.S. — *Nyarubanja Na Sheria*. Nairobi: East African Literature Bureau, 1976.

Ogot, B.A. — *History of the Southern Luo, Migration and Settlement 1500–1900*, Vol. 1. Nairobi: East African Publishing House, 1967.

Ogot, B.A. (ed.) — *Zamani: A Survey of East African History*. Nairobi: East African Publishing House, 1969.

Pelt, P. van — *Bantu Customs in Mainland Tanzania*. Tabora: TMP Book Department, 1974.

Peters, K. — *New Light on Dark Africa*. London: Ward, Lock & Co., 1891.

Phatak, K.M. — 'A Note on the German Two-Rupee Coin and the Maria Theresa Dollar'. *Tanganyika Notes and Records*, Vol. 57 (September 1961), 177–80.

Postam, M.N. — *The Cambridge Economic History of Europe*. Cambridge: Cambridge University Press, 1971.

Rehse, H. — *Kiziba Land und Leute*. Stuttgart: Verlag von Strecker & Schröder, 1919.

Reining, P.C. — 'Haya Land Tenure: Land Holding and Tenancy'. *Anthropological Quarterly*, Vol. 35 (April 1962), 58–73.

Rines, M. (editor) — *Marketing Handbook*. Gower Publishing Ltd., 1981.

Roberts, A.D. — 'Baganda', *Journal of African History*, Vol. III, 2 (1962), 435–40.

Rostow, W.W. — *The Stages of Economic Growth: A Non-Communist Manifesto*. Cambridge University Press, 1961.

Sadleir, T.R. — *The Co-operative Movement in Tanganyika*. Dar es Salaam: Government Printer, 1961.

Schweitzer, G. — *Emin Pasha. His Life and Work*, Vol. II. Westminster: Archibald Constable & Co., 1898.

Seligman, C.G. — *Races of Africa*. London: London University Press, 1957.

Smith, A. — 'The Missionary Contribution to Education (Tanganyika) to 1914'. *Tanganyika Notes and Records*, No. 60 (March 1963), 91–119.

Speke, J.H. — *Journal of the Discovery of the Source of the Nile*. Edinburgh and London: William Blackwood, 1863.

Speke, J.H. — *What Led to the Discovery of the Source of the Nile*. London: William Blackwood, 1864.

Stanley, H.M. — *The Exploration and Discoveries of Henry Morton Stanley*. London: William Kimberlay, 1861.

Stanley, H.M. — *Through the Dark Continent*. London, 1878.

Steinhart, E.I. — *Conflict and Collaboration: The Kingdoms of Western Uganda 1890–1907*. Princeton: Princeton University Press.

Svendsen, K.E. and Teisen, M. — *Self-reliant Tanzania*. Dar es Salaam: Tanzania Publishing House, 1969.

Swahili Research, Institute of — Zamani Mpaka Suku Hizi. Arusha: East Africa Publications Ltd., 1981.

Taasisi, Ya Uchunguzi Wa Kiswahili — *Kamusi ya Kiswahili Sanifu*. Dar es Salaam: Oxford University Press, 1981.

Tibazarwa, C.M. — *Economic Impact on Tanzania of East African Common Market*. Ph.D. dissertation at Claremont University Center, awaiting publication by Kenya Literature Bureau.

Unstead, R.J. — *Kings, Barons and Serfs: A Pictorial History 1086–1200*, Vol. II. Aylesbury: Hazel Watson & Viney Ltd.

Wallerstein, I. — 'The Evolving Role of the African Scholar in African Studies'. *Canadian Journal of African Studies Revue*, Vol. 17 (1983), 9–16.

Werlen, J. — *Edini Omuli Buhaya*. Bunena: Rumuli Press.

Wilson, D.A. — *East African History*. Nairobi: Evans Brothers Ltd., 1967.

Yonge, B.E. — 'The Stranding of Sybil'. *Tanganyika Notes and Records*, No. 75 (1974), 29–35.

ANNEX I

LIST OF BAKAMA DURING THE ENFURA PERIOD AND AFTER

CHIEFDOMS COVERED:
A. BUGABO
B. KARAGWE
C. KIHANJA
D. KIZIBA
E. MARUKU
F. MISSENYI

INFORMATION LISTED:
1. Name of Mukama
2. Headquarters or capital of chiefdom
3. Remarks where appropriate

Note:
1. Tables for Ihangiro and Kyamutwara chiefdoms are presented in Chapter IV.
2. Sources:
   – Interviews with Goti Ntambala, Otto Sulemani Kolomba and the late Raphael Kyandyoga of Muleba District;
   – Published references: Hans Cory, H. Rehse, A.G.M. Ishumi, J.F. Kaijage, I. Katoke and J. Werlen (for references, see main text).

A. BUGABO

1. Name: KALAMAGI
   Capital: Bugabo Village
   Remarks: Kalamagi fled Buzinza after being accused of intrigues against the ruler there and arrived in Buhaya with his mother, KAMBUGU, his charming sister, MATITI, and three brothers, MUTASHABA, BENGONZO and MUKOTA. When MATITI became wife of Mukama KAHIGI I of Kyamutwara, KALAMAGI was made a subchief (mwami) of Bugabo and this position was inherited by his son, BUYENJE and subsequent offspring, including RUGAMBWA, BUGIMBI, KANGARAGWA and NKWERE. NKWERE was in power when the Germans arrived in Buhaya. KALAMAGI's brother, MUTASHABA, became mwami of Itahwa and among his great grandsons were RUSHUMA, father of KITEKERE

whose son, KAITABA, became the first effective Bankango ruler of Kyamutwara. When KALEMERA IV married two of RUSHUMA's sister, KWEZI and ISHARAZA, the Bankango clan increased its influence in the kingdom.

2.	Name:	BUYENJE
	Capital:	Bugabo Village
	Remarks:	He was actually a subchief (mwami) and, from the time of KALAMAGI down to that of KANGARAGWA, the power of the rulers was that of a subchief working directly under the Mukama of Kyamutwara.
3.	Name:	RUGAMBWA
	Remarks:	A subchief
4.	Name:	BUGIMBI
	Remarks:	A subchief
5.	Name:	KANGARAGWA
	Remarks:	A subchief
6.	Name:	NKWERE
	Capital:	Kalema
	Remarks:	First recognized independent Bankango Mukama of Bugabo.
7.	Name:	KAHYOZA
	Capital:	Kalema
	Remarks:	Reigned approximately between 1860 and 1895 and was in power when the European colonizers arrived. He was a popular ruler.
8.	Name:	RUTAHIGWA
	Remarks:	Ruled from 1895 to 1899 and though with a non-Enfura (commoner) mother, he outwitted his half-brother, KAMPAYANI, and occupied the throne.
9.	Name:	RUGACHWA
	Remarks:	Son of RUTAHIGWA. Ruled from 1899 to 1927.
10.	Name:	GABRIEL LUTALEMWA
	Remarks:	First ruled under the regency of Lweikiza but later proved to be incapable of ruling.

11.	Name:	LWEIKIZA
	Remarks:	From being a courtier, he took over the throne in 1937 and ruled until 1943.
12.	Name:	GALIKANI LWEGELERA
	Remarks:	Son of LWEIKIZA. Ruled from 1943 until Independence.
13.	Name:	EDWARD R. RUGAIGANISA
	Remarks:	Titular Mukama during the post-Independence era.

B. KARAGWE

1.	Name:	RUHINDA KIBONABAGABE
	Capital:	Bweranyange, which for centuries remained the capital.
	Remarks:	He was born in Bunyòro and is believed to have been the son of the last Bachwezi god-king, WAMARA, and a commoner mother, NJUNAKI. Founder of the Bahinda dynasties in the Interlacustrine Region.
2.	Name:	NTARE I
	Remarks:	The names of the Karagwe rulers alternated for centuries between RUHINDA and NTARE.
3.	Name:	RUHINDA II
4.	Name:	NTARE II
5.	Name:	RUHINDA III
6.	Name:	NTARE III
7.	Name:	RUHINDA IV
8.	Name:	NTARE IV
9.	Name:	RUHINDA V
10.	Name:	RUSATIRA
11.	Name:	MEHIGA
12.	Name:	KALEMERA BWIRANGENDA

13. Name: NTARE V KIITABANYORO
Remarks: He ousted the invaders from Bunyoro.

14. Name: RUHINDA VI ORUSHONGO

15. Name: NDAGARA I RUZINGA MICHUCHU
Remarks: He was associated with the metal industry and is presumed to have reigned from 1820 to 1855.

16. Name: RUMANYIKA I RUGOROGOKA RWA KAKINDO. Sometimes called ORUGUNDU or RWA NDAGARA
Remarks: First documented Mukama of Karagwe and was visited by European explorers such as J.H. Speke and H.M. Stanley. He reigned during the period 1853–83.

17. Name: KAYENJE (KALEMERA II)
Remarks: He reigned from 1883 to 1885 and was killed by lightning after barely two years on the throne.

18. Name: NYAMUKUBA (NDAGARA II)
Remarks: Son of KAYENJE, he was a minor when he succeeded his father.

19. Name: KANYOROZI (NTARE VI)
Capital: Bugene
Remarks: Son of KAYENJE and grandson of RUMANYIKA, he was a minor and had a triumvirate regency comprising KAKETO, BAKAHUGA and KYOBYA. He was publicly executed by the Germans in 1914.

20. Name: DAUD RUMANYIKA
Capital: Bugene
Remarks: He was direct in line of succession from NDAGARA, being the son of NTARE VI and grandson of NDAGARA II. He was deposed in 1939 by the British.

21. Name: BURCHARD I. RUHINDA
Capital: Bugene
Remarks: He was the grandson of KAKOKO, who was only a regent. He remained in power from 1939 until after Independence and died in 1983.

C. KIHANJA

1. Name: KINYONYI
Capital: Kigaze, and later Bulembo
Remarks: Son of BWOGI II of Kyamutwara and prospective heir to the throne but was ousted by KAITABA KA KITEKERE after supporting the latter's stepbrother, KAJURUNGA. He fled to Buganda where he died. While in exile, he had a son, MUGANGUZI, who later became Mukama RUGOMORA. KINYONYI sought the aid of the Baganda to invade Kyamutwara but he was unsuccessful because KAITABA managed to hide.

2. Name: RUGOMORA III (MUGANGUZI)
Remarks: Son of KINYONYI, born when his father was in exile in Buganda, he was brought home to be a Mukama in order to appease the Bahamba loyalty for a Mhinda king. He joined KAITABA to fight KAJURUNGA, though later on, KAJURUNGA's son, KAMILO, became an ally of KAITABA and was crowned king and built a palace at Itahwa. RUGOMORA was backed by KABAKA SUNA of Buganda. During the truce that ensued, RUGOMORA died and was succeeded by his son, KAHIGI II in 1890 when the Germans were establishing a colony in Buhaya.

3. Name: KAHIGI II KA BULEMBO
Remarks: Initially, he had his palace at Bulembo in Upper Kihanja but later shifted it to Kanazi. His Bulembo palace had been surrounded by a wall or embankment, presumably to improve his defence against Mukotani of Kyamutwara. Son of Rugomora II, he became Mukama in 1890 and died in 1916. He was a favourite of the German administration.

4. Name: ALFRED KALEMERA
Capital: Kanazi
Remarks: Son of KAHIGI, he had a somewhat colourless reign He ascended the throne in 1916 and died in 1943.

5. Name: BENJAMINI RUGOMORA IV
Capital: Kanazi
Remarks: Popularly known as BENJAMINI MUTEMBEI, he was the son of KAHIGI II. As he had an Enfura

mother, he was preferred politically to his half-brother, LORENTI. His other attractions included his youthfulness (he was in his mid-thirties when he ascended the throne), his sound formal schooling and his status as a salaried employee in Dar es Salaam at the time of his appointment as Mukama. Unfortunately, he reigned for only 11 months and allegedly died of poisoning.

6. Name: BWOGI III
Capital: Kanazi
Remarks: Another son of KAHIGI III, he reigned from 1944 till his death in 1958.

7. Name: PETER M.K. NYARUBAMBA II
Capital: Kanazi
Remarks: Reigned from 1958 to Independence when he became a titular Mukama.

D. KIZIBA

1. Name: KIBI (alias NYAKIIRU, KAGANDA, WUNYI)
Capital: Kanyigo, Kigarama
Remarks: Son of KINTU and grandson of KYOMYA and a great cousin of RUHINDA KIBONABAGABE. According to the legend, RUHINDA's grandfather, NDAHURA, and KIBI's grandfather, KYOMYA, were stepbrothers, the sons of ISIMBWA. KIBI's father, KINTU, conquered the kingdoms of Kitara and Buddu, and later, Kiziba. On his arrival in Kiziba (known then as Bunjarwe), KIBI conspired with KANYAMAISHWA, son of the Bantu king, NTUMWA, to usurp the throne by assassinating the king, though ultimately, KIBI killed KANYAMAISHWA and ruled by himself.

2. Name: ISHAMURA-NJOBE
Capital: Kanyigo
Remarks: The son of KANYAMAISHWA, he ruled for a short time.

3. Name: ISHAMURA-NYAKABINGA
Capital: Kanyigo
Remarks: Self-styled son of KIBI. He killed ISHAMURA-NJOBE and took over the throne. He succeeded in

consolidating the Babiito dynasty in Kiziba.

4. Name: WANUMI
Capital: Kanyigo (Nshumba/Byazi)
Remarks: He had a nervous breakdown and was succeeded by his son, MATWI.

5. Name: MATWI
Capital: Bugandika (Runyabikinde)
Remarks: He fought and killed his brother, BWANAMBA, in order to seize the throne.

6. Name: MAGEMBE I
Capital: Bugandika (Ruti)

7. Name: MUZINGA
Capital: Buyango

8. Name: MWIGARA
Capital: Buyango

9. Name: BURUNGU I
Capital: Buyango (Ntunda)
Remarks: He was excessively cruel for he blinded relatives, burnt wives and flogged subjects.

10. Name: MAGEMBE II
Capital: Bwanjai (Mweyanjale)
Remarks: He was a charismatic, popular but warlike king.

11. Name: MBONEKO I
Capital: Kitobo (Buganzi)
Remarks: He was chiefly involved in a power struggle with his own brothers.

12. Name: NYARWANGU
Capital: Kitobo (Igoma)
Remarks: Son of MBONEKO, he ruled for only one month.

13. Name: RUHANGARAZI I
Capital: Kitobo
Remarks: Son of MBONEKO.

14. Name: RUTAJWAHA
Capital: Buyango

15. Name: BURUNGU II
Capital: Kitobo (Bukele)
Remarks: He was non-progressive and of an unreliable character.

16. Name: KIBI II (RUTAIRWA II)
Capital: Bwanjai
Remarks: Cousin of BURUNGU.

17. Name: RUHANGARAZI II
Capital: Bwanjai
Remarks: He was too peaceful and did not even try to stop the invaders.

18. Name: MUTATEMBWA
Capital: Bwanjai (Kantale)
Remarks: The first widely-known and documented Mukama of Kiziba. Son of RUHANGARAZI II, he reigned during the period 1870–1903 when the Germans were colonizing the country. He is described as a strong, wise and valiant Mukama.

19. Name: MUTAHANGARWA
Capital: Bwanjai, and then Gera
Remarks: Son of MUTATEMBWA, he had to fight a prolonged civil war with his brother before he could establish himself as ruler of Kiziba. His rule is closely associated with the increasing influence of German rule in the region.

20. Name: MBONEKO II (EDWARD GEORGE)
Remarks: Son of MUTAHANGARWA, he ruled from 1917 to 1927 when he died. He had had a good formal education.

21. Name: WILLIAM MUTAKUBWA
Capital: Gera
Remarks: He was still at school when he was appointed to succeed his father, MBONEKO, in 1927. He was, however, dethroned by the British administration in 1937.

22. Name: NESTOR LUTINWA
Remarks: Son of MUTAHANGARWA, he was crowned on 3 May 1937 and held the title until he died in 1983.

E. MARUKU

1. Name: KAJURUNGA
   Capital: Kanyangereko
   Remarks: Former rightful king of Kyamutwara but was ousted and expelled by his cousin, KAITABA, and was restored only to be given a strip of land called Maruku.

2. Name: BWOGI
   Capital: Itahwa
   Remarks: He was subdued by KAITABA of Kyamutwara who detained him at Itahwa.

3. Name: KISHEBUKA
   Capital: Maruku
   Remarks: He came to the throne in 1891, though he had to flee from the Germans to Kibumbiro but succeeded in regaining his throne in 1907.

4. Name: DAUD RUGOMORA
   Capital: Maruku
   Remarks: Still a minor when he ascended the throne in 1917, he did not assume complete reign until 1925. He remained on the throne until after Independence.

F. MISSENYI

1. Name: WAKARA
   Capital: Bunyoro
   Remarks: He was not a Mukama as such but he is important because he is the source of the dynasty.

2. Name: KAGORO
   Capital: Bunyoro
   Remarks: Died in Buganda at Kyonga.

3. Name: NYAMUTURA
   Remarks: Died in Kyango.

4. Name: RWEKIIKA I
   Remarks: Died at Mayanja in Buganda.

5. Name: KAGORO II
   Remarks: The first Mwami (subchief in Missenyi).

6. Name: NYAMUTURA II

7. Name: KAGORO III
Remarks: He succeeded his brother, KAGORO II, as Mwami.

8. Name: KYAMUKUMA I
Remarks: Brother of KAGORO III.

9. Name: RWEKIIKA II
Remarks: The first effective Mukama of Missenyi, having been installed by the Germans in 1902.

10. Name: SULEMANI KAKOKO WAKARA II
Remarks: He ruled during the period 1913–19. Being a minor, he had a regency to run the country. However, he ran away from school in Buganda and so lost his title to the throne.

11. Name: PAULO LWAMUJONGO NYAMUTURA III
Remarks: He ruled during the period 1919–55.

12. Name: SERAPION KYAMUKUMA II
Remarks: He ruled from 1955 until Independence.

ANNEX II

NOTES ON SOME MAJOR ECONOMIC PLANTS IN BAHAYA HISTORY

KEY: THE LOCAL NAME IS FOLLOWED BY THE ENGLISH NAME (. . . .) AND THE LATIN NAME [. . . .]

	PLANT	NOTES
1.	Bitoke (banana) [*Musa paradisiaca*]	The banana fruit is the most important food of the Bahaya. The prevalent species, which is presumed to be non-indigenous, is *Musa paradisiaca* or plantain. The native species, *Musa ensente*, is not economically important. The plant belongs to the herbaceous category of the *Musaceae* family.
2.	Bigando, bilibwa (cassava, manioc) [*Manihot esculenta crantz* or *Manihot utilissima*]	A semi-ligneous bush belonging to the *Euphorbiaceae* family. It is widely used in Buhaya as food.
3.	Barai, kashuli (large yams, l'igname) [*Diascorea batatas*]	Yams are of the *Dioscoreaceae monocotyledon* family. The tubers are used as food.
4.	Nfuma, Bitakuli, ndiibwa (sweet potatoes) [*Ipomea batatas*]	This is a creeping herbaceous plant belonging to the Convolvulus family. Sweet potatoes are widely used for food and their importance increases during dry years.
5.	Numbu	A plant apparently belonging to the potato (*Solanum tuberosum*) family, though it is sometimes described as being close to the turnip. It was once widely cultivated in the region. Planted in September, it would be harvested in February. The tubers, which measure less than 2 inches, are oblongish with thin skin and can be eaten raw or cooked.

6.	Bikwara (colocasia, taro) [*Colocasia esculenta*]	Colocasia of different types are grown in the region.
7.	Buroi (fingermillet) [*Eleusine coracana*]	At one time, fingermillet formed a staple food for Buhaya and it is still widely used, particularly the Gaertner variety. The tiny grain of eleusine has the quality of storability and nutrition, being rich in proteins, fat, calcium, iron, phosphorous and starch.
8.	Mugusha (bittermillet) [*Sorghum vulgare*]	Bittermillet is added to banana juice to produce banana wine.
9.	Bichori (maize) [*Zea mais*]	The traditional variety is small but highly multicoloured and grows well in the space between banana plants.
10.	Mpelege, biimba (beans) [*Phaseolus vulgaris*]	Beans of different sizes and colours are grown in the region and are almost invariably used at every meal.
11.	Nkole, nkaiga (cowpeas) [*Vigna unguiculata*]	Cowpeas feature in ancient stories of the tribe and are valued for their leaves, pods and beans.
12.	Nshoro (earthnut or bambara nut) [*Voandzeie subterranea*]	This is widely grown and is cooked like beans or roasted like groundnuts.
13.	Binyobwa (groundnut) [*Arachis hypogaea*]	When ground, it is used as a cooking oil. It is also roasted or cooked like beans.
14.	Murondo	A creeping plant, possibly of the vanilla family, whose roots are cooked with different foods to provide aroma.
15.	Mwani (coffee) [*Coffea*]	The plant belongs to the *Rubiaceae* family. The two major varieties of *arabica* and *robusta* are both grown in Buhaya.

16.	Tabai (tobacco) [*Nicotiana tabacum*]	Old stories refer to tobacco. The native variety has smaller leaves and can be grown on poor soil.
17.	Ebishalalago (cattail) [*Typha latifolia*]	This plant grows in marshes and is used for making mats. Its ashes are sometimes dissolved to produce cooking salt.
18.	Ebinuma (sedge) [*Carex vesicaria*]	This plant is dried and used for making mats.
19.	Obufunjo (umbrella plant) [*Cyperus alternifolius*]	The stem of the plant is used in various types of basketwork.
20.	Obufunjo (bulrush) [*Scirpus palutris*]	This plant is used for making carpets and mats.
21.	Ebishalunga (common reed) [*Phragmites communis*]	The stem of the plant is used for making traditional flutes. When the hollow stem is flattened out, it can be woven into various types of sheets used for building and drying crops.
22.	Ebifunjo obugala (papyrus) [*Cyperus papyrus*]	Its pine-like leaves are used as a substitute for grass in thatching and carpeting floors. The white part of its stem is used in ceremonies. The plastic-like outer skin is used for making mats.
23.	Obuti bw'entukulu (osier or willow) [*Salix viminalis*]	The slender stem of the plant is used for making baskets of the wickerwork type.
24.	Orwongu lw'ebishus (gourd plant) [*Lagenaria*]	This creeping plant produces large and hard-shelled fruits used for making vessels, utensils and containers.

25.	Olubingo (elephant grass) [*Pennisetum purpureum*]	Elephant grass was used for many purposes and it was particularly important in the construction of the Mshonge hut. The cleaned stems of the grass were woven together to form the walls of the hut.
26.	Omulehe (not available) [*Terminalia superba*]	A tree whose timber was used for carving different objects, including dug-out canoes and wooden food containers.

INDEX